HIPOTHYROIDISM COOKBOOK

MEGA BUNDLE – 4 Manuscripts in 1 – 160+ Bariatric - friendly recipes including breakfast, side dishes, and desserts for a delicious and tasty diet

TABLE OF CONTENTS

2

This document is geared towards providing exact and reliable information in regards to the topic and issue covered. The publication is sold with the idea that the publisher is not required to render accounting, officially permitted, or otherwise, qualified services. If advice is necessary, legal or professional, a practiced individual in the profession should be ordered.

- From a Declaration of Principles which was accepted and approved equally by a Committee of the American Bar Association and a Committee of Publishers and Associations.

Introduction

Hipothyroidism recipes for personal enjoyment but also for family enjoyment. You will love them for sure for how easy it is to prepare them.

ROAST RECIPES

ROASTED ZUCCHINI

Serves: **3-4**

Prep Time: **10**   Minutes

Cook Time: **20**   Minutes

Total Time: **30**   Minutes

INGREDIENTS

- 2 lb. zucchini
- 2 tablespoons olive oil
- 1 tsp curry powder
- 1 tsp salt

DIRECTIONS

1. Preheat the oven to 400 F
2. Cut everything in half lengthwise
3. Toss everything with olive oil and place onto a prepared baking sheet
4. Roast for 18-20 minutes at 400 F or until golden brown
5. When ready remove from the oven and serve

10

ROASTED SQUASH

Serves: **3-4**

Prep Time: **10**   Minutes

Cook Time: **20**   Minutes

Total Time: **30**   Minutes

INGREDIENTS

-   2 delicata squashes
-   2 tablespoons olive oil
-   1 tsp curry powder
-   1 tsp salt

DIRECTIONS

1. Preheat the oven to 400 F
2. Cut everything in half lengthwise
3. Toss everything with olive oil and place onto a prepared baking sheet
4. Roast for 18-20 minutes at 400 F or until golden brown
5. When ready remove from the oven and serve

ZUCCHINI SOUP

Serves:	**4**	
Prep Time:	**10**	Minutes
Cook Time:	**20**	Minutes
Total Time:	**30**	Minutes

INGREDIENTS

- 1 tablespoon olive oil
- 1 lb. zucchini
- ¼ red onion
- ½ cup all-purpose flour
- ¼ tsp salt
- ¼ tsp pepper
- 1 can vegetable broth
- 1 cup heavy cream

DIRECTIONS

1. In a saucepan heat olive oil and sauté zucchini until tender
2. Add remaining ingredients to the saucepan and bring to a boil
3. When all the vegetables are tender transfer to a blender and blend until smooth
4. Pour soup into bowls, garnish with parsley and serve

NOODLE SOUP

Serves: **4**

Prep Time: **10**   Minutes

Cook Time: **20**   Minutes

Total Time: **30**   Minutes

INGREDIENTS

- 2-3 cups water
- 1 can chicken broth
- 1 tablespoon olive oil
- ¼ red onion
- ¼ cup celery
- ¼ tsp salt
- ¼ tsp black pepper
- 5-6 oz. fusilli pasta
- 2 cups chicken breast
- 2 tablespoons parsley

DIRECTIONS

1. In a pot boil water with broth
2. In a saucepan heat oil, add carrot, pepper, celery, onion, salt and sauté until tender
3. Add broth mixture to the mixture and pasta

4. Cook until al dente and stir in chicken breast, cook until chicken breast is tender
5. When ready remove from heat, stir in parsley and serve

ROASTED RED PEPPER SOUP

Serves: *6*
Prep Time: *30*   Minutes

Cook Time: *30*   Minutes

Total Time: *60*   Minutes

INGREDIENTS

- 4 cups vegetable broth
- 1 can green chiles
- 2 tsp cumin
- 2 tbs fresh cilantro
- 1 tbs lemon juice
- 4 ounces cream cheese
- 2 tbs olive oil
- 2 onions
- 1 jar roasted red peppers
- 2 tsp salt
- 1 tsp coriander
- 4 cups sweet potatoes

DIRECTIONS

1. Heat the oil in a pan.
2. Cook the onions until soft, then add the peppers, green chiles, coriander, cumin, and salt and cook for 3 minutes.

3. Stir in the roasted peppers juice, peeled and cubed potatoes, and the vegetable broth.

4. Bring to a boil, then reduce the heat and cook for 15 minutes.

5. Stir in the lemon juice and cilantro.

6. Blend half of the soup with the cream cheese, then add back into the soup, serve immediately.

POTATO SOUP

Serves: **4-6**

Prep Time: **10** Minutes

Cook Time: **50** Minutes

Total Time: **60** Minutes

INGREDIENTS

- 1 onion
- 2-3 carrots
- 2 tablespoons flour
- 5-6 large potatoes
- 2 cups milk
- 2 cups bouillon
- 1 cup water
- 2 cups milk
- 1 tsp salt
- 1 tsp pepper

DIRECTIONS

1. In a saucepan melt butter and sauce carrots, garlic and onion for 4-5 minutes
2. Add flour, milk, potatoes, bouillon and cook for another 15-20 minutes

3. Add pepper and remaining ingredients and cook on low heat for 20-30 minutes

4. When ready remove from heat and serve

TILAPIA WITH PECAN ROSEMARY

Serves: **4**

Prep Time: **20**   Minutes

Cook Time: **20**   Minutes

Total Time: **40**   Minutes

INGREDIENTS

- Cayenne pepper
- 1/3 cup breadcrumbs
- 2 tsp rosemary
- 1 ½ tsp olive oil
- 1 egg white
- 1/3 cup pecans
- 4 tilapia fillets
- ½ tsp brown sugar
- 1/8 tsp salt

DIRECTIONS

1. Preheat the oven to 350F.
2. Stir together the sugar, cayenne pepper, rosemary, pecans, breadcrumbs, and salt.
3. Add the olive oil and toss.
4. Bake for 10 minutes.

5. Whisk the egg white in a bowl and dip the fish into it then into the pecan mixture.

6. Bake for 10 minutes.

7. Serve immediately.

CHICKEN THIGHS WITH BRUSSELS SPROUTS AND POTATOES

Serves: **4**

Prep Time: **15**   Minutes

Cook Time: **30**   Minutes

Total Time: **45**   Minutes

INGREDIENTS

- 2 tsp salt
- 1 tsp thyme
- 1 lb chicken thighs
- 1 lb potatoes
- 3 tbs olive oil
- 1 lemon
- 1 orange
- 1 tsp black pepper
- 2 cloves garlic
- 4 shallots
- 1 ½ tbs paprika
- 2 lb Brussels sprouts

DIRECTIONS

1. Preheat the oven to 450F.
2. Toss the Brussels sprouts, potatoes, shallots, lemon and orange slices with 1 tbs oil, 1 tsp salt, and ½ tsp pepper.

3. Pour into a baking dish.

4. Mix the garlic, remaining salt and pepper, thyme, lemon and orange zest, paprika, and 2 tsp oil in a bowl.

5. Toss the chicken into the mixture.

6. Place the chicken over the Brussels sprouts.

7. Roast for 25 minutes, then serve.

CHICKEN STIR FRY

Serves: **2**

Prep Time: **10** Minutes

Cook Time: **10** Minutes

Total Time: **20** Minutes

INGREDIENTS

- 2 bell peppers
- 2 chicken breasts
- 1 tsp cumin
- 1 tsp cayenne pepper
- 1 tsp olive oil
- ½ tsp paprika
- 2 cups broccoli florets

DIRECTIONS

1. Heat the oil in a pan.
2. Add the diced chicken and cook until browned.
3. Add the broccoli and peppers and cook for 5-10 minutes.
4. Add the spices and a little water.
5. Cook for another few minutes.

MEATBALLS

Serves: *8*

Prep Time: *15*   Minutes

Cook Time: *20*   Minutes

Total Time: *35*   Minutes

INGREDIENTS

- 3 tbs ketchup
- ½ cup breadcrumbs
- 2 garlic cloves
- 2 tsp salt
- 1 lb ground beef
- ½ cup onion
- 1 tsp pepper
- 1 ½ tbs parsley
- 1 egg
- ½ cup cheese

DIRECTIONS

1. Preheat the oven to 400F.
2. Mix all of the ingredients in a bowl.
3. Form balls and place them on a greased cookie sheet.
4. Cook for 20 minutes, allow to cool, then serve.

CHICKEN SALAD SLIDERS

Serves: **4**

Prep Time: **10**   Minutes

Cook Time: **0**   Minutes

Total Time: **10**   Minutes

INGREDIENTS

- ¼ cup almonds
- 1 cup apples
- ¼ cup dried cranberries
- 1 tsp salt
- 4 buns
- ½ lb shredded rotisserie chicken
- ¾ cup Greek yogurt
- 1 cup grapes

DIRECTIONS

1. Combine all of the ingredients in a bowl, except the buns.
2. Place the mixture onto the buns and secure with a toothpick, serve immediately.

CAULIFLOWER RICE

Serves: **4**

Prep Time: **10**   Minutes

Cook Time: **20**   Minutes

Total Time: **30**   Minutes

INGREDIENTS

- 2 tbs soy sauce
- ½ tsp sesame oil
- ½ onion
- 2 cloves garlic
- 1 cup carrots
- 1 tsp black pepper
- 1 cauliflower
- 1 egg
- 2 Tbs oil
- 2 green onions
- 2 tsp salt
- 1 cup peas

DIRECTIONS

1. Mince the cauliflower.
2. Cook the onion and garlic in the oil in a pan.
3. Add the cauliflower and sauté.

4. Add the peas and carrots and stir until combined.
5. Add the sesame oil, soy sauce, beaten egg, and black pepper.
6. Stir until well cooked.
7. Add green onions, season, stir and serve.

CHICKEN THIGHS WITH BUTTERNUT SQUASH

Serves: *6*
Prep Time: *20*   Minutes

Cook Time: *30*   Minutes

Total Time: *50*   Minutes

INGREDIENTS

- ½ lb bacon
- Pepper
- 3 cup Butternut Squash
- 2 tbs oil
- 6 chicken thighs
- Sage
- Salt

DIRECTIONS

1. Preheat the oven to 425F.
2. Fry the bacon until crispy.
3. Sauté the butternut squash in the bacon grease.
4. Season and cook until soft, then remove.
5. Cook the chicken thighs for 10 minutes.
6. Flip the thighs over and add the butternut all around.
7. Place the skillet in the oven.
8. Bake for 15 minutes.

9. Serve topped with the bacon and sage.

Serves: *9*

Prep Time: *20* Minutes

Cook Time: *30* Minutes

Total Time: *50* Minutes

INGREDIENTS

- 3 cup cheese
- 2/3 cup water
- 1 can tomatoes
- ½ cup green pepper
- 1 lb ground beef
- taco seasoning
- 1 can black beans
- ½ cup chopped onion
- 6 tortillas
- 1 can refried beans

DIRECTIONS

1. Cook the beef, onion, and pepper over medium heat.
2. Add the taco seasoning and water and bring to a boil.
3. Stir in the tomatoes and black beans.
4. Simmer for 10 minutes.

5. Place 2 tortillas into a baking dish and spread half of the mixture over.

6. Sprinkle 1 cup cheese and repeat layers.

7. Top with cheese.

8. Cook until the cheese it melted for about 30 minutes.

9. Serve immediately.

GREEN PESTO PASTA

Serves: 2

Prep Time: 5   Minutes

Cook Time: 15   Minutes

Total Time: 20   Minutes

INGREDIENTS

- 4 oz. spaghetti
- 2 cups basil leaves
- 2 garlic cloves
- ¼ cup olive oil
- 2 tablespoons parmesan cheese
- ½ tsp black pepper

DIRECTIONS

1. Bring water to a boil and add pasta
2. In a blend add parmesan cheese, basil leaves, garlic and blend
3. Add olive oil, pepper and blend again
4. Pour pesto onto pasta and serve when ready

OLIVE OIL & HERBS SALMON

Serves: **4**

Prep Time: **15**   Minutes

Cook Time: **40**   Minutes

Total Time: **55**   Minutes

INGREDIENTS

- ½ cup oil
- 1 ½ lb salmon
- ¼ cup dill fronds
- ¼ cup tarragon leaves
- 1 lemon zest
- 1 shallot
- Salt
- Pepper

DIRECTIONS

1. Preheat the oven to 250F.
2. Cook the salmon in the oil in a large pan.
3. Process the dill, lemon zest, shallot and tarragon in a food processor.
4. Blend in 2 tbs of oil and pour the paste over the salmon.
5. Bake for 30 minutes and serve with green salad.

Serves: *4*

Prep Time: *10*   Minutes

Cook Time: *30*   Minutes

Total Time: *40*   Minutes

INGREDIENTS

- 5 thyme sprigs
- Salt
- Pepper
- 2 lb chicken thighs
- Oil
- 1 lemon

DIRECTIONS

1. Preheat the oven to 400F.
2. Drizzle oil over the chicken and season with salt and pepper.
3. Cook over medium heat for 15 minutes.
4. When crispy, flip over and scatter lemon slices and thyme over.
5. Roast for another 15 minutes.
6. Serve immediately.

GARLIC ZUCCHINI

Serves: **4**
Prep Time: **20** Minutes

Cook Time: **30** Minutes

Total Time: **50** Minutes

INGREDIENTS

- 3 tbs basil
- 1/3 cup oil
- ¼ cup red wine vinegar
- 2 lb zucchini
- Salt
- Pepper
- ¼ cup parsley
- 3 cloves garlic

DIRECTIONS

1. Sprinkle the zucchini with salt, let stand for 30 minutes, then rinse.
2. Mix the basil, parsley, and garlic in a bowl.
3. Fry the zucchini in the oil for about 5 minutes.
4. Transfer the zucchini to a plate and top with the herb mixture and the vinegar.
5. Season with salt and pepper.

CHEESE MACARONI

Serves: **1**

Prep Time: **10** Minutes

Cook Time: **20** Minutes

Total Time: **30** Minutes

INGREDIENTS

- 1 lb. macaroni
- 1 cup cheddar cheese
- 1 cup Monterey Jack cheese
- 1 cup mozzarella cheese
- ¼ tsp salt
- ¼ tsp pepper

DIRECTIONS

1. In a pot bring water to a boil
2. Add pasta and cook until al dente
3. In a bowl combine all cheese together and add it to the pasta
4. When ready transfer to a bowl, add salt, pepper and serve

POTATO CASSEROLE

Serves: 2

Prep Time: 10   Minutes

Cook Time: 20   Minutes

Total Time: 30   Minutes

INGREDIENTS

- 5-6 large potatoes
- ¼ cup sour cream
- ½ cup butter
- 5-6 bacon strips
- 1-2 cups mozzarella cheese
- ¼ cup heavy cream

DIRECTIONS

1. Place the potatoes in a pot with boiling water, cook until tender
2. Place the potatoes in a bowl, add sour cream, butter, cheese and mix well
3. In a baking dish place the bacon strips and cover with potato mixture
4. Add remaining mozzarella cheese on top
5. Bake at 325 F for 15-18 minutes or until the mozzarella is fully melted
6. When ready remove from the oven and serve

CHEESE STUFFED SHELLS

Serves: **2**

Prep Time: **10** Minutes

Cook Time: **30** Minutes

Total Time: **40** Minutes

INGREDIENTS

- 2-3 cups macaroni
- 2 cups cream cheese
- 1 cup spaghetti sauce
- 1 cup onions
- 1 cup mozzarella cheese

DIRECTIONS

1. In a pot boil water and add shells
2. Cook for 12-15 minutes
3. In a baking dish add spaghetti sauce
4. In a bowl combine cream cheese, onion and set aside
5. Add cream cheese to the shells and place them into the baking dish
6. Bake at 325 F for 30 minutes or until golden brown
7. When ready remove from the oven and serve

CHICKEN ALFREDO

Serves: 2

Prep Time: *10* Minutes

Cook Time: *20* Minutes

Total Time: *30* Minutes

INGREDIENTS

- 2-3 chicken breasts
- 1 lb. rotini
- 1 cup parmesan cheese
- 1 cup olive oil
- 1 tsp salt
- 1 tsp black pepper
- 1 tsp parsley

DIRECTIONS

1. In a pot add the rotini and cook on low heat for 12-15 minutes
2. In a frying pan heat olive oil, add chicken, salt, parsley, and cook until the chicken is brown
3. Drain the rotini and place the rotini in pan with chicken
4. Cook for 2-3 minutes
5. When ready remove from heat and serve with parmesan cheese on top

Serves: *2*
Prep Time: *10* Minutes

Cook Time: *20* Minutes

Total Time: *30* Minutes

INGREDIENTS

- 6-7 oz. penne pasta
- 2-3 bacon slices
- ¼ cup red onion
- 2 cups asparagus
- 1 cup chicken broth
- 2-3 cups spinach leaves
- ¼ cup parmesan cheese

DIRECTIONS

1. Cook pasta until al dente
2. In a skillet cook bacon until crispy and set aside
3. In a pan add onion, asparagus, broth and cook on low heat for 5-10 minutes
4. Add spinach, cheese, pepper, pasta and cook for another 5-6 minutes
5. When ready sprinkle bacon and serve

TOMATO WRAP

Serves: **4**
Prep Time: **5**   Minutes

Cook Time: **15**   Minutes

Total Time: **20**   Minutes

INGREDIENTS

- 1 cup corn
- 1 cup tomatoes
- 1 cup pickles
- 1 tablespoon olive oil
- 1 tablespoon mayonnaise
- 6-7 turkey slices
- 2-3 whole-wheat tortillas
- 1 cup romaine lettuce

DIRECTIONS

1. In a bowl combine tomatoes, pickles, olive oil, corn and set aside
2. Place the turkey slices over the tortillas and top with tomato mixture and mayonnaise
3. Roll and serve

THYME COD

Serves: *2*
Prep Time: *5*   Minutes

Cook Time: *15*   Minutes

Total Time: *20*   Minutes

INGREDIENTS

- 1 tablespoon olive oil
- ½ red onion
- 1 can tomatoes
- 2-3 springs thyme
- 2-3 cod fillets

DIRECTIONS

1. In a frying pan heat olive oil and sauté onion, stir in tomatoes, spring thyme and cook for 5-6 minutes
2. Add cod fillets, cover and cook for 5-6 minutes per side
3. When ready remove from heat and serve

VEGGIE STIR-FRY

Serves: 2
Prep Time: *10* Minutes

Cook Time: *20* Minutes

Total Time: *30* Minutes

INGREDIENTS

- 1 tablespoon cornstarch
- 1 garlic clove
- ¼ cup olive oil
- ¼ head broccoli
- ¼ cup show peas
- ½ cup carrots
- ¼ cup green beans
- 1 tablespoon soy sauce
- ½ cup onion

DIRECTIONS

1. In a bowl combine garlic, olive oil, cornstarch and mix well
2. Add the rest of the ingredients and toss to coat
3. In a skillet cook vegetables mixture until tender
4. When ready transfer to a plate garnish with ginger and serve

Serves: **4**

Prep Time: **10** Minutes

Cook Time: **3** Minutes

Total Time: **40** Minutes

INGREDIENTS

- 1 ½ tsp vinegar
- ½ tbs butter
- Salt
- Pepper
- 1 lb asparagus
- ¼ cup mint leaves
- 4 ounces radishes
- 1 tbs oil

DIRECTIONS

1. Cut the asparagus into pieces.
2. Cook the asparagus for 3 minutes in the butter.
3. Slice the radishes and toss with the asparagus in a bowl.
4. Mix the oil and the vinegar and pour the mixture over the vegetables.
5. Season with salt and pepper.
6. Slice the mint and toss with the vegetables, serve cold.

CRANBERRY SALAD

Serves: **2**
Prep Time: **5**   Minutes

Cook Time: **15**   Minutes

Total Time: **20**   Minutes

INGREDIENTS

- ½ cup celery
- 1 packet Knox Gelatin
- 1 cup cranberry juice
- 1 can berry cranberry sauce
- 1 cup sour cream

DIRECTIONS

1. In a pan add juice, gelatin, cranberry sauce and cook on low heat
2. Add sour cream, celery and continue to cook
3. Pour mixture into a pan
4. Serve when ready

Serves: 2
Prep Time: 5   Minutes

Cook Time: 5   Minutes

Total Time: 10   Minutes

INGREDIENTS

- 1 tablespoon mayonnaise
- 1 tablespoon lemon juice
- 1 apple
- 1 cup red grapes
- ½ cup cranberries
- ½ cup walnuts
- 12 cup celery
- 6 lettuce leaves

DIRECTIONS

1. In a bowl combine all ingredients together and mix well
2. Serve with dressing

CRANBERRY SALAD

Serves: **2**

Prep Time: **5**   Minutes

Cook Time: **5**   Minutes

Total Time: **10**   Minutes

INGREDIENTS

- 1 can unsweetened pineapple
- 1 package cherry gelatin
- 1 tablespoon lemon juice
- ½ cup artificial sweetener
- 1 cup cranberries
- 1 orange
- 1 cup celery
- ½ cup pecans

DIRECTIONS

1. In a bowl combine all ingredients together and mix well
2. Serve with dressing

GRILLED VEGETABLE SALAD

Serves: 2

Prep Time: 5   Minutes

Cook Time: 5   Minutes

Total Time: *10*   Minutes

INGREDIENTS

- ¼ lb. asparagus
- 1 zucchini
- 1 yellow squash
- ¼ red onion
- 1 red bell pepper
- ¼ cup olive oil
- ¼ cup red wine vinegar
- 2 garlic cloves
- Salt

DIRECTIONS

1. Cut into thin strips and grill all vegetables
2. In a bowl mix all ingredients and mix well
3. Serve with salad dressing

RUSSIAN CABBAGE SALAD

Serves: **2**

Prep Time: **5** Minutes

Cook Time: **5** Minutes

Total Time: **10** Minutes

INGREDIENTS

- 2 lb. cabbage
- 2 carrots
- 2 beets
- 2 garlic cloves
- ¼ tsp black pepper
- ¼ cup olive oil

DIRECTIONS

1. In a bowl combine all ingredients together and mix well
2. Serve with dressing

ROQUEFORT SALAD

Serves: **2**

Prep Time: **5** Minutes

Cook Time: **5** Minutes

Total Time: **10** Minutes

INGREDIENTS

- 1 head leaf lettuce
- 2 pears
- 4 oz. Roquefort cheese
- 1 avocado
- ¼ cup green onions
- ¼ cup pecans
- ¼ cup olive oil
- 1 tsp mustard
- 1 garlic clove
- ¼ tsp salt

DIRECTIONS

1. In a bowl combine all ingredients together and mix well
2. Serve with dressing

BLACK BEAN SALAD

Serves: **2**
Prep Time: **5**   Minutes

Cook Time: **5**   Minutes

Total Time: **10**   Minutes

INGREDIENTS

- 1 can black beans
- 1 can corn
- 4 green onion
- 1 red bell pepper
- 2 tomatoes
- 1 lime
- ¼ cup salad dressing

DIRECTIONS

1. In a bowl combine all ingredients together and mix well
2. Serve with dressing

CRANBERRY SALAD

Serves: 2

Prep Time: 5   Minutes

Cook Time: 5   Minutes

Total Time: 10   Minutes

INGREDIENTS

- 1 can unsweetened pineapple
- 1 package cherry gelatin
- 1 tablespoon lemon juice
- ½ cup artificial sweetener
- 1 cup cranberries
- 1 orange
- 1 cup celery
- ½ cup pecans

DIRECTIONS

1. In a bowl mix all ingredients and mix well
2. Serve with dressing

ARTICHOKE AND WHITE BEAN SALAD

Serves: 2

Prep Time: 5   Minutes

Cook Time: 5   Minutes

Total Time: **10**   Minutes

INGREDIENTS

- 2 cups white beans
- ¼ can artichoke hearts
- ¼ cup red bell pepper
- ¼ cup black olives
- ½ cup red onion
- ¼ cup parsley
- Mint leaves
- ¼ cup olive oil

DIRECTIONS

1. In a bowl combine all ingredients together and mix well
2. Serve with dressing

BEEF STEW

Serves: **4**
Prep Time: **15**   Minutes

Cook Time: **45**   Minutes

Total Time: **60**   Minutes

INGREDIENTS

- 2 lb. beef
- 1 tsp salt
- 4 tablespoons olive oil
- 2 red onions
- 2 cloves garlic
- 1 cup white wine
- 2 cups beef broth
- 1 cup water
- 3-4 bay leaves
- ¼ tsp thyme
- 1 lb. potatoes

DIRECTIONS

1. Chop all ingredients in big chunks
2. In a large pot heat olive oil and add ingredients one by one

3. Cook for 5-6 or until slightly brown
4. Add remaining ingredients and cook until tender, 35-45 minutes
5. Season while stirring on low heat
6. When ready remove from heat and serve

Serves: **4**

Prep Time: **15**   Minutes

Cook Time: **45**   Minutes

Total Time: **60**   Minutes

INGREDIENTS

- 4-5 slices bacon
- 2 lb. beef
- ¼ cup flour
- ½ tsp black pepper
- 4 carrots
- ½ cup beef broth

DIRECTIONS

1. Chop all ingredients in big chunks
2. In a large pot heat olive oil and add ingredients one by one
3. Cook for 5-6 or until slightly brown
4. Add remaining ingredients and cook until tender, 35-45 minutes
5. Season while stirring on low heat
6. When ready remove from heat and serve

CORN CASSEROLE

Serves: **4**

Prep Time: **10**   Minutes

Cook Time: **15**   Minutes

Total Time: **25**   Minutes

INGREDIENTS

- ½ cup cornmeal
- ½ cup butter
- 2 eggs
- 1 cup milk
- ½ cup heavy cream
- 3 cups corn
- ¼ tsp smoked paprika

DIRECTIONS

1. Sauté the veggies and set aside
2. Preheat the oven to 425 F
3. Transfer the sautéed veggies to a baking dish, add remaining ingredients to the baking dish
4. Mix well, add seasoning and place the dish in the oven

5. Bake for 12-15 minutes or until slightly brown
6. When ready remove from the oven and serve

ARTICHOKE CASSEROLE

Serves: **4**

Prep Time: **10** Minutes

Cook Time: **15** Minutes

Total Time: **25** Minutes

INGREDIENTS

- 1 cup cooked rice
- 1 cup milk
- 1 cup parmesan cheese
- 4 oz. cream cheese
- 1 lb. cooked chicken breast
- 1 cup spinach
- 1 can artichoke hearts
- 1 cup mozzarella cheese

DIRECTIONS

1. Sauté the veggies and set aside
2. Preheat the oven to 425 F
3. Transfer the sautéed veggies to a baking dish, add remaining ingredients to the baking dish
4. Mix well, add seasoning and place the dish in the oven
5. Bake for 12-15 minutes or until slightly brown
6. When ready remove from the oven and serve

PIZZA RECIPES

CASSEROLE PIZZA

Serves: **6-8**

Prep Time: **10** Minutes

Cook Time: **15** Minutes

Total Time: **25** Minutes

INGREDIENTS

- 1 pizza crust
- ½ cup tomato sauce
- ¼ black pepper
- 1 cup zucchini slices
- 1 cup mozzarella cheese
- 1 cup olives

DIRECTIONS

1. Spread tomato sauce on the pizza crust
2. Place all the toppings on the pizza crust
3. Bake the pizza at 425 F for 12-15 minutes
4. When ready remove pizza from the oven and serve

Serves:	**4-6**
Prep Time:	**10** Minutes
Cook Time:	**15** Minutes
Total Time:	**25** Minutes

INGREDIENTS

- 2 cups butternut squash
- ¼ tsp salt
- 1 pizza crust
- 5-6 tablespoons alfredo sauce
- 1 tsp olive oil
- 4-5 cups baby spinach
- 2-3 oz. goat cheese

DIRECTIONS

1. Place the pizza crust on a baking dish and spread the alfredo sauce
2. In a skillet sauté spinach and place it over the pizza crust
3. Add goat cheese, butternut squash, olive oil and salt
4. Bake pizza at 425 F for 8-10 minutes
5. When ready remove from the oven and serve

SECOND COOKBOOK

BLUEBERRY PANCAKES

Serves: **4**

Prep Time: **10**   Minutes

Cook Time: **20**   Minutes

Total Time: **30**   Minutes

INGREDIENTS

- 1 cup whole wheat flour
- ¼ tsp baking soda
- ¼ tsp baking powder
- 1 cup blueberries
- 2 eggs
- 1 cup milk

DIRECTIONS

1. In a bowl combine all ingredients together and mix well
2. In a skillet heat olive oil
3. Pour ¼ of the batter and cook each pancake for 1-2 minutes per side
4. When ready remove from heat and serve

PEACH PANCAKES

Serves: *4*

Prep Time: *10*   Minutes

Cook Time: *30*   Minutes

Total Time: *40*   Minutes

INGREDIENTS

- 1 cup whole wheat flour
- ¼ tsp baking soda
- ¼ tsp baking powder
- 1 cup mashed peaches
- 2 eggs
- 1 cup milk

DIRECTIONS

1. In a bowl combine all ingredients together and mix well
2. In a skillet heat olive oil
3. Pour ¼ of the batter and cook each pancake for 1-2 minutes per side
4. When ready remove from heat and serve

BANANA PANCAKES

Serves: *4*

Prep Time: *10*   Minutes

Cook Time: *20*   Minutes

Total Time: *30*   Minutes

INGREDIENTS

- 1 cup whole wheat flour
- ¼ tsp baking soda
- ¼ tsp baking powder
- 1 cup mashed banana
- 2 eggs
- 1 cup milk

DIRECTIONS

1. In a bowl combine all ingredients together and mix well
2. In a skillet heat olive oil
3. Pour ¼ of the batter and cook each pancake for 1-2 minutes per side
4. When ready remove from heat and serve

PLUMS PANCAKES

Serves: *4*

Prep Time: *10*   Minutes

Cook Time: *20*   Minutes

Total Time: *30*   Minutes

INGREDIENTS

- 1 cup whole wheat flour
- ¼ tsp baking soda
- ¼ tsp baking powder
- 1 cup mashed plums
- 2 eggs
- 1 cup milk

DIRECTIONS

1. In a bowl combine all ingredients together and mix well
2. In a skillet heat olive oil
3. Pour ¼ of the batter and cook each pancake for 1-2 minutes per side
4. When ready remove from heat and serve

PANCAKES

Serves: **4**

Prep Time: **10** Minutes

Cook Time: **30** Minutes

Total Time: **40** Minutes

INGREDIENTS

- 1 cup whole wheat flour
- ¼ tsp baking soda
- ¼ tsp baking powder
- 2 eggs
- 1 cup milk

DIRECTIONS

1. In a bowl combine all ingredients together and mix well
2. In a skillet heat olive oil
3. Pour ¼ of the batter and cook each pancake for 1-2 minutes per side
4. When ready remove from heat and serve

MUSHROOM OMELETTE

Serves: **1**

Prep Time: **5**   Minutes

Cook Time: **10**   Minutes

Total Time: **15**   Minutes

INGREDIENTS

- 2 eggs
- ¼ tsp salt
- ¼ tsp black pepper
- 1 tablespoon olive oil
- ¼ cup cheese
- ¼ tsp basil
- 1 cup mushrooms

DIRECTIONS

1. In a bowl combine all ingredients together and mix well
2. In a skillet heat olive oil and pour the egg mixture
3. Cook for 1-2 minutes per side
4. When ready remove omelette from the skillet and serve

OLIVE OMELETTE

Serves: **1**

Prep Time: **5** Minutes

Cook Time: **10** Minutes

Total Time: **15** Minutes

INGREDIENTS

- 2 eggs
- ¼ tsp salt
- ¼ tsp black pepper
- 1 tablespoon olive oil
- ¼ cup cheese
- ½ cup olives
- ¼ tsp basil

DIRECTIONS

1. In a bowl combine all ingredients together and mix well
2. In a skillet heat olive oil and pour the egg mixture
3. Cook for 1-2 minutes per side
4. When ready remove omelette from the skillet and serve

ZUCCHINI OMELETTE

Serves: *1*

Prep Time: *5*   Minutes

Cook Time: *10*   Minutes

Total Time: *15*   Minutes

INGREDIENTS

- 2 eggs
- ¼ tsp salt
- ¼ tsp black pepper
- 1 tablespoon olive oil
- ¼ cup cheese
- ¼ tsp basil
- 1 cup zucchini

DIRECTIONS

1. In a bowl combine all ingredients together and mix well
2. In a skillet heat olive oil and pour the egg mixture
3. Cook for 1-2 minutes per side
4. When ready remove omelette from the skillet and serve

BASIL OMELETTE

Serves: **1**

Prep Time: **5**   Minutes

Cook Time: **10** Minutes

Total Time: **15** Minutes

INGREDIENTS

- 2 eggs
- ¼ tsp salt
- ¼ tsp black pepper
- 1 tablespoon olive oil
- ¼ cup cheese
- ¼ tsp basil
- 1 cup red onion

DIRECTIONS

1. In a bowl combine all ingredients together and mix well
2. In a skillet heat olive oil and pour the egg mixture
3. Cook for 1-2 minutes per side
4. When ready remove omelette from the skillet and serve

MUSHROOM OMELETTE

Serves: **1**

Prep Time: **5**   Minutes

Cook Time: **10**   Minutes

Total Time: **15**   Minutes

INGREDIENTS

- 2 eggs
- ¼ tsp salt
- ¼ tsp black pepper
- 1 tablespoon olive oil
- ¼ cup cheese
- ¼ tsp basil
- 1 cup mushrooms

DIRECTIONS

1. In a bowl combine all ingredients together and mix well
2. In a skillet heat olive oil and pour the egg mixture
3. Cook for 1-2 minutes per side
4. When ready remove omelette from the skillet and serve

CHEESE OMELETTE

Serves: **1**

Prep Time: **5**   Minutes

Cook Time: **10** Minutes

Total Time: **15** Minutes

INGREDIENTS

- 2 eggs
- ¼ tsp salt
- ¼ tsp black pepper
- 1 tablespoon olive oil
- ¼ cup cheese
- ¼ tsp basil
- 1 cup tomatoes

DIRECTIONS

1. In a bowl combine all ingredients together and mix well
2. In a skillet heat olive oil and pour the egg mixture
3. Cook for 1-2 minutes per side
4. When ready remove omelette from the skillet and serve

STRAWBERRIES OATMEAL

Serves: 2
Prep Time: 5   Minutes

Cook Time: 10   Minutes

Total Time: 15   Minutes

INGREDIENTS

- 2 cups oats
- 1 cup strawberries
- 1 tablespoon chia seeds
- 1 banana
- 2 cups almond milk
- 1 tablespoon maple syrup

DIRECTIONS

1. Mash banana and strawberries together, set aside
2. In a saucepan add the rest of the ingredients and bring to a boil
3. Reduce heat and cook for 4-5 minutes
4. When ready transfer to the mashed banana mixture and mix well
5. Serve when ready

BANANA OATMEAL

Serves: *2*

Prep Time: *5*   Minutes

Cook Time: *10*   Minutes

Total Time: *15*   Minutes

INGREDIENTS

- 1 cup oats
- 2 cup almond milk
- 1 tablespoon maple syrup
- 1 banana
- 1 tsp vanilla extract
- ¼ tsp cinnamon
- 1 tablespoon chia seeds

DIRECTIONS

1. Place all ingredients into a saucepan and bring to a boil
2. Simmer for 5-6 minutes
3. When ready remove from heat
4. Transfer to a bowl, top with walnuts and serve

CHERRY-ALMOND OATMEAL

Serves: *1*

Prep Time: *10*   Minutes

Cook Time: *10*   Minutes

Total Time: *20*   Minutes

INGREDIENTS

- ¼ cup gluten free oats
- ¼ cup water
- ¼ cup almond milk
- 1 banana
- 1 tablespoon brown sugar
- ¼ tsp vanilla extract
- ½ cup cherries
- ¼ cup almonds

DIRECTIONS

1. In a saucepan add oats, water, banana, milk and cook for 4-5 minutes
2. When ready remove from heat and add remaining ingredients
3. Mix well and serve

SPINACH SCRAMBLE

Serves: 2

Prep Time: *10*   Minutes

Cook Time: *30*   Minutes

Total Time: *40*   Minutes

INGREDIENTS

- 1 tablespoon olive oil
- 1 onion
- 1 cup spinach
- 1 avocado
- 4 eggs
- 2 cups cheese
- ¼ tsp salt

DIRECTIONS

1. In a skillet sauté onion until soft
2. In a bowl beat the eggs with salt
3. Add remaining ingredients and mix well
4. Place the mixture into a prepare baking dish
5. Bake at 325 F for 25-30 minutes
6. When ready remove from the oven and serve

BREAKFAST MIX

Serves: *1*

Prep Time: 5   Minutes

Cook Time: 5   Minutes

Total Time: *10*   Minutes

INGREDIENTS

- 1 cup corn cereal
- 1 cup rice cereal
- ¼ cup cocoa cereal
- ¼ cup rice cakes

DIRECTIONS

1. In a bowl combine all ingredients together
2. Serve with milk

SAUSAGE BREAKFAST SANDWICH

Serves: 2

Prep Time: 5   Minutes

Cook Time: 15   Minutes

Total Time: 20   Minutes

INGREDIENTS

- ¼ cup egg substitute
- 1 muffin
- 1 turkey sausage patty
- 1 tablespoon cheddar cheese

DIRECTIONS

1. In a skillet pour egg and cook on low heat
2. Place turkey sausage patty in a pan and cook for 4-5 minutes per side
3. On a toasted muffin place the cooked egg, top with a sausage patty and cheddar cheese
4. Serve when ready

BREAKFAST GRANOLA

Serves: 2

Prep Time: 5   Minutes

Cook Time: 30   Minutes

Total Time: 35   Minutes

INGREDIENTS

- 1 tsp vanilla extract
- 1 tablespoon honey
- 1 lb. rolled oats
- 2 tablespoons sesame seeds
- ¼ lb. almonds
- ¼ lb. berries

DIRECTIONS

1. Preheat the oven to 325 F
2. Spread the granola onto a baking sheet
3. Bake for 12-15 minutes, remove and mix everything
4. Bake for another 12-15 minutes or until slightly brown
5. When ready remove from the oven and serve

PANCAKES

BLUEBERRY PANCAKES

Serves: **4**

Prep Time: **10**   Minutes

Cook Time: **20**   Minutes

Total Time: **30**   Minutes

INGREDIENTS

- 1 cup whole wheat flour
- ¼ tsp baking soda
- ¼ tsp baking powder
- 1 cup blueberries
- 2 eggs
- 1 cup milk

DIRECTIONS

1. In a bowl combine all ingredients together and mix well
2. In a skillet heat olive oil
3. Pour ¼ of the batter and cook each pancake for 1-2 minutes per side
4. When ready remove from heat and serve

PEACH PANCAKES

Serves: *4*
Prep Time: *10* Minutes

Cook Time: *30* Minutes

Total Time: *40* Minutes

INGREDIENTS

- 1 cup whole wheat flour
- ¼ tsp baking soda
- ¼ tsp baking powder
- 1 cup mashed peaches
- 2 eggs
- 1 cup milk

DIRECTIONS

1. In a bowl combine all ingredients together and mix well
2. In a skillet heat olive oil
3. Pour ¼ of the batter and cook each pancake for 1-2 minutes per side
4. When ready remove from heat and serve

BANANA PANCAKES

Serves: **4**

Prep Time: **10**   Minutes

Cook Time: **20**   Minutes

Total Time: **30**   Minutes

INGREDIENTS

- 1 cup whole wheat flour
- ¼ tsp baking soda
- ¼ tsp baking powder
- 1 cup mashed banana
- 2 eggs
- 1 cup milk

DIRECTIONS

1. In a bowl combine all ingredients together and mix well
2. In a skillet heat olive oil
3. Pour ¼ of the batter and cook each pancake for 1-2 minutes per side
4. When ready remove from heat and serve

PLUMS PANCAKES

Serves: **4**

Prep Time: **10** Minutes

Cook Time: **20** Minutes

Total Time: **30** Minutes

INGREDIENTS

- 1 cup whole wheat flour
- ¼ tsp baking soda
- ¼ tsp baking powder
- 1 cup mashed plums
- 2 eggs
- 1 cup milk

DIRECTIONS

1. In a bowl combine all ingredients together and mix well
2. In a skillet heat olive oil
3. Pour ¼ of the batter and cook each pancake for 1-2 minutes per side
4. When ready remove from heat and serve

PANCAKES

Serves: *4*

Prep Time: *10*   Minutes

Cook Time: *30*   Minutes

Total Time: *40*   Minutes

INGREDIENTS

- 1 cup whole wheat flour
- ¼ tsp baking soda
- ¼ tsp baking powder
- 2 eggs
- 1 cup milk

DIRECTIONS

1. In a bowl combine all ingredients together and mix well
2. In a skillet heat olive oil
3. Pour ¼ of the batter and cook each pancake for 1-2 minutes per side
4. When ready remove from heat and serve

COOKIES

BREAKFAST COOKIES

Serves: *8-12*

Prep Time: 5   Minutes

Cook Time: *15*   Minutes

Total Time: *20*   Minutes

INGREDIENTS

- 1 cup rolled oats
- ¼ cup applesauce
- ½ tsp vanilla extract
- 3 tablespoons chocolate chips
- 2 tablespoons dried fruits
- 1 tsp cinnamon

DIRECTIONS

1. Preheat the oven to 325 F
2. In a bowl combine all ingredients together and mix well
3. Scoop cookies using an ice cream scoop
4. Place cookies onto a prepared baking sheet
5. Place in the oven for 12-15 minutes or until the cookies are done
6. When ready remove from the oven and serve

CLEMENTINE SMOOTHIE

Serves: *1*

Prep Time: 5   Minutes

Cook Time: 5   Minutes

Total Time: *10*   Minutes

INGREDIENTS

- 4 oz. clementine juice
- 2 oz. oats
- 2 oz. blueberries
- 2 pears
- 1 tablespoon honey
- 1 tsp mixed spice

DIRECTIONS

1. In a blender place all ingredients and blend until smooth
2. Pour smoothie in a glass and serve

AVOCADO SMOOTHIE

Serves: *1*
Prep Time: *5*   Minutes

Cook Time: *5*   Minutes

Total Time: *10*   Minutes

INGREDIENTS

- 1 banana
- 2 tablespoons cacao powder
- 1 tsp coconut oil
- 1 avocado
- 1 tsp vanilla extract
- 2 tablespoons honey
- 1 cup ice

DIRECTIONS

1. In a blender place all ingredients and blend until smooth
2. Pour smoothie in a glass and serve

PEAR SMOOTHIE

Serves: *1*
Prep Time: 5   Minutes

Cook Time: 5   Minutes

Total Time: *10*   Minutes

INGREDIENTS

- 2 pears
- 1 banana
- 1 cup almond milk
- ½ cup vanilla yoghurt
- 1 tsp cinnamon

DIRECTIONS

1. In a blender place all ingredients and blend until smooth
2. Pour smoothie in a glass and serve

Serves: *1*
Prep Time: 5   Minutes

Cook Time: 5   Minutes

Total Time: *10*   Minutes

INGREDIENTS

- 1 banana
- 1 tsp coffee
- 1 tsp cinnamon
- 1 tsp honey
- 1 cup milk

DIRECTIONS

1. In a blender place all ingredients and blend until smooth
2. Pour smoothie in a glass and serve

BANANA SMOOTHIE

Serves: *1*

Prep Time: *5*   Minutes

Cook Time: *5*   Minutes

Total Time: *10*   Minutes

INGREDIENTS

- 2 tablespoons cocoa powder
- 1 cup ice
- 1 banana
- 1 cup skimmed milk

DIRECTIONS

1. In a blender place all ingredients and blend until smooth
2. Pour smoothie in a glass and serve

GREEN SMOOTHIE

Serves: *1*

Prep Time: 5   Minutes

Cook Time: 5   Minutes

Total Time: *10*   Minutes

INGREDIENTS

- 1 banana
- 1 apple
- 1 kiwi
- 2 oz. spinach

DIRECTIONS

1. In a blender place all ingredients and blend until smooth
2. Pour smoothie in a glass and serve

KALE SMOOTHIE

Serves: *1*
Prep Time: 5   Minutes

Cook Time: 5   Minutes

Total Time: *10*   Minutes

INGREDIENTS

- 2 oz. spinach leaves
- 1 cup soy milk
- 1 tablespoon peanut butter
- 1 tablespoon chia seeds
- 1 banana

DIRECTIONS

1. In a blender place all ingredients and blend until smooth
2. Pour smoothie in a glass and serve

GREEN JUICE SMOOTHIE

Serves: **1**

Prep Time: **5**   Minutes

Cook Time: **5**   Minutes

Total Time: **10** Minutes

INGREDIENTS

- 2 apples
- 2 celery sticks
- 1 cucumber
- ½ cup kale leaves
- ¼ lemon

DIRECTIONS

1. In a blender place all ingredients and blend until smooth
2. Pour smoothie in a glass and serve

SPICY SMOOTHIE

Serves: **1**

Prep Time: 5   Minutes

Cook Time: 5   Minutes

Total Time: **10**   Minutes

INGREDIENTS

- 1 banana
- 2 oz. baby spinach
- 1 cup mango
- ¼ tsp jalapeno pepper
- 1 cup water

DIRECTIONS

1. In a blender place all ingredients and blend until smooth
2. Pour smoothie in a glass and serve

COCONUT SMOOTHIE

Serves: *1*

Prep Time: 5   Minutes

Cook Time: 5   Minutes

Total Time: *10* Minutes

INGREDIENTS

- 1 mango
- 1 banana
- 1 cup coconut milk
- 1 cup pineapple chunks
- 2 tablespoons coconut flakes

DIRECTIONS

1. In a blender place all ingredients and blend until smooth
2. Pour smoothie in a glass and serve

MUFFINS

SIMPLE MUFFINS

Serves: **8-12**

Prep Time: **10** Minutes

Cook Time: **20** Minutes

Total Time: **30** Minutes

INGREDIENTS

- 2 eggs
- 1 tablespoon olive oil
- 1 cup milk
- 2 cups whole wheat flour
- 1 tsp baking soda
- ¼ tsp baking soda
- 1 cup pumpkin puree
- 1 tsp cinnamon
- ¼ cup molasses

DIRECTIONS

1. In a bowl combine all wet ingredients
2. In another bowl combine all dry ingredients
3. Combine wet and dry ingredients together
4. Pour mixture into 8-12 prepared muffin cups, fill 2/3 of the cups

5. Bake for 18-20 minutes at 375 F
6. When ready remove from the oven and serve

GINGERBREAD MUFFINS

Serves: *8-12*

Prep Time: *10*   Minutes

Cook Time: *20*   Minutes

Total Time: *30*   Minutes

INGREDIENTS

- 2 eggs
- 1 tablespoon olive oil
- 1 cup milk
- 2 cups whole wheat flour
- 1 tsp baking soda
- ¼ tsp baking soda
- 1 tsp ginger
- 1 tsp cinnamon
- ¼ cup molasses

DIRECTIONS

1. In a bowl combine all wet ingredients
2. In another bowl combine all dry ingredients
3. Combine wet and dry ingredients together
4. Fold in ginger and mix well
5. Pour mixture into 8-12 prepared muffin cups, fill 2/3 of the cups

6. Bake for 18-20 minutes at 375 F
7. When ready remove from the oven and serve

KIWI MUFFINS

Serves: **8-12**
Prep Time: **10**   Minutes

Cook Time: **20**   Minutes

Total Time: **30**   Minutes

INGREDIENTS

- 2 eggs
- 1 tablespoon olive oil
- 1 cup milk
- 2 cups whole wheat flour
- 1 tsp baking soda
- ¼ tsp baking soda
- 1 tsp cinnamon
- 1 cup mashed kiwi

DIRECTIONS

1. In a bowl combine all wet ingredients
2. In another bowl combine all dry ingredients
3. Combine wet and dry ingredients together
4. Pour mixture into 8-12 prepared muffin cups, fill 2/3 of the cups
5. Bake for 18-20 minutes at 375 F
6. When ready remove from the oven and serve

BLUEBERRY MUFFINS

Serves: *8-12*

Prep Time: *10*   Minutes

Cook Time: *20*   Minutes

Total Time: *30*   Minutes

INGREDIENTS

- 2 eggs
- 1 tablespoon olive oil
- 1 cup milk
- 2 cups whole wheat flour
- 1 tsp baking soda
- ¼ tsp baking soda
- 1 tsp cinnamon
- 1 cup blueberries

DIRECTIONS

1. In a bowl combine all wet ingredients
2. In another bowl combine all dry ingredients
3. Combine wet and dry ingredients together
4. Pour mixture into 8-12 prepared muffin cups, fill 2/3 of the cups
5. Bake for 18-20 minutes at 375 F
6. When ready remove from the oven and serve

PLUM MUFFINS

Serves: **8-12**

Prep Time: **10**   Minutes

Cook Time: **20**   Minutes

Total Time: **30**   Minutes

INGREDIENTS

- 2 eggs
- 1 tablespoon olive oil
- 1 cup milk
- 2 cups whole wheat flour
- 1 tsp baking soda
- ¼ tsp baking soda
- 1 tsp cinnamon
- 1 cup mashed plums

DIRECTIONS

1. In a bowl combine all wet ingredients
2. In another bowl combine all dry ingredients
3. Combine wet and dry ingredients together
4. Pour mixture into 8-12 prepared muffin cups, fill 2/3 of the cups
5. Bake for 18-20 minutes at 375 F
6. When ready remove from the oven and serve

CHOCOLATE MUFFINS

Serves: *8-12*

Prep Time: *10*   Minutes

Cook Time: *20*   Minutes

Total Time: *30*   Minutes

INGREDIENTS

- 2 eggs
- 1 tablespoon olive oil
- 1 cup milk
- 2 cups whole wheat flour
- 1 tsp baking soda
- ¼ tsp baking soda
- 1 tsp cinnamon
- 1 cup chocolate chips

DIRECTIONS

1. In a bowl combine all wet ingredients
2. In another bowl combine all dry ingredients
3. Combine wet and dry ingredients together
4. Fold in chocolate chips and mix well
5. Pour mixture into 8-12 prepared muffin cups, fill 2/3 of the cups
6. Bake for 18-20 minutes at 375 F

PRUNES MUFFINS

Serves: *8-12*

Prep Time: *10*   Minutes

Cook Time: *20*   Minutes

Total Time: *30*   Minutes

INGREDIENTS

- 2 eggs
- 1 tablespoon olive oil
- 1 cup milk
- 2 cups whole wheat flour
- 1 tsp baking soda
- 1 cup mashed prunes
- ¼ tsp baking soda
- 1 tsp cinnamon
- 1 cup mashed prunes

DIRECTIONS

1. In a bowl combine all wet ingredients
2. In another bowl combine all dry ingredients
3. Combine wet and dry ingredients together
4. Pour mixture into 8-12 prepared muffin cups, fill 2/3 of the cups
5. Bake for 18-20 minutes at 375 F

THIRD COOKBOOK

CHOCOLATE COCONUT OATS

Serves: *4*

Prep Time: *10* Minutes

Cook Time: *10* Minutes

Total Time: *20* Minutes

INGREDIENTS

- 1 cup oats
- 2 tablespoons chia seeds
- 2 tablespoons maple syrup
- 1 vanilla extract
- 1 tablespoon cocoa powder
- 1 cup water
- 2/3 cup coconut milk
- 2 tablespoons water

DIRECTIONS

1. In a bowl mix oat with water and place it in the fridge overnight
2. In the morning add chia seeds and coconut milk
3. Transfer mixture to a skillet and cook for 5 minutes
4. Remove and move into serving bowl and add vanilla extract, cacao powder and maple syrup

Serves: **4**

Prep Time: **10** Minutes

Cook Time: **10** Minutes

Total Time: **20** Minutes

INGREDIENTS

- 1 cup Quinoa
- ½ cup coconut milk yogurt
- 1 pinch ground cinnamon
- 1 cup Grain Free Muesli

DIRECTIONS

1. Cook the quinoa according to the indications, nd set aside
2. Drizzle the quinoa with coconut milk yogurt and top with grain free muesli
3. Add cinnamon to each bowl and serve

SWEET POTATO

Serves: **4**

Prep Time: **10** Minutes

Cook Time: **30** Minutes

Total Time: **40** Minutes

INGREDIENTS

- 3 sweet potatoes
- 8 tablespoons almond milk
- 1 tablespoon mint leaves
- 1 tablespoon lemon zest
- 1 tablespoon coconut oil
- 1 pinch salt
- 1 pinch ground cinnamon
- 3 tablespoons vanilla cereal

DIRECTIONS

1. Preheat oven to 350 F and line a baking sheet with parchment paper
2. Place the sweet potatoes on the baking sheet
3. Rub the sweet potato with coconut oil and sprinkle salt and pepper
4. Roast for 30 minutes

5. Remove the sweet potatoes from the oven and cut into small pieces
6. Top with coconut oil, lemon zest and cereal mixture

BANANA SPLIT

Serves: 2

Prep Time: *10* Minutes

Cook Time: *10* Minutes

Total Time: *20* Minutes

INGREDIENTS

- 2 bananas
- 1 cup strawberries
- 1 cup blackberries
- 1 cup chopped pineapple
- 1 cup coconut milk
- 1 tablespoon whole grain granola
- ¼ ounce roasted coconut chips

DIRECTIONS

1. Slice the bananas and place them into a bowl
2. Divide the strawberries, blackberries and pineapple and place it in the bottom of the bowl
3. Top with yogurt and divide the granola and coconut chips between the bananas

CHAI-SPICED PEAR OATMEAL

Serves: *2*

Prep Time: *10*   Minutes

Cook Time: *30*   Minutes

Total Time: *40*   Minutes

INGREDIENTS

- 1 cup oats
- ½ tsp ground cinnamon
- 1 tsp maple syrup
- 1 tablespoon walnut halves
- 2 tsp coconut oil
- 1 Anjou pear spiralized with blade
- 1 cup almond milk
- ½ tsp vanilla extract

DIRECTIONS

1. In a saucepan boil water and add oats for another 10 minutes
2. In a skillet heat coconut oil over medium heat and add almond milk, pear noodles, cinnamon, maple syrup and vanilla extract
3. Stir to simmer for about 10-15 minutes
4. In another skillet place walnuts and cook for 5-6 minutes, remove from pan when ready

5. Place the oatmeal in a bowl and top with pear mixture and toasted walnuts

CHOCOLATE BREAD

Serves: **2**

Prep Time: **10** Minutes

Cook Time: **30** Minutes

Total Time: **40** Minutes

INGREDIENTS

- Coconut oil
- 1 cup oat flour
- ½ cup almond flour
- 1 tablespoon flaxseeds
- 5 tablespoons water
- ½ cup almond milk
- 1 tsp baking powder
- 1 tsp baking soda
- 1 tsp vanilla extract
- ½ cup maple syrup
- 1 banana
- ½ cup cocoa powder

DIRECTIONS

1. Preheat oven to 300 F
2. Mix water with flax and water and set aside

3. In a bowl mash the banana and add remaining ingredients
4. Transfer the mixture to a loaf pan and bake for 40 minutes
5. Remove from the oven and let it cool
6. Slice the bread and serve

Serves: **2**

Prep Time: **10**   Minutes

Cook Time: **60**   Minutes

Total Time: **70**   Minutes

INGREDIENTS

- 1 cup hazelnut flour
- 1 peach
- 8 tablespoons water
- 6 tablespoons olive oil
- ¾ tsp salt
- 1 tsp cacao powder
- ½ tsp cinnamon
- 1 cup water
- ¼ tsp ginger
- ½ tablespoons coconut flakes
- 1 cup coconut flour
- 2 tablespoons flaxseeds
- 1 tablespoon cherries

DIRECTIONS

1. Preheat oven to 325 F

2. In a bowl mix water with flaxseeds
3. In another bowl mix all the ingredients, excepting coconut flakes and form a ball
4. Transfer the dough to a baking sheet with parchment paper
5. Sprinkle with coconut flakes and bake for 50 minutes
6. Remove and let it cool before serving

ALMOND BUTTER

Serves: **4**

Prep Time: **10** Minutes

Cook Time: **30** Minutes

Total Time: **40** Minutes

INGREDIENTS

- 1 cup pitted dates
- 2 bananas
- 1 cup almond flour
- 1 cup oats
- 2 tablespoons almond butter
- 2 tablespoons cherries
- 1 tsp sesame seeds

DIRECTIONS

1. In a food processor puree the dates until well combined
2. Add bananas and puree them also
3. Add oats, almond butter, almond flour, and puree until well combined
4. Transfer to the fridge for 25-30 minutes
5. Remove from fridge and add cherries and mix and also sesame seeds

6. Roll into small balls and place them on a baking sheet and bake for 20-25 minutes
7. Remove from oven and let them cool before serving

Serves: *1*

Prep Time: *5*   Minutes

Cook Time: *5*   Minutes

Total Time: *10*   Minutes

INGREDIENTS

- ½ cup dried raisins
- ½ cup dried pecans
- ¼ cup almonds
- 1 cup coconut milk
- 1 tsp cinnamon

DIRECTIONS

3. In a bowl combine all ingredients together
4. Serve with milk

CRANBERRY BREAKFAST MIX

Serves: *1*

Prep Time: 5   Minutes

Cook Time: 5   Minutes

Total Time: *10*   Minutes

INGREDIENTS

- ½ cup cranberries
- ½ cup dried pecans
- ¼ cup oats
- 1 tablespoon corn cereal
- 1 tsp cinnamon

DIRECTIONS

1. In a bowl combine all ingredients together
2. Serve with milk

BREAKFAST MIX

Serves: **1**

Prep Time: **5**   Minutes

Cook Time: **5**   Minutes

Total Time: **10**   Minutes

INGREDIENTS

- 1 cup oats
- 1 cup mix dried fruits
- 1 tsp cinnamon
- 1 cup coconut milk

DIRECTIONS

1. In a bowl combine all ingredients together
2. Serve with milk

ACAI PANCAKES

Serves: **4**

Prep Time: **10** Minutes

Cook Time: **20** Minutes

Total Time: **30** Minutes

INGREDIENTS

- 1 cup whole wheat flour
- ¼ tsp baking soda
- ¼ tsp baking powder
- 1 cup acai
- 2 eggs
- 1 cup milk

DIRECTIONS

1. In a bowl combine all ingredients together and mix well
2. In a skillet heat olive oil
3. Pour ¼ of the batter and cook each pancake for 1-2 minutes per side
4. When ready remove from heat and serve

AKEE PANCAKES

Serves: **4**

Prep Time: **10** Minutes

Cook Time: **30** Minutes

Total Time: **40** Minutes

INGREDIENTS

- 1 cup whole wheat flour
- ¼ tsp baking soda
- ¼ tsp baking powder
- 1 cup akee
- 2 eggs
- 1 cup milk

DIRECTIONS

1. In a bowl combine all ingredients together and mix well
2. In a skillet heat olive oil
3. Pour ¼ of the batter and cook each pancake for 1-2 minutes per side
4. When ready remove from heat and serve

APPLE PANCAKES

Serves: **4**

Prep Time: **10** Minutes

Cook Time: **20** Minutes

Total Time: **30** Minutes

INGREDIENTS

- 1 cup whole wheat flour
- ¼ tsp baking soda
- ¼ tsp baking powder
- 1 cup mashed apple
- 2 eggs
- 1 cup milk

DIRECTIONS

1. In a bowl combine all ingredients together and mix well
2. In a skillet heat olive oil
3. Pour ¼ of the batter and cook each pancake for 1-2 minutes per side
4. When ready remove from heat and serve

AVOCADO PANCAKES

Serves: *4*

Prep Time: *10*   Minutes

Cook Time: *20*   Minutes

Total Time: *30*   Minutes

INGREDIENTS

- 1 cup whole wheat flour
- ¼ tsp baking soda
- ¼ tsp baking powder
- 1 cup avocado
- 2 eggs
- 1 cup milk

DIRECTIONS

1. In a bowl combine all ingredients together and mix well
2. In a skillet heat olive oil
3. Pour ¼ of the batter and cook each pancake for 1-2 minutes per side
4. When ready remove from heat and serve

SIMPLE PANCAKES

Serves: **4**

Prep Time: **10** Minutes

Cook Time: **30** Minutes

Total Time: **40** Minutes

INGREDIENTS

- 1 cup whole wheat flour
- ¼ tsp baking soda
- ¼ tsp baking powder
- 2 eggs
- 1 cup milk

DIRECTIONS

1. In a bowl combine all ingredients together and mix well
2. In a skillet heat olive oil
3. Pour ¼ of the batter and cook each pancake for 1-2 minutes per side
4. When ready remove from heat and serve

GINGERBREAD MUFFINS

Serves: *8-12*

Prep Time: *10*   Minutes

Cook Time: *20*   Minutes

Total Time: *30*   Minutes

INGREDIENTS

- 2 eggs
- 1 tablespoon olive oil
- 1 cup milk
- 2 cups whole wheat flour
- 1 tsp baking soda
- ¼ tsp baking soda
- 1 tsp ginger
- 1 tsp cinnamon
- ¼ cup molasses

DIRECTIONS

1. In a bowl combine all wet ingredients
2. In another bowl combine all dry ingredients
3. Combine wet and dry ingredients together
4. Pour mixture into 8-12 prepared muffin cups, fill 2/3 of the cups
5. Bake for 18-20 minutes at 375 F, when ready remove and serve

BLACKBERRY MUFFINS

Serves: *8-12*

Prep Time: *10*   Minutes

Cook Time: *20*   Minutes

Total Time: *30*   Minutes

INGREDIENTS

- 2 eggs
- 1 tablespoon olive oil
- 1 cup milk
- 2 cups whole wheat flour
- 1 tsp baking soda
- ¼ tsp baking soda
- 1 tsp cinnamon
- 1 cup blackberry

DIRECTIONS

1. In a bowl combine all wet ingredients
2. In another bowl combine all dry ingredients
3. Combine wet and dry ingredients together
4. Pour mixture into 8-12 prepared muffin cups, fill 2/3 of the cups
5. Bake for 18-20 minutes at 375 F
6. When ready remove from the oven and serve

CHERRY MUFFINS

Serves: *8-12*

Prep Time: *10*   Minutes

Cook Time: *20*   Minutes

Total Time: *30*   Minutes

INGREDIENTS

- 2 eggs
- 1 tablespoon olive oil
- 1 cup milk
- 2 cups whole wheat flour
- 1 tsp baking soda
- ¼ tsp baking soda
- 1 tsp cinnamon
- 1 cup cherries

DIRECTIONS

1. In a bowl combine all wet ingredients
2. In another bowl combine all dry ingredients
3. Combine wet and dry ingredients together
4. Pour mixture into 8-12 prepared muffin cups, fill 2/3 of the cups
5. Bake for 18-20 minutes at 375 F
6. When ready remove from the oven and serve

COCONUT MUFFINS

Serves: *8-12*

Prep Time: *10*   Minutes

Cook Time: *20*   Minutes

Total Time: *30*   Minutes

INGREDIENTS

- 2 eggs
- 1 tablespoon olive oil
- 1 cup milk
- 2 cups whole wheat flour
- 1 tsp baking soda
- ¼ tsp baking soda
- 1 tsp cinnamon
- 1 cup coconut flakes

DIRECTIONS

1. In a bowl combine all wet ingredients
2. In another bowl combine all dry ingredients
3. Combine wet and dry ingredients together
4. Pour mixture into 8-12 prepared muffin cups, fill 2/3 of the cups
5. Bake for 18-20 minutes at 375 F
6. When ready remove from the oven and serve

CHOCOLATE MUFFINS

Serves:	*8-12*	
Prep Time:	*10*	Minutes
Cook Time:	*20*	Minutes
Total Time:	*30*	Minutes

INGREDIENTS

- 2 eggs
- 1 tablespoon olive oil
- 1 cup milk
- 2 cups whole wheat flour
- 1 tsp baking soda
- ¼ tsp baking soda
- 1 tsp cinnamon
- 1 cup chocolate chips

DIRECTIONS

1. In a bowl combine all wet ingredients
2. In another bowl combine all dry ingredients
3. Combine wet and dry ingredients together
4. Pour mixture into 8-12 prepared muffin cups, fill 2/3 of the cups
5. Bake for 18-20 minutes at 375 F
6. When ready remove from the oven and serve

RAISIN MUFFINS

Serves: *8-12*

Prep Time: *10*   Minutes

Cook Time: *20*   Minutes

Total Time: *30*   Minutes

INGREDIENTS

- 2 eggs
- 1 tablespoon olive oil
- 1 cup milk
- 2 cups whole wheat flour
- 1 tsp baking soda
- ¼ tsp baking soda
- 1 tsp cinnamon
- 1 cup dates

DIRECTIONS

1. In a bowl combine all wet ingredients
2. In another bowl combine all dry ingredients
3. Combine wet and dry ingredients together
4. Pour mixture into 8-12 prepared muffin cups, fill 2/3 of the cups
5. Bake for 18-20 minutes at 375 F
6. When ready remove from the oven and serve

SIMPLE OMELETTE

Serves: **1**
Prep Time: **5**   Minutes

Cook Time: **10** Minutes

Total Time: **15** Minutes

INGREDIENTS

- 2 eggs
- ¼ tsp salt
- ¼ tsp black pepper
- 1 tablespoon olive oil
- ¼ cup cheese
- ¼ tsp basil

DIRECTIONS

1. In a bowl combine all ingredients together and mix well
2. In a skillet heat olive oil and pour the egg mixture
3. Cook for 1-2 minutes per side
4. When ready remove omelette from the skillet and serve

ASPARAGUS OMELETTE

Serves: *1*

Prep Time: 5   Minutes

Cook Time: *10*   Minutes

Total Time: *15*   Minutes

INGREDIENTS

- 2 eggs
- ¼ tsp salt
- ¼ tsp black pepper
- 1 tablespoon olive oil
- ¼ cup cheese
- ¼ tsp basil
- 1 cup asparagus

DIRECTIONS

1. In a bowl combine all ingredients together and mix well
2. In a skillet heat olive oil and pour the egg mixture
3. Cook for 1-2 minutes per side
4. When ready remove omelette from the skillet and serve

BLACK BEANS OMELETTE

Serves: *1*

Prep Time: *5* Minutes

Cook Time: *10* Minutes

Total Time: *15* Minutes

INGREDIENTS

- 2 eggs
- ¼ tsp salt
- ¼ tsp black pepper
- 1 tablespoon olive oil
- ¼ cup cheese
- ¼ tsp basil
- 1 cup red onion
- 1 cup black beans

DIRECTIONS

1. In a bowl combine all ingredients together and mix well
2. In a skillet heat olive oil and pour the egg mixture
3. Cook for 1-2 minutes per side
4. When ready remove omelette from the skillet and serve

LENTIL OMELETTE

Serves: *1*
Prep Time: 5   Minutes

Cook Time: *10* Minutes

Total Time: *15* Minutes

INGREDIENTS

- 2 eggs
- ¼ tsp salt
- ¼ tsp black pepper
- 1 tablespoon olive oil
- ¼ cup cheese
- ¼ tsp basil
- 1 cup lentils

DIRECTIONS

1. In a bowl combine all ingredients together and mix well
2. In a skillet heat olive oil and pour the egg mixture
3. Cook for 1-2 minutes per side
4. When ready remove omelette from the skillet and serve

ENDIVE OMELETTE

Serves: **1**

Prep Time: **5** Minutes

Cook Time: **10** Minutes

Total Time: **15** Minutes

INGREDIENTS

- 2 eggs
- ¼ tsp salt
- ¼ tsp black pepper
- 1 tablespoon olive oil
- ¼ cup cheese
- ¼ tsp basil
- 1 cup endive

DIRECTIONS

1. In a bowl combine all ingredients together and mix well
2. In a skillet heat olive oil and pour the egg mixture
3. Cook for 1-2 minutes per side
4. When ready remove omelette from the skillet and serve

PEAR TART

Serves: **6-8**

Prep Time: **25**   Minutes

Cook Time: **25**   Minutes

Total Time: **50**   Minutes

INGREDIENTS

- 1 lb. pears
- 2 oz. brown sugar
- ½ lb. flaked almonds
- ¼ lb. porridge oat
- 2 oz. flour
- ¼ lb. almonds
- pastry sheets
- 2 tablespoons syrup

DIRECTIONS

1. Preheat oven to 400 F, unfold pastry sheets and place them on a baking sheet
2. Toss together all ingredients together and mix well
3. Spread mixture in a single layer on the pastry sheets
4. Before baking decorate with your desired fruits

5. Bake at 400 F for 22-25 minutes or until golden brown
6. When ready remove from the oven and serve

CARDAMOM TART

Serves: *6-8*

Prep Time: *25*   Minutes

Cook Time: *25*   Minutes

Total Time: *50*   Minutes

INGREDIENTS

- 4-5 pears
- 2 tablespoons lemon juice
- pastry sheets

CARDAMOMO FILLING

- ½ lb. butter
- ½ lb. brown sugar
- ½ lb. almonds
- ¼ lb. flour
- 1 ¼ tsp cardamom
- 2 eggs

DIRECTIONS

1. Preheat oven to 400 F, unfold pastry sheets and place them on a baking sheet
2. Toss together all ingredients together and mix well
3. Spread mixture in a single layer on the pastry sheets
4. Before baking decorate with your desired fruits

5. Bake at 400 F for 22-25 minutes or until golden brown
6. When ready remove from the oven and serve

PEACH PECAN PIE

Serves: **8-12**

Prep Time: **15**   Minutes

Cook Time: **35**   Minutes

Total Time: **50**   Minutes

INGREDIENTS

- 4-5 cups peaches
- 1 tablespoon preserves
- 1 cup sugar
- 4 small egg yolks
- ¼ cup flour
- 1 tsp vanilla extract

DIRECTIONS

1. Line a pie plate or pie form with pastry and cover the edges of the plate depending on your preference
2. In a bowl combine all pie ingredients together and mix well
3. Pour the mixture over the pastry
4. Bake at 400-425 F for 25-30 minutes or until golden brown
5. When ready remove from the oven and let it rest for 15 minutes

BUTTERFINGER PIE

Serves: *8-12*

Prep Time: *15*   Minutes

Cook Time: *35*   Minutes

Total Time: *50*   Minutes

INGREDIENTS

- pastry sheets
- 1 package cream cheese
- 1 tsp vanilla extract
- ¼ cup peanut butter
- 1 cup powdered sugar (to decorate)
- 2 cups Butterfinger candy bars
- 8 oz whipped topping

DIRECTIONS

1. Line a pie plate or pie form with pastry and cover the edges of the plate depending on your preference
2. In a bowl combine all pie ingredients together and mix well
3. Pour the mixture over the pastry
4. Bake at 400-425 F for 25-30 minutes or until golden brown
5. When ready remove from the oven and let it rest for 15 minutes

STRAWBERRY PIE

Serves: *8-12*

Prep Time: *15*   Minutes

Cook Time: *35*   Minutes

Total Time: *50*   Minutes

INGREDIENTS

- pastry sheets
- 1,5 lb. strawberries
- 1 cup powdered sugar
- 2 tablespoons cornstarch
- 1 tablespoon lime juice
- 1 tsp vanilla extract
- 2 eggs
- 2 tablespoons butter

DIRECTIONS

1. Line a pie plate or pie form with pastry and cover the edges of the plate depending on your preference
2. In a bowl combine all pie ingredients together and mix well
3. Pour the mixture over the pastry
4. Bake at 400-425 F for 25-30 minutes or until golden brown
5. When ready remove from the oven and let it rest for 15 minutes

APPLE-GINGER SMOOTHIE

Serves: **1**

Prep Time: **5** Minutes

Cook Time: **5** Minutes

Total Time: **10** Minutes

INGREDIENTS

- 1 apple
- 1 cup almond milk
- 1 cup kale
- 1 tsp ginger

DIRECTIONS

1. In a blender place all ingredients and blend until smooth
2. Pour smoothie in a glass and serve

POMEGRANATE SMOOTHIE

Serves: *1*

Prep Time: 5   Minutes

Cook Time: 5   Minutes

Total Time: *10*   Minutes

INGREDIENTS

- 1 cucumber
- 1 pomegranate
- 1 cup ice
- 1 cup almond milk

DIRECTIONS

1. In a blender place all ingredients and blend until smooth
2. Pour smoothie in a glass and serve

Serves: **1**

Prep Time: **5**   Minutes

Cook Time: **5**   Minutes

Total Time: **10**   Minutes

INGREDIENTS

- 1 mango
- 1 cup strawberries
- 1 cup coconut milk
- 1 cup ice

DIRECTIONS

1. In a blender place all ingredients and blend until smooth
2. Pour smoothie in a glass and serve

CARAMEL SMOOTHIE

Serves: *1*

Prep Time: 5   Minutes

Cook Time: 5   Minutes

Total Time: *10*   Minutes

INGREDIENTS

- 1 cup caramel powder
- 1 cup almond milk
- 1 tsp cinnamon

DIRECTIONS

1. In a blender place all ingredients and blend until smooth
2. Pour smoothie in a glass and serve

BASIL SMOOTHIE

Serves: *1*

Prep Time: 5 Minutes

Cook Time: 5 Minutes

Total Time: *10* Minutes

INGREDIENTS

- 1 cup blueberries
- 1 cup water
- 2 basil leaves
- ½ cup coconut milk
- 1 tablespoon peanut butter

DIRECTIONS

1. In a blender place all ingredients and blend until smooth
2. Pour smoothie in a glass and serve

PROTEIN SMOOTHIE

Serves: *1*
Prep Time: *5*   Minutes

Cook Time: *5*   Minutes

Total Time: *10* Minutes

INGREDIENTS

- 1 cup blueberries
- 1 cup cauliflower
- 1 cup vanilla yoghurt
- 1 cup protein powder

DIRECTIONS

1. In a blender place all ingredients and blend until smooth
2. Pour smoothie in a glass and serve

Serves: *1*

Prep Time: *5*   Minutes

Cook Time: *5*   Minutes

Total Time: *10*   Minutes

INGREDIENTS

- 1 nectarine
- 2 oz. cauliflower
- 2 oz. swiss chard
- 1 tablespoon almond butter

DIRECTIONS

1. In a blender place all ingredients and blend until smooth
2. Pour smoothie in a glass and serve

PISTACHIOS ICE-CREAM

Serves: **6-8**

Prep Time: **15** Minutes

Cook Time: **15** Minutes

Total Time: **30** Minutes

INGREDIENTS

- 4 egg yolks
- 1 cup heavy cream
- 1 cup milk
- 1 cup sugar
- 1 vanilla bean
- 1 tsp almond extract
- 1 cup cherries
- ½ cup pistachios

DIRECTIONS

1. In a saucepan whisk together all ingredients
2. Mix until bubbly
3. Strain into a bowl and cool
4. Whisk in favorite fruits and mix well
5. Cover and refrigerate for 2-3 hours

6. Pour mixture in the ice-cream maker and follow manufacturer instructions
7. Serve when ready

VANILLA ICE-CREAM

Serves: *6-8*

Prep Time: *15*   Minutes

Cook Time: *15*   Minutes

Total Time: *30*   Minutes

INGREDIENTS

- 1 cup milk
- 1 tablespoon cornstarch
- 1 oz. cream cheese
- 1 cup heavy cream
- 1 cup brown sugar
- 1 tablespoon corn syrup
- 1 vanilla bean

DIRECTIONS

1. In a saucepan whisk together all ingredients
2. Mix until bubbly
3. Strain into a bowl and cool
4. Whisk in favorite fruits and mix well
5. Cover and refrigerate for 2-3 hours
6. Pour mixture in the ice-cream maker and follow manufacturer instructions
7. Serve when ready

FOURTH COOKBOOK

SIDE DISHES

QUINOA FALAFEL

Serves: **6-8**

Prep Time: **15**   Minutes

Cook Time: **25**   Minutes

Total Time: **40**   Minutes

INGREDIENTS

- 2 cups cooked quinoa
- 2 cups chickpeas
- 1 onion
- 1 tablespoon tahini
- 4 garlic cloves
- 1 cup parsley
- 2 tsp cumin
- 1 tsp coriander
- 2 tablespoons olive oil
- 1 tablespoon lemon juice

TAHINI SAUCE

- 1 cup water
- 1 cup tahini
- 1 garlic clove
- pinch of salt

DIRECTIONS

1. In a blender add garlic, parsley, coriander, lemon juice, onion and blend until smooth

2. Add the remaining ingredients and blend again

3. Form patties and freeze patties for 15-20 minutes

4. In a frying pan place the patties and fry until golden brown

5. When ready transfer patties to a plate and serve with tahini sauce

VEGAN RAMEN

Serves: **6**

Prep Time: **10** Minutes

Cook Time: **20** Minutes

Total Time: **30** Minutes

INGREDIENTS

- 4 cups vegetable broth
- 2 tablespoon soy sauce
- 2 clove garlic
- 1 tsp miso paste
- 1 cup mushrooms
- 1 cup tofu
- 1 cup broccoli florets
- 1 cup ramen noodles
- 1 cup sprouts
- ½ red onion
- ¼ cup cilantro
- 1 tablespoon sesame seeds

DIRECTIONS

1. In a pan sauté garlic, onion and set aside
2. In a pot add broth and sautéed onion, garlic and stir in miso paste

3. Transfer everything to a blender and blend until smooth
4. Add salt soy sauce and blend again
5. In a pan fry mushrooms, noodles, broccoli, sprouts, and tofu
6. Stir in broth and sesame seeds
7. When ready serve fried vegetables with the garlic mixture

ROASTED CAULIFLOWER

Serves: 2

Prep Time: *10* Minutes

Cook Time: *30* Minutes

Total Time: *40* Minutes

INGREDIENTS

- 1 cauliflower head

BBQ SAUCE

- ¼ cup tomato sauce
- 1 tsp garam masala
- 1 tablespoon peanut butter
- 1 tsp olive oil
- 1 tsp Worchester sauce
- 1 tsp soy sauce
- 1 clove garlic
- 1 black pepper

DIRECTIONS

1. In a bowl combine all ingredients for the sauce and whisk well
2. Place the cauliflower in a baking dish and bake for 20-25 minutes at 225 F or until brown
3. When ready remove from the oven and serve with bbq sauce

GARLIC TOFU

Serves: *4*

Prep Time: *10*   Minutes

Cook Time: *20*   Minutes

Total Time: *30*   Minutes

INGREDIENTS

- 1 cup tofu
- 1 cup cooked brown rice
- 1 tablespoon chives
- 1 tablespoon olive oil
- 1 tsp vegan butter
- ¼ cup hoisin sauce
- 1 tablespoon soy sauce
- 2 cloves garlic
- 1 tsp sesame seeds

DIRECTIONS

1. In a bowl combine hoisin sauce, garlic and mix well
2. Add tofu, toss well and refrigerate overnight
3. In a skillet heat olive oil and add tofu and spread on a single layer
4. Add remaining ingredients, sprinkle sesame seeds and cook until browned

5. When ready remove from the pan and serve with brown rice

BUDDHA BOWL

Serves: **4**

Prep Time: **10** Minutes

Cook Time: **30** Minutes

Total Time: **40** Minutes

INGREDIENTS

- 1 cup buckwheat

DRESSING

- 1 tablespoon nutritional yeast
- 1 tsp mustard
- salt
- 1 clove garlic

DIRECTIONS

1. Place the buckwheat into a bowl and add 1-2 cups of water
2. In a blender all the ingredients for the dressing and blend until smooth
3. Divide the buckwheat between 2-3 plates and serve with dressing
4. Add toppings like tomatoes, bell pepper or radish sprouts

VEGAN RICE BACON

Serves: **4**

Prep Time: **10** Minutes

Cook Time: **30** Minutes

Total Time: **40** Minutes

INGREDIENTS

- 2 rice paper sheets
- 1 tablespoon water
- 1 tablespoon olive oil
- 1 tablespoon soy sauce
- ¼ tsp onion powder
- ¼ tsp cumin powder
- 1 tsp tomato sauce
- 1 tsp agave syrup

DIRECTIONS

1. In a bowl combine all ingredients together excepting the rice paper
2. Dip the rice paper into a large plate with water
3. Cut the paper into strips and lay the strips onto a baking tray
4. Brush with sauce from the blender and bake for 10-12 minutes at 300 F
5. When ready remove from the oven and serve

FALAFEL BITES

Serves: **12**

Prep Time: **5**   Minutes

Cook Time: **15**   Minutes

Total Time: **20**   Minutes

INGREDIENTS

- 1 cup chickpeas
- 1 onion
- ¼ cup parsley
- 2 cloves garlic
- 1 tsp baking soda
- 1 tablespoon flour
- 1 tsp cumin
- ¼ tsp coriander

DIRECTIONS

1. In a blender add all the ingredients and blend until smooth
2. In a pan heat olive oil and form small patties
3. Cook each falafel until crispy
4. When ready remove and serve

ZUCCHINI FRIES

Serves: *6*

Prep Time: *10*   Minutes

Cook Time: *20*   Minutes

Total Time: *30*   Minutes

INGREDIENTS

- 2 zucchinis
- ¼ cup breadcrumbs
- ¼ cup vegan cheese
- olive oil
- tahini
- pesto
- ketchup

DIRECTIONS

1. Cut zucchinis into thin strips
2. In a bowl add vegan cheese, breadcrumbs, salt and mix well
3. Dip each zucchini strip into the mixture
4. Place the strips onto a parchment paper
5. Bake for 18-20 minutes at 350 F
6. When ready remove from the oven and serve

ZUCCHINI DAL

Serves: 2

Prep Time: 5   Minutes

Cook Time: 20   Minutes

Total Time: 25   Minutes

INGREDIENTS

- 2 cups water
- ½ cup red lentils
- 1 zucchini
- 1 onion
- 2 tablespoons curry powder
- 1 tablespoon olive oil
- salt

DIRECTIONS

1. In a pot add zucchini, onion, pepper and sauté for 5-6 minutes
2. Ad lentils, water and the remaining ingredients
3. Cook on low heat for 15-18 minutes
4. When ready from heat, add scallions and serve

CHICKPEA PATTIES

Serves: **12**

Prep Time: **5** Minutes

Cook Time: **15** Minutes

Total Time: **20** Minutes

INGREDIENTS

- 2 lb. chickpeas
- ¼ cup parsley
- ½ red onion
- 2 tablespoons yeast flakes
- 2 tablespoons rosemary leaves
- olive oil

DIRECTIONS

1. Place chickpea in a blender and blend until smooth
2. Add remaining ingredients and blend again
3. Remove the mixture from the blender and form small patties

ONION SOUP

Serves: **4**

Prep Time: **10**   Minutes

Cook Time: **20**   Minutes

Total Time: **30**   Minutes

INGREDIENTS

- 6 spring onions
- ½ red onion
- 1 potato
- 1 tablespoon olive oil
- Salt
- ¼ tsp coriander

DIRECTIONS

1. In a pot place the potatoes, water and boil until the potatoes are soft
2. In another pot heat olive oil and sauté spring onions and onion until soft
3. Add boiled potatoes to the pot where are the sauté onions
4. Add coriander, salt, pepper and stir well
5. Blend the soup until the soup is creamy
6. When ready pour into bowls and serve

ZUCCHINI SOUP

Serves: **6**

Prep Time: **10** Minutes

Cook Time: **25** Minutes

Total Time: **35** Minutes

INGREDIENTS

- 1 onion
- 1 tsp olive oil
- 1 zucchini
- 1 cup corn
- 1 cup broth
- 1 cup soy yogurt
- 1 tsp red pepper flakes
- 1 tablespoon cilantro
- 1 tablespoon parmesan

DIRECTIONS

1. In a skillet sauté onion until soft
2. Add zucchinis, corn and sauté for 5-6 minutes
3. Stir in water, vegetable broth, black pepper and salt
4. Bring everything to a boil and cook for 8-10 minutes
5. Add soy yogurt, cilantro, red pepper flakes and cook for another 5-6 minutes

SAUERKRAUT SOUP

Serves: **4**

Prep Time: **10**   Minutes

Cook Time: **30**   Minutes

Total Time: **40**   Minutes

INGREDIENTS

- 2 celery sticks
- 1 onion
- 2 carrots
- 2 potatoes
- 1 cup mushrooms
- 1 cup sauerkraut
- 6 cups vegetable broth
- 1 tablespoon olive oil
- 1 cup tofu
- 1 bay leaf

DIRECTIONS

1. In a pot heat olive oil and add tofu
2. Cook until crispy and set aside
3. Sauté onion and mushrooms for 2-3 minutes
4. Add vegetable broth and the rest of the ingredients

5. Bring everything to a boil and simmer on low heat for 18-20 minutes

6. When the soup is ready remove the bay leaf and transfer soup to a blender

7. Blend until smooth and serve with tofu slices on top

Serves: **6**

Prep Time: **10**   Minutes

Cook Time: **35**   Minutes

Total Time: **45**   Minutes

INGREDIENTS

- 1 onion
- 1 carrot
- 1 cup celery
- 4 cups vegetable broth
- ¼ cup rice
- ½ cup tofu
- 1 tablespoon dill
- 1 lemon

EGG MIXTURE

- 1 cup coconut milk
- 1 cup tofu
- 2 tablespoons lemon juice
- 1 tsp salt
- 1 tsp black pepper
- 1 tsp nutritional yeast

DIRECTIONS

1. In a pot heat olive oil and add carrots, celery, onion and sauté until vegetables are soft

2. Add rice, vegetable broth and cook until the rice absorbs the liquid

3. In a blender add the ingredients for the egg mixture and blend until smooth

4. Pour the egg mixture into the soup and stir well

5. Add tofu, dill and any remaining ingredients to the soup

6. Cover and cook until the soup is ready

SALMON PIZZA

Serves: **6-8**
Prep Time: **10**   Minutes

Cook Time: **15**   Minutes

Total Time: **25**   Minutes

INGREDIENTS

- 1 pizza crust
- 1 shallot
- 1 parmesan cheese
- ½ red onion
- 2 tablespoons olive oil
- ½ lb. smoked salmon
- ½ lemon

DIRECTIONS

1. Spread tomato sauce on the pizza crust
2. Place all the toppings on the pizza crust
3. Bake the pizza at 425 F for 12-15 minutes
4. When ready remove pizza from the oven and serve

GREEN OLIVE PIZZA

Serves: **6-8**

Prep Time: **10** Minutes

Cook Time: **15** Minutes

Total Time: **25** Minutes

INGREDIENTS

- 1 onion
- 1 pizza crust
- 1 cup green olives
- 1 clove garlic
- ½ lb. potatoes
- ½ lb. taleggio

DIRECTIONS

1. Spread tomato sauce on the pizza crust
2. Place all the toppings on the pizza crust
3. Bake the pizza at 425 F for 12-15 minutes
4. When ready remove pizza from the oven and serve

CAULIFLOWER PIZZA

Serves: *6-8*
Prep Time: *10*   Minutes

Cook Time: *15*   Minutes

Total Time: *25*   Minutes

INGREDIENTS

- 1 pizza crust
- 2 oz. parmesan cheese
- 1 tablespoon olive oil
- 4-5 basil leaves
- 1 cup mozzarella cheese
- 1 cup cauliflower

DIRECTIONS

1. Spread tomato sauce on the pizza crust
2. Place all the toppings on the pizza crust
3. Bake the pizza at 425 F for 12-15 minutes
4. When ready remove pizza from the oven and serve

ARTICHOKE AND SPINACH PIZZA

Serves: **6-8**

Prep Time: **10**   Minutes

Cook Time: **15**   Minutes

Total Time: **25**   Minutes

INGREDIENTS

- 1 pizza crust
- 1 garlic clove
- ½ lb. spinach
- ½ lb. soft cheese
- 2 oz. artichoke hearts
- 1 cup mozzarella cheese
- 1 tablespoon olive oil

DIRECTIONS

1. Spread tomato sauce on the pizza crust
2. Place all the toppings on the pizza crust
3. Bake the pizza at 425 F for 12-15 minutes
4. When ready remove pizza from the oven and serve

BEANS FRITATTA

Serves: **2**
Prep Time: **10** Minutes

Cook Time: **20** Minutes

Total Time: **30** Minutes

INGREDIENTS

- ½ lb. black beans
- 1 tablespoon olive oil
- ½ red onion
- ¼ tsp salt
- 2 eggs
- 2 oz. cheddar cheese
- 1 garlic clove
- ¼ tsp dill

DIRECTIONS

1. In a bowl whisk eggs with salt and cheese
2. In a frying pan heat olive oil and pour egg mixture
3. Add remaining ingredients and mix well
4. Serve when ready

SPINACH FRITATTA

Serves: *2*

Prep Time: *10* Minutes

Cook Time: *20* Minutes

Total Time: *30* Minutes

INGREDIENTS

- ½ lb. spinach
- 1 tablespoon olive oil
- ½ red onion
- ¼ tsp salt
- 2 eggs
- 2 oz. cheddar cheese
- 1 garlic clove
- ¼ tsp dill

DIRECTIONS

1. In a bowl whisk eggs with salt and cheese
2. In a frying pan heat olive oil and pour egg mixture
3. Add remaining ingredients and mix well
4. Serve when ready

Serves: **2**

Prep Time: **10** Minutes

Cook Time: **20** Minutes

Total Time: **30** Minutes

INGREDIENTS

- 1 cup Asian greens
- 1 tablespoon olive oil
- ½ red onion
- ¼ tsp salt
- 2 eggs
- 2 oz. cheddar cheese
- 1 garlic clove
- ¼ tsp dill

DIRECTIONS

1. In a bowl whisk eggs with salt and cheese
2. In a frying pan heat olive oil and pour egg mixture
3. Add remaining ingredients and mix well
4. Serve when ready

SALAMI FRITATTA

Serves: **2**

Prep Time: **10** Minutes

Cook Time: **20** Minutes

Total Time: **30** Minutes

INGREDIENTS

- 8-10 slices salami
- 1 tablespoon olive oil
- ½ red onion
- ¼ tsp salt
- 2 eggs
- 2 oz. parmesan cheese
- 1 garlic clove
- ¼ tsp dill

DIRECTIONS

1. In a bowl whisk eggs with salt and parmesan cheese
2. In a frying pan heat olive oil and pour egg mixture
3. Add remaining ingredients and mix well
4. When salami and eggs are cooked remove from heat and serve

BROCCOLI FRITATTA

Serves: **2**

Prep Time: **10** Minutes

Cook Time: **20** Minutes

Total Time: **30** Minutes

INGREDIENTS

- 1 cup broccoli
- 2 eggs
- 1 tablespoon olive oil
- ½ red onion
- ¼ tsp salt
- 2 oz. cheddar cheese
- 1 garlic clove
- ¼ tsp dill

DIRECTIONS

1. In a bowl whisk eggs with salt and cheese
2. In a frying pan heat olive oil and pour egg mixture
3. Add remaining ingredients and mix well
4. Serve when ready

VEGETARIAN CARBONARA

Serves: *2*

Prep Time: *10*   Minutes

Cook Time: *20*   Minutes

Total Time: *30*   Minutes

INGREDIENTS

- ¼ cup olive oil
- 1 tablespoon Worcestershire sauce
- 1 garlic clove
- 15 oz. spaghetti
- 1 cup water
- 2 eggs
- 1 tsp salt
- ½ cup parmesan cheese

DIRECTIONS

1. In a pot boil spaghetti until al dente
2. In another bowl whisk eggs with salt
3. Whisk ¼ cup pasta with egg mixture, garlic and pour a Dutch oven
4. When ready remove to a plate, add parmesan cheese and serve

KALE & QUINOA BOWL

Serves: *2*

Prep Time: *10* Minutes

Cook Time: *20* Minutes

Total Time: *30* Minutes

INGREDIENTS

- 1 cup cooked quinoa
- 1 bunch kale
- 2 tablespoons olive oil
- 1 cup tomatoes
- Juice from ½ lemon
- ¼ cup parmesan cheese

DIRECTIONS

1. Set cooked quinoa aside
2. In a pan heat olive oil and add kale
3. Add water and cook until tender
4. Place the cooked kale in a bowl
5. Add quinoa, tomatoes and lemon juice
6. Top with parmesan cheese and serve

AVOCADO TOAST

Serves: *1*

Prep Time: 5   Minutes

Cook Time: 5   Minutes

Total Time: *10*   Minutes

INGREDIENTS

- 2 slices gluten free toast
- 1 avocado
- 1 cup smoked salmon
- 6-8 basil leaves
- ¼ tsp salt

DIRECTIONS

1. Top bread with avocado and salmon
2. Add basil leaves, salt and top with another bread slice
3. Serve when ready

Serves: **2**
Prep Time: **10** Minutes

Cook Time: **10** Minutes

Total Time: **20** Minutes

INGREDIENTS

- 1 tablespoon butter
- 4 slices bread
- 6 oz. brie cheese
- 2 figs

DIRECTIONS

1. In a pan heat olive oil
2. Divide the figs and cheese between 2 bread slices
3. Top with the other bread slices
4. Place in the pan and cover with a lid
5. Cook for 3-4 minutes per side on low heat
6. When ready remove from heat and serve

ROASTED SQUASH

Serves: **3-4**

Prep Time: **10** Minutes

Cook Time: **20** Minutes

Total Time: **30** Minutes

INGREDIENTS

- 2 delicata squashes
- 2 tablespoons olive oil
- 1 tsp curry powder
- 1 tsp salt

DIRECTIONS

1. Preheat the oven to 400 F
2. Cut everything in half lengthwise
3. Toss everything with olive oil and place onto a prepared baking sheet
4. Roast for 18-20 minutes at 400 F or until golden brown
5. When ready remove from the oven and serve

BRUSSELS SPROUT CHIPS

Serves: 2
Prep Time: *10*   Minutes

Cook Time: *20*   Minutes

Total Time: *30*   Minutes

INGREDIENTS

- 1 lb. brussels sprouts
- 1 tablespoon olive oil
- 1 tablespoon parmesan cheese
- 1 tsp garlic powder
- 1 tsp seasoning

DIRECTIONS

1. Preheat the oven to 425 F
2. In a bowl toss everything with olive oil and seasoning
3. Spread everything onto a prepared baking sheet
4. Bake for 8-10 minutes or until crisp
5. When ready remove from the oven and serve

PASTA

SIMPLE SPAGHETTI

Serves: 2

Prep Time: 5   Minutes

Cook Time: 15   Minutes

Total Time: 20   Minutes

INGREDIENTS

- 10 oz. spaghetti
- 2 eggs
- ½ cup parmesan cheese
- 1 tsp black pepper
- Olive oil
- 1 tsp parsley
- 2 cloves garlic

DIRECTIONS

1. In a pot boil spaghetti (or any other type of pasta), drain and set aside
2. In a bowl whish eggs with parmesan cheese
3. In a skillet heat olive oil, add garlic and cook for 1-2 minutes
4. Pour egg mixture and mix well
5. Add pasta and stir well

6. When ready garnish with parsley and serve

CHICKEN PASTA

Serves: **2**

Prep Time: **5** Minutes

Cook Time: **15** Minutes

Total Time: **20** Minutes

INGREDIENTS

- 1 lb. cooked chicken breast
- 8 oz. pasta
- 2 tablespoons butter
- 1 tablespoon garlic
- 1 tablespoon flour
- ½ cup milk
- ½ cup heavy cream
- 1 jar red bell peppers
- 2 tablespoons basil

DIRECTIONS

1. In a pot boil spaghetti (or any other type of pasta), drain and set aside
2. Place all the ingredients for the sauce in a pot and bring to a simmer
3. Add pasta and mix well
4. When ready garnish with parmesan cheese and serve

SHRIMP PASTA

Serves: 2
Prep Time: 5   Minutes

Cook Time: 15   Minutes

Total Time: 20   Minutes

INGREDIENTS

- ¼ cup mayonnaise
- ¼ cup sweet chili sauce
- 1 tablespoon lime juice
- 1 garlic clove
- 8 z. pasta
- 1 lb. shrimp
- ¼ tsp paprika

DIRECTIONS

1. In a pot boil spaghetti (or any other type of pasta), drain and set aside
2. Place all the ingredients for the sauce in a pot and bring to a simmer
3. Add pasta and mix well
4. When ready garnish with parmesan cheese and serve

PASTA WITH OLIVES AND TOMATOES

Serves: 2

Prep Time: 5   Minutes

Cook Time: 15   Minutes

Total Time: 20   Minutes

INGREDIENTS

- 8 oz. pasta
- 3 tablespoons olive oil
- 2 cloves garlic
- 5-6 anchovy fillets
- 2 cups tomatoes
- 1 cup olives
- ½ cup basil leaves

DIRECTIONS

1. In a pot boil spaghetti (or any other type of pasta), drain and set aside
2. Place all the ingredients for the sauce in a pot and bring to a simmer
3. Add pasta and mix well
4. When ready garnish with parmesan cheese and serve

GREEN SALAD WITH THAI DRESSING

Serves: 2
Prep Time: 5   Minutes

Cook Time: 5   Minutes

Total Time: *10*   Minutes

INGREDIENTS

- 2 cucumber
- 10 cups salad greens
- 2 cups sunflower sprouts
- 2 stalks celery

DRESSING

- ½ cup lime juice
- 2 tablespoons fish sauce
- ¼ tsp honey
- 1 clove garlic
- 1 tablespoon cilantro

DIRECTIONS

1. In a bowl combine all ingredients together and mix well
2. Serve with dressing

Serves: 2

Prep Time: 5   Minutes

Cook Time: 5   Minutes

Total Time: 10   Minutes

INGREDIENTS

- 6 oz. bacon
- 1 bunches of kale
- ¾ cup dried cranberries
- ½ cup olive oil
- ½ cup red onion

DIRECTIONS

1. In a bowl combine all ingredients together and mix well
2. Serve with salad dressing

Serves: 2

Prep Time: 5   Minutes

Cook Time: 5   Minutes

Total Time: 10   Minutes

INGREDIENTS

- 3 tablespoons lime juice
- 2 tablespoons olive oil
- ¼ cup cilantro
- ¼ tsp cracked pepper
- 1 pinch salt

DIRECTIONS

1. In a bowl combine all ingredients together and mix well
2. Serve with salad dressing

FENNEL SALAD

Serves: **2**

Prep Time: **5** Minutes

Cook Time: **5** Minutes

Total Time: **10** Minutes

INGREDIENTS

- 1 lb. fennel
- juice 1 lemon
- ½ tsp salt
- 1 tablespoon olive oil

DIRECTIONS

1. In a bowl combine all ingredients together and mix well
2. Serve with salad dressing

CRANBERRY SALAD

Serves: 2

Prep Time: 5   Minutes

Cook Time: 5   Minutes

Total Time: 10   Minutes

INGREDIENTS

- 2 cups kale
- 1 tablespoon coconut oil
- 2 cups spinach
- ½ cup dried cranberries
- 1 tablespoon sliced almonds
- 1 tablespoon water

DIRECTIONS

1. In a bowl combine all ingredients together and mix well
2. Serve with salad dressing

GREEN SALAD

Serves: **2**

Prep Time: **5** Minutes

Cook Time: **5** Minutes

Total Time: **10** Minutes

INGREDIENTS

- 12 cup salad greens
- 1 bunch radishes
- ½ onion
- 1 cucumber

ITALIAN DRESSING

- 5 tablespoons olive oil
- ½ cup apple cider vinegar
- ½ tsp oregano leaves
- ½ tsp rosemary
- ½ tsp marjoram leaves
- ½ tsp thyme leaves
- 1 clove garlic

DIRECTIONS

1. In a bowl combine all ingredients together and mix well
2. Serve with salad dressing

CUCUMBER SALAD

Serves: **4**

Prep Time: **5**   Minutes

Cook Time: **5**   Minutes

Total Time: **10**   Minutes

INGREDIENTS

- 1 cucumber
- 1 tsp salt
- 3 green onions
- 1 tablespoon cilantro
- ½ cup lemon juice
- ½ cup olive oil
- 1 tsp lemon zest
- ¼ tsp cracked pepper

DIRECTIONS

1. In a bowl mix all ingredients and mix well
2. Serve with salad dressing

APRICOT SALAD

Serves: **4**

Prep Time: **5**   Minutes

Cook Time: **5**   Minutes

Total Time: **10**   Minutes

INGREDIENTS

- 2 apricots
- 5 cups arugula

BALSAMIC VINAIGRETTE

- ½ cup balsamic vinegar
- ½ cup olive oil
- 3 tsp mustard
- 1 tablespoon chives

DIRECTIONS

1. In a bowl mix all ingredients and mix well
2. Serve with salad dressing

MORNING SALAD

Serves: 2

Prep Time: 5   Minutes

Cook Time: 5   Minutes

Total Time: **10**   Minutes

INGREDIENTS

- 1 onion
- 1 tsp cumin
- 1 tablespoon olive oil
- 1 avocado
- ¼ lb. cooked lentils
- 1 oz. walnuts
- Coriander
- ¼ lb. feta cheese
- Salad dressing of choice
- 8-10 baby carrots

DIRECTIONS

1. In a bowl combine all ingredients together and mix well
2. Add dressing and serve

THANK YOU FOR READING THIS BOOK!

1/20 Magpie lark   Bridgstreet

Australian
Poems
You Need to Know

Edited by Jamie Grant
Foreword by Phillip Adams

hardie grant books

MELBOURNE · LONDON

Foreword

THE PUZZLES AND PERILS OF POETRY

I have no right to be introducing this book of poetry. Or any
book of poetry. I've no poet's license. My ignorance of poetry
is exceeded only by my incomprehension of cricket or quantum
mechanics.

The other arts range from the self-evident to the reasonably
easy. Take pottery, which sounds like poetry and sometimes is.
Probably the oldest art of all retains its earthiness. No matter how
odd the shape or crazy the glaze, a pot remains recognisably potty.

Architecture, from the humpy to the corporate tower, speaks
for itself. In a whisper or a shout.

Painting? Much of it requires no effort. The Altamira
caves and the Impressionists offer the reassurance of instant
recognition, although I still require a cultural sherpa when
tackling the mountains of mystery that comprise the visual
arts of the twentieth and twenty-first centuries. What does it all
mean? If anything? Does it matter if most of the pictures deemed
'modern' are framed silences? Puzzles without answers?

Music is the most assertive of the arts. Only deafness can
protect you from its siren song. Penetrating the autonomic nervous
system via the eardrums, it manipulates our emotions whether we
like it or not. Though appalled by its marching rhythms, a pacifist
can be as stirred by martial music as the silliest of patriots – just as
I'm often angered by my helpless response to the mawkish muzak
that ambushes you in a lift or shopping mall.

Prose is a doddle, as easy to write as to read. My own career
attests to that. Since my first published utterances fifty-eight
years ago, I've poured out countless millions of words for every
medium. Prose is, by and large, written down talk. Mine, certainly
for 90 per cent of my 'writing', wasn't. I've simply mumbled into
dictaphones.

But poetry? All my life it defeated me – along with whistling
through my teeth and playing chess. How marvellous chess looks!
How posh and profound it appears and how unfathomable are its
rules. While I'd love to hail a taxi with a whistle, I'd kill to play
chess. And too much poetry operates – to a would-be reader like
me – on the same level of unattainable skill as whistling or check-
mating.

No, not the bush poetry to be found in the nineteenth century
Bulletin by Lawson or Patterson. My cattle dogs could understand
that, along with the sheep. And even I could make sense of Kipling

or Tennyson. But when confronted with any modern poet more complex than Dylan Thomas, I despaired. Ezra Pound, even when writing in what seems to be English, employed an extraterrestrial vocabulary. I'd need the aid of code-breakers at Bletchley Park or an Enigma machine to begin to understand Ezra. And I told him so – when visiting his grave on Venice's Cemetery Island. Am I the only person who made the trek to complain?

Having grizzled to Pound I made a teenage trek to Mary Gilmore, to thank the patron saint of Australian communism for one amazing line – 'but this bread is my son's bread' – and a little later would pay homage to Judith Wright for words that haunted me, and to a friend, Lawrence Collinson. (Does anyone else remember poor dead Lawrence, one of the *Overland* poets?) A couple of years back, on my little wireless program, I told Philip Hodgins that his descriptions of river redgums reclining on the Murray's banks were amongst the finest words I'd ever read – infinitely more vivid than the eucalyptic outpourings of Heysen or the Heidelberg school.

I always held poets in awe because I couldn't understand them. Yet from childhood on I stumbled upon poets I could understand, who used two or three words where I'd waste a paragraph trying to distill a feeling, an image, an idea. I'd bow to the power and pleasure that came out of words that weren't poured onto the page like mine – leaking from a hydrant – but were considered and wrestled with. Intensifying the experience of reading to the power of ten. No hydrant for the poet. Their words seem to come from an eye-dropper – or a hypodermic syringe.

Then, a few months back, the manuscript of this collection arrived. And I was surprised how much of the poetry between its covers was familiar to me – that I'd absorbed so much more of it than I'd realised or remembered. That the *Bulletin* tradition is alive and kicking, that Australia continues to produce poets who both invite and encourage understanding – and that our poets, every bit as much as our painters or film-makers (who take too much of the credit) have not only described but created the country I love. Instead of being awed by obscurity I am grateful for a clarity of vision that makes HDTV look murky in comparison.

I now declare this book well and truly open – so that I can read it all again.

Phillip Adams

Introduction

ᏽ

Not long ago, an opinion poll was conducted by the ABC with the aim of determining Australia's best loved poems. The outcome was the opposite of what was intended: a list which was an awkward blend of the banal yet familiar and the respected but unread. Of course a poll is not the best way to settle a question of aesthetics; poetry is hardly susceptible to the scientific method, and, besides, there must have been quite a few respondents who gave untruthful answers to the questions posed.

The failure of the poll is my justification for the system used here. The selection made represents the opinion of one person only, with all the prejudices, accidental omissions and blind spots one individual must be prone to, and that individual is me. There has been no attempt to be fair or comprehensive or respectable or historically representative. Instead, I have simply chosen a hundred Australian poems I, as a reader, have been unable to forget.

There will inevitably be some other readers' favourites missing, particularly as I have restricted my choice to one poem for each author. If I had attempted to literally present the first one hundred in a list of this country's most popular poems, there might not be many more than a dozen poets included in the collection, from Henry Lawson to Les Murray. The broader range which results from my self-imposed restriction should enable other readers to make some pleasurable discoveries.

In arriving at this selection, I have made discoveries of my own, even though I began with no other criterion than my own enjoyment. As the poems have been arranged in order of their authors' dates of birth, it is noticeable that particular themes and subjects have been taken up as if to represent the spirit of the time, as for example in the late nineteenth century, when it seemed every poet had to write about bushrangers.

Another discovery, for me, has been to observe the evolution of our poets' approach to verse form, from the early ballad metres to the iambic dimeter quatrains usually associated with Mary Gilmore's best known poems (she is represented here by something quite different) which can be seen in the poems of Dorothea MacKellar and Lesbia Harford, before the regular structures of the poets born between the wars begin to give way to free verse.

Alert readers will observe that many of the poems are connected in some way to other poems in the collection, whether this means comparing AF York's 'The Bullocky's Love-song' with Judith Wright's 'Bullocky', or contrasting three poems with the word 'country' in their title by three near-contemporaries, Kenneth Slessor, AD Hope and Douglas Stewart, or considering the very different poems about sport by Thomas E Spencer, JAR MacKellar, Bruce Dawe, Evan Jones and Clive James.

The two world wars prompted some of the most powerful writing to be found in this collection, understandably, for there can be no more powerful subject than war; but John Manifold's great poem about the fighting in Crete in the 1940s is also a poem about Australia's cultural and literary traditions. By contrast, the most frequent theme among the poets born after the start of the Second World War is the family recollection, whether of parents, grandparents or other relatives. Autobiographical poetry is almost unknown in Australia before the middle of the twentieth century.

The poets of the nineteenth century may deal with different themes, in very different ways, to the poets who are writing now, but it is surprising how many of the poems in the first half of this collection are relevant, and salutary, today. Those who are concerned about global warming would do well to recall the perennial favourite 'Said Hanrahan', while diners in today's fashionable restaurants can see from Marcus Clarke's 'The Wail of the Waiter' that people have been eating out in Melbourne for more than a century and a half.

Above all, it is significant that a large proportion of the poems I have chosen are distinctly funny. Many words have been expended, by politicians and intellectuals alike, in efforts to define the Australian national character, and events and achievements from Gallipoli to the America's Cup, from art, music, cinema and science, have been imbued with symbolic meaning in pursuit of an elusive definition. It seems to me that all these would-be definitions point in the wrong direction. The most striking achievement of our culture, and the distinctive element of our national character, lies in the Australian sense of humour.

That sense of humour is often described as 'dry', like
the Australian landscape, but it also includes an element
of cheerful exaggeration, and a liking for the reversal of
expectations. It amuses Australians that our most iconic
military venture was a failure, but it also amuses us that
we have produced triumphs where none was anticipated,
whether through a stroke of ingenuity such as a winged keel
or by winning a race by being the last left standing. There is
no better summary of the essence of our humour than in Les
Murray's poem 'The Quality of Sprawl', which is why I have
chosen that poem over dozens of other Murray poems with
an equal claim for inclusion in this collection.

The key to understanding Australia's national character
is to be found in our sense of humour, and the key to our
sense of humour is located, ultimately, in the best of our
poetry. For all the awards and international acclaim given
to our novelists and film-makers, it is our poetry which is
the indispensable element in the rich and varied culture of
Australia. Thus it is my hope that this collection will be just
as indispensable as an addition to every Australian home.

Jamie Grant

Contents

୧୨

AP   'Goats'   Bridget Kennedy

Convict and Stockrider

❧

The Red Page

❧

Gundagai to Ironbark

❧

Bastard and Bushranger

Drought, Dusk and War

Country Story

*

Melbourne and Sydney

❧

Beyond Sprawl

❧

The Generation of XYZ

CHAPTER 1

Convict and Stockrider

20/20   Cockatoo   Bridgford

A Convict's Tour to Hell

❧

FRANCIS MACNAMARA ('FRANK THE POET')

(1811–1880)

❧

Composed at Stroud A.A. Co. Establishment Station
New South Wales

> *Nor can the foremost of the sons of men*
> *Escape my ribald and licentious pen.*
> Swift

Composed and written
October 23rd day, Anno 1839

You prisoners of New South Wales,
Who frequent watchhouses and gaols
A story to you I will tell
'Tis of a convict's tour to hell.

Whose valour had for years been tried
On the highway before he died
At length he fell to death a prey
To him it proved a happy day
Downwards he bent his course I'm told
Like one destined for Satan's fold
And no refreshment would he take
'Till he approached the Stygian lake
A tent he then began to fix
Contiguous to the River Styx
Thinking that no one could molest him
He leaped when Charon thus addressed him
Stranger I say from whence art thou,
And thy own name, pray tell me now,
Kind sir I come from Sydney gaol
My name I don't mean to conceal
And since you seem anxious to know it
On earth I was called Frank the Poet.
Are you that person? Charon cried,
I'll carry you to the other side.
Five or sixpence I mostly charge
For the like passage in my barge
So stranger do not troubled be
For you shall have a passage free
Frank seeing no other succour nigh
With the invitation did comply
And having a fair wind and tide

They soon arrived at the other side
And leaving Charon at the ferry
Frank went in haste to Purgatory
And rapping loudly at the gate
Of Limbo, or the Middle State
Pope Pius the 7th soon appeared
With gown, beads, crucifix and beard
And gazing at the Poet the while
Accosts him in the following style
Stranger art thou a friend or foe
Your business here I fain would know
Quoth the Poet for Heaven I'm not fitted
And here I hope to be admitted
Pius rejoined, vain are your hopes
This place was made for Priests and Popes
'Tis a world of our own invention
But friend I've not the least intention
To admit such a foolish elf
Who scarce knows how to bless himself
Quoth Frank were you mad or insane
When first you made this world of pain?
For I can see nought but fire
A share of which I can't desire
Here I see weeping wailing gnashing
And torments of the newest fashion
Therefore I call you silly elf
Who made a rod to whip yourself
And may you like all honest neighbours
Enjoy the fruit of all your labours
Frank then bid the Pope farewell
And hurried to that place called Hell
And having found the gloomy gate
Frank rapped aloud to know his fate
He louder knocked and louder still
When the Devil came, pray what's your will?
Alas cried the Poet I've come to dwell
With you and share your fate in Hell
Says Satan that can't be, I'm sure
For I detest and hate the poor
And none shall in my kingdom stand
Except the grandees of the land.
But Frank I think you are going astray
For convicts never come this way
But soar to Heaven in droves and legions

A place so called in the upper regions
So Frank I think with an empty purse
You shall go further and fare worse
Well cried the Poet since 'tis so
One thing of you I'd like to know
As I'm at present in no hurry
Have you one here called Captain Murray?
Yes Murray is within this place
Would you said Satan see his face?
May God forbid that I should view him
For on board the *Phoenix* Hulk I knew him
Who is that Sir in yonder blaze
Who on fire and brimstone seems to graze?
'Tis Captain Logan of Moreton Bay
And Williams who was killed the other day
He was overseer at Grosse Farm
And done poor convicts no little harm
Cook who discovered New South Wales
And he that first invented gaols
Are both tied to a fiery stake
Which stands in yonder boiling lake
Hark do you hear this dreadful yelling
It issues from Doctor Wardell's dwelling
And all those fiery seats and chairs
Are fitted up for Dukes and Mayors
And nobles of Judicial orders
Barristers Lawyers and Recorders
Here I beheld legions of traitors
Hangmen gaolers and flagellators
Commandants, Constables and Spies
Informers and Overseers likewise
In flames of brimstone they were toiling
And lakes of sulphur round them boiling
Hell did resound with their fierce yelling
Alas how dismal was their dwelling
Then Major Morriset I espied
And Captain Cluney by his side
With a fiery belt they were lashed together
As tight as soles to upper leather
Their situation was most horrid
For they were tyrants down at the Norrid
Prostrate I beheld a petitioner
It was the Company's Commissioner
Satan said he my days are ended

For many years I've superintended
The An. Company's affairs
And I punctually paid all arrears
Sir should you doubt the hopping Colonel
At Carrington you'll find my journal
Legibly penned in black and white
To prove that my accounts were right
And since I've done your will on earth
I hope you'll put me in a berth
Then I saw old Serjeant Flood
In Vulcan's hottest forge he stood
He gazed at me his eyes with ire
Appeared like burning coals of fire
In fiery garments he was arrayed
And like an Arabian horse he brayed
He on a bloody cutlass leaned
And to a lamp-post he was chained
He loudly called out for assistance
Or begged me to end his existence
Cheer up said I be not afraid
Remember No. 3 Stockade
In the course of time you may do well
If you behave yourself in Hell
Your heart on earth was fraught with malice
Which oft drove convicts to the gallows
But you'll now atone for all the blood
Of prisoners shed by Serjeant Flood.
Then I beheld that well known Trapman
The Police Runner called Izzy Chapman
Here he was standing on his head
In a river of melted boiling lead.
Alas he cried behold me stranger
I've captured many a bold bushranger
And for the same I'm suffering here
But lo, now yonder snakes draw near
On turning round I saw slow worms
And snakes of various kinds and forms
All entering at his mouth and nose
To devour his entrails as I suppose
Then turning round to go away
Bold Lucifer bade me to stay
Saying Frank by no means go man
Till you see your old friend Dr Bowman
'Yonder he tumbles groans and gnashes

He gave you many a thousand lashes
And for the same he does bewail
For Osker with an iron flail
Thrashes him well you may depend
And will till the world comes to an end
Just as I spoke a coach and four
Came in full post haste to the door
And about six feet of mortal sin
Without leave or licence trudged in
At his arrival three cheers were given
Which rent I'm sure the highest Heaven
And all the inhabitants of Hell
With one consent rang the great bell
Which never was heard to sound or ring
Since Judas sold our Heavenly King
Drums were beating flags were hoisting
There never before was such rejoicing
Dancing singing joy or mirth
In Heaven above or on the earth
Straightway to Lucifer I went
To know what these rejoicings meant
Of sense cried Lucifer I'm deprived
Since Governor Darling has arrived
With fire and brimstone I've ordained him
And Vulcan has already chained him
And I'm going to fix an abode
For Captain Rossi, he's on the road
Frank don't go 'till you see the novice
The magistrate from the Police Office
Oh said the Poet I'm satisfied
To hear that he is to be tied
And burned in this world of fire
I think 'tis high time to retire
And having travelled many days
O'er fiery hills and boiling seas
At length I found that happy place
Where all the woes of mortals cease
And rapping loudly at the wicket
Cried Peter, where's your certificate
Or if you have not one to show
Pray who in Heaven do you know?
Well I know Brave Donohue
Young Troy and Jenkins too
And many others whom floggers mangled

And lastly were by Jack Ketch strangled
Peter, says Jesus, let Frank in
For he is thoroughly purged from sin
And although in convict's habit dressed
Here he shall be a welcome guest.
Isaiah go with him to Job
And put on him a scarlet robe
St Paul go to the flock straightway
And kill the fatted calf today
And go tell Abraham and Abel
In haste now to prepare the table
For we shall have a grand repast
Since Frank the Poet has come at last
Then came Moses and Elias
John the Baptist and Mathias
With many saints from foreign lands
And with the Poet they all join hands
Thro' Heaven's Concave their rejoicings rang
And hymns of praise to God they sang
And as they praised his glorious name
I woke and found 'twas but a dream.

The Beautiful Squatter

CHARLES HARPUR

(1813–1868)

Where the wandering Barwin delighteth the eye,
Befringed with the myall and golden-bloomed gorse,
Oh a beautiful Squatter came galloping by,
With a beard on his chin like the tail of his horse!
And his locks trained all round to so equal a pitch,
That his mother herself, it may truly be said,
Had been puzzled in no small degree to find which
Was the front, or the back, or the sides of his head.

Beside a small fire 'neath a fair-spreading tree,
(A cedar I think — but perhaps 'twas a gum)
What vision of Love did that Squatter now see,
In the midst of a catch so to render him dumb?
Why, all on the delicate herbage asquat,
And smiling to see him so flustered and mute,
'Twas the charming Miss Possumskin having a chat
With the elegant Lady of Lord Bandycoot.

The Squatter dismounted — what else could he do?
And meaning her tender affections to win,
'Gan talking of dampers and blankets quite new
With a warmth that soon ruined poor Miss Possumskin!
And Lord Bandycoot also, while dining that day
On a baked kangaroo of the kind that is red,
At the very third bite to King Dingo did say —
O, how heavy I feel all at once in the head!

But alas for the Belles of the Barwin! the Youth
Galloped home, to forget all his promises fair!
Whereupon Lady Bandycoot told the whole truth
To her Lord, and Miss Possumskin raved in despair!
And mark the result! royal Dingo straightway,
And his Warriors, swore to avenge them in arms:
And that Beautiful Squatter one beautiful day,
Was waddied to death in the bloom of his charms.

Taking the Census

∾

CHARLES R THATCHER

(1831–1882)

∾

*A New Original Song, as written and sung by
Thatcher, with deafening applause,
at the 'Shamrock'.
(Air—'Miser's Man')*

When the census is taken, of course,
    All the elderly females are furious,
They don't like to tell their real age,
    For gov'ment they say is too curious:
I got hold of a chap that went round,
    For I wanted to twig their rum capers,
So I tipped him a crown on the sly
    To let me look over his papers.

There's that elderly dame, Mother Baggs,
    Has marked down her age twenty-seven,
Although she's possessed of five kids,
    The eldest of which is eleven;
Miss Fluffen says she's thirty-two,
    But to tell such a story is naughty,
She's a regular frumpish old maid,
    And if she's a year old she's forty.

There's another thing struck me as queer,
    As the papers I sat overhauling,
Beneath occupation, thinks I,
    I'll soon find out each person's calling;
But the first I looked at made me grin,
    My wash'woman, old Mother Archer,
Beneath occupation I found
    Had described herself as a clear starcher.

The chemist's assistant up here,
    When his paper I happened to see, sirs,
'Pon my honour had had the vile cheek
    To mark after his name M.D., sirs,
And Bolus, that wretched old quack,
    Whom folks here regard with suspicion,
When his paper I looked at, I found
    He'd put himself down a physician!

Here's a *barberous* custom you'll say,
    No less than three diff'rent hairdressers,
In the papers which they have filled up
    Have described themselves all as *professors*;
In Heidelberg district I find
    My bounceable friend, Harry Potter,
In the paper that he has sent in,
    Tries to make us believe he's a squatter.

My friend said he called on two girls,
    Who are noted for cutting rum capers,
They live in an elegant crib,
    And he knocked at the door for their papers;
They handed him what he required,
    He read, but exclaimed with vexation,
'The instructions you haven't fulfilled—
    'You've not put down your occupation.'

'Well, Poll, that's a good 'un,' says one,
    And both of them burst out a-laughing,
But the young man exclaimed precious quick
    'I can't stay all day while you're chaffing;'
'Occupation' says she, with a scream,
    (Her laughter was pretty near killing her),
'Poll, I'm blowed if I knows what you are,
    But, young man, shove me down as a milliner.'

The Sick Stockrider

❧

ADAM LINDSAY GORDON

(1833–1870)

❧

Hold hard, Ned! Lift me down once more, and lay me in the shade.
Old man, you've had your work cut out to guide
Both horses, and to hold me in the saddle when I swayed,
All through the hot, slow, sleepy, silent ride.

The dawn at Moorabinda was a mist-wrack dull and dense;
The sunrise was a sullen, sluggish lamp;
I was dozing in the gateway at Arbuthnot's boundary fence;
I was dreaming on the Limestone cattle camp.

We crossed the creek at Carricksford and, sharply through the haze,
And suddenly, the sun shot flaming forth:
To southward lay Katâwa, with the sand-peaks all ablaze,
And the flushed fields of Glen Lomond lay to north.

Now westward winds the bridle-path that leads to Lindisfarm,
And yonder looms the double-headed Bluff:
From the far side of the first hill, when the skies are clear and calm,
You can see Sylvester's woolshed fair enough.

Five miles we used to call it from our homestead to the place
Where the big tree spans the roadway like an arch;
'Twas here we ran the dingo down that gave us such a chase
Eight years ago—or was it nine?—last March.

'Twas merry in the glowing morn, among the gleaming grass,
To wander as we've wandered many a mile,
And blow the cool tobacco cloud and watch the white wreaths pass,
Sitting loosely in the saddle all the while.

'Twas merry 'mid the backwoods, when we spied the station roofs,
To wheel the wild scrub cattle at the yard,
With a running fire of stockwhips and a fiery run of hoofs
—Oh, the hardest day was never then too hard!

Ay, we had a glorious gallop after Starlight and his gang
When they bolted from Sylvester's on the flat!
How the sun-dried reed-beds crackled, how the flint-strewn ranges rang
To the strokes of Mountaineer and Acrobat!

Hard behind them in the timber—harder still across the heath—
Close beside them through the tea-tree scrub we dashed;

And the golden-tinted fern leaves, how they rustled underneath,
And the honeysuckle osiers, how they crashed!

We led the hunt throughout, Ned, on the chestnut and the grey,
And the troopers were three hundred yards behind
While we emptied our six-shooters on the bushrangers at bay
In the creek, with stunted box-tree for a blind.

There you grappled with the leader, man to man and horse to horse,
And you rolled together when the chestnut reared:
He blazed away and missed you in that shallow water-course—
A narrow shave!—his powder singed your beard.

In these hours when life is ebbing, how those days when life was young
Come back to us! how clearly I recall
Even the yarns Jack Hall invented, and the songs Jem Roper sung
—And where are now Jem Roper and Jack Hall?

Ay, nearly all our comrades of the old colonial school,
Our ancient boon companions, Ned, are gone:
Hard livers for the most part! somewhat reckless as a rule!—
It seems that you and I are left alone.

There was Hughes, who got in trouble through that business with the cards—
It matters little what became of him;
But a steer ripped up MacPherson in the Cooraminta yards
And Sullivan was drowned at Sink-or-Swim.

And Mostyn—poor Frank Mostyn!—died at last a fearful wreck,
In the horrors at the upper Wandinong;
And Carisbrooke, the rider, at the Horsefall broke his neck—
Faith, the wonder was he saved his neck so long!

Ah, those days and nights we squandered at the Logans' in the glen!
The Logans, man and wife, have long been dead:
Elsie's tallest girl seems taller than your 'little Elsie' then
And Ethel is a woman grown and wed.

I've had my share of pastime, and I've done my share of toil,
And life is short—the longest life a span:
I care not now to tarry for the corn or for the oil,
Or for the wine that maketh glad the heart of man.

For good undone, and gifts misspent, and resolutions vain,
'Tis somewhat late to trouble: this I know—
I should live the same life over, if I had to live again;
And the chances are I go where most men go.

The deep blue skies wax dusky, and the tall green trees grow dim,
The sward beneath me seems to heave and fall;
And sickly, smoky shadows through the sleepy sunlight swim
And on the very sun's face weave their pall.

Let me slumber in the hollow where the wattle blossoms wave,
With never stone or rail to fence my bed:
Should the sturdy station children pull the bush flowers on my grave
I may chance to hear them romping overhead.

'Go, do as you are bid,' I cried, 'we wait for no reply;
Go! let us have tea early, and another rabbit pie!'
Oh, that I had stopped his answer! But it came out with a run:
'Last-a week-a plenty puppy; this-a week-a puppy done!'
James Brunton Stephens, 'My Other Chinee Cook'

CHAPTER 2

The Red Page

And the folk are jubilating as they never did before;
For we played Molongo cricket—and McDougal topped the score!
Thomas E Spencer, 'How McDougal Topped the Score'

6/20   Magpie   Bridgefoot

My Other Chinee Cook

JAMES BRUNTON STEPHENS

(1835–1902)

Yes, I got another Johnny; but he was to Number One
As a Satyr to Hyperion, as a rushlight to the sun;
He was lazy, he was cheeky, he was dirty, he was sly,
But he had a single virtue, and its name was rabbit pie.

Now those who say the bush is dull are not so far astray,
For the neutral tints of station life are anything but gay;
But with all its uneventfulness, I solemnly deny
That the bush is unendurable along with rabbit pie.

We had fixed one day to sack him, and agreed to moot the
     point
When my lad should bring our usual regale of cindered joint,
But instead of cindered joint we saw and smelt, my wife and
     I,
Such a lovely, such a beautiful, oh! such a rabbit pie!

There was quite a new expression on his lemon-coloured face,
And the unexpected odour won him temporary grace,
For we tacitly postponed the sacking-point till by-and-by,
And we tacitly said nothing save the one word, 'rabbit pie!'

I had learned that pleasant mystery should simply be endured,
And forebore to ask of Johnny where the rabbits were
     procured!
I had learnt from Number One to stand aloof from how
     and why,
And I threw myself upon the simple fact of rabbit pie.

And when the pie was opened, what a picture did we see!
They lay in beauty side by side, they filled our home with
     glee!
How excellent, how succulent, back, neck, and leg, and thigh!
What a noble gift is manhood! What a trust is rabbit pie!

For a week this thing continued, rabbit pie from day to day;
Though where he got the rabbits John would ne'er vouchsafe
     to say;
But we never seemed to tire of them, and daily could descry
Subtle shades of new delight in each successive rabbit pie.

Sunday came; by rabbit reckoning, the seventh day of the
    week;
We had dined, we sat in silence, both our hearts(?) too full
    to speak,
When in walks Cousin George, and, with a sniff, says he,
    'Oh my!
What a savoury suggestion! What a smell of rabbit pie!'

'Oh, why so late, George?' says my wife, 'the rabbit pie is
    gone;
But you *must* have one for tea, though. Ring the bell, my
    dear, for John.'
So I rang the bell for John, to whom my wife did signify,
'Let us have an early tea, John, and another rabbit pie.'

But John seemed taken quite aback, and shook his funny
    head,
And uttered words I comprehended no more than the dead;
'Go, do as you are bid,' I cried, 'we wait for no reply;
Go! let us have tea early, and another rabbit pie!'

Oh, that I had stopped his answer! But it came out with a
    run:
'Last-a week-a plenty puppy; this-a week-a puppy done!'
Just then my wife, my love, my life, the apple of mine eye,
Was seized with what seemed mal-de-mer—'sick transit'
    rabbit pie!

And George! By George, he laughed, and then he howled
    like any bear!
The while my wife contorted like a mad 'convulsionnaire';
And I—I rushed on Johnny, and I smote him hip and thigh,
And I never saw him more, nor tasted more of rabbit pie.

And the childless mothers met me, as I kicked him from the
    door,
With loud maternal wailings and anathemas galore;
I must part with pretty Tiny, I must part with little Fly,
For I'm sure they know the story of the so-called 'rabbit pie'.

Bell-birds

❧

HENRY KENDALL

(1839–1882)

❧

By channels of coolness the echoes are calling,
And down the dim gorges I hear the creek falling:
It lives in the mountain where moss and the sedges
Touch with their beauty the banks and the ledges.
Through breaks of the cedar and sycamore bowers
Struggles the light that is love to the flowers;
And, softer than slumber, and sweeter than singing,
The notes of the bell-birds are running and ringing.

The silver-voiced bell-birds, the darlings of daytime!
They sing in September their songs of the May-time;
When shadows wax strong, and the thunder-bolts hurtle,
They hide with their fear in the leaves of the myrtle;
When rain and the sunbeams shine mingled together,
They start up like fairies that follow fair weather;
And straightway the hues of their feathers unfolden
Are the green and the purple, the blue and the golden.

October, the maiden of bright yellow tresses,
Loiters for love in these cool wildernesses;
Loiters, knee-deep, in the grasses, to listen,
Where dripping rocks gleam and the leafy pools glisten:
Then is the time when the water-moons splendid
Break with their gold, and are scattered or blended
Over the creeks, till the woodlands have warning
Of songs of the bell-bird and wings of the Morning.

Welcome as waters unkissed by the summers
Are the voices of bell-birds to thirsty far-comers.
When fiery December sets foot in the forest,
And the need of the wayfarer presses the sorest,
Pent in the ridges for ever and ever
The bell-birds direct him to spring and to river,
With ring and with ripple, like runnels whose torrents
Are toned by the pebbles and leaves in the currents.

Often I sit, looking back to a childhood,
Mixt with the sights and the sounds of the wildwood,
Longing for power and the sweetness to fashion,
Lyrics with beats like the heart-beats of Passion;—

Songs interwoven of lights and of laughters
Borrowed from bell-birds in far forest-rafters;
So I might keep in the city and alleys
The beauty and strength of the deep mountain valleys:
Charming to slumber the pain of my losses
With glimpses of creeks and a vision of mosses.

Are You the Cove?

JOSEPH FURPHY ('TOM COLLINS')

(1843–1912)

'Are you the Cove?' he spoke the words
As swagmen only can;
The Squatter freezingly inquired,
'What do you mean, my man?'

'Are you the Cove?' his voice was stern,
His look was firm and keen;
Again the Squatter made reply,
'I don't know what you mean.'

'O! dash my rags! let's have some sense—
You ain't a fool, by Jove,
Gammon you dunno what I mean;
I mean—are you the Cove?'

'Yes, I'm the Cove,' the Squatter said;
The Swagman answered, 'Right,
I thought as much: show me some place
Where I can doss tonight.'

How McDougal Topped the Score

THOMAS E SPENCER

(1845–1910)

A peaceful spot is Piper's Flat. The folk that live around—
They keep themselves by keeping sheep and turning up the ground;
But the climate is erratic, and the consequences are
The struggle with the elements is everlasting war.
We plough, and sow, and harrow—then sit down and pray for rain;
And then we all get flooded out and have to start again.
But the folk are now rejoicing as they ne'er rejoiced before,
For we've played Molongo cricket, and McDougal topped the score!

Molongo had a head on it, and challenged us to play
A single-innings match for lunch—the losing team to pay.
We were not great guns at cricket, but we couldn't well say no,
So we all began to practise, and we let the reaping go.
We scoured the Flat for ten miles round to muster up our men,
But when the list was totalled we could only number ten.
Then up spoke big Tim Brady: he was always slow to speak,
And he said—'What price McDougal, who lives down at Cooper's Creek?'

So we sent for old McDougal, and he stated in reply
That he'd never played at cricket, but he'd half a mind to try.
He couldn't come to practise—he was getting in his hay,
But he guessed he'd show the beggars from Molongo how to play.
Now, McDougal was a Scotchman, and a canny one at that,
So he started in to practise with a paling for a bat.
He got Mrs Mac to bowl to him, but she couldn't run at all,
So he trained his sheep-dog, Pincher, how to scout and fetch the ball.

Now, Pincher was no puppy; he was old, and worn, and grey;
But he understood McDougal, and—accustomed to obey—
When McDougal cried out 'Fetch it!' he would fetch it in a trice,
But until the word was 'Drop it!' he would grip it like a vice.
And each succeeding night they played until the light grew dim:
Sometimes McDougal struck the ball—sometimes the ball struck him.
Each time he struck, the ball would plough a furrow in the ground;
And when he missed, the impetus would turn him three times round.

The fatal day at length arrived—the day that was to see
Molongo bite the dust, or Piper's Flat knocked up a tree!
Molongo's captain won the toss, and sent his men to bat,
And they gave some leather-hunting to the men of Piper's Flat.

When the ball sped where McDougal stood, firm planted in his track,
He shut his eyes, and turned him round, and stopped it—with his back!
The highest score was twenty-two, the total sixty-six,
When Brady sent a yorker down that scattered Johnson's sticks.

Then Piper's Flat went in to bat, for glory and renown,
But, like the grass before the scythe, our wickets tumbled down.
'Nine wickets down for seventeen, with fifty more to win!'
Our captain heaved a heavy sigh, and sent McDougal in.
'Ten pounds to one you'll lose it!' cried a barracker from town;
But McDougal said, 'I'll tak' it, mon!' and planked the money down.
Then he girded up his moleskins in a self-reliant style,
Threw off his hat and boots and faced the bowler with a smile.

He held the bat the wrong side out, and Johnson with a grin
Stepped lightly to the bowling crease, and sent a 'wobbler' in;
McDougal spooned it softly back, and Johnson waited there,
But McDougal, crying 'Fetch it!' started running like a hare.
Molongo shouted 'Victory! He's out as sure as eggs',
When Pincher started through the crowd, and ran through Johnson's legs.
He seized the ball like lightning; then he ran behind a log,
And McDougal kept on running, while Molongo chased the dog!

They chased him up, they chased him down, they chased him round, and then
He darted through the sliprail as the scorer shouted 'Ten!'
McDougal puffed; Molongo swore; excitement was intense;
As the scorer marked down twenty, Pincher cleared a barbed-wire fence.
'Let us head him!' shrieked Molongo. 'Brain the mongrel with a bat!'
'Run it out! Good old McDougal!' yelled the men of Piper's Flat.
And McDougal kept on jogging, and then Pincher doubled back,
And the scorer counted 'Forty' as they raced across the track.

McDougal's legs were going fast, Molongo's breath was gone—
But still Molongo chased the dog—McDougal struggled on.
When the scorer shouted 'fifty' then they knew the chase could cease;
And McDougal gasped out 'Drop it!' as he dropped within his crease.
Then Pincher dropped the ball, and as instinctively he knew
Discretion was the wiser plan, he disappeared from view;
And as Molongo's beaten men exhausted lay around
We raised McDougal shoulder-high, and bore him from the ground.

We bore him to McGinniss's, where lunch was ready laid,
And filled him up with whisky-punch, for which Molongo paid.
We drank his health in bumpers and we cheered him three times three,
And when Molongo got its breath Molongo joined the spree,
And the critics say they never saw a cricket match like that,
When McDougal broke the record in the game at Piper's Flat;

And the folk are jubilating as they never did before;
For we played Molongo cricket—and McDougal topped the score!

The Wail of the Waiter (A Tavern Catch)

MARCUS CLARKE

(1846–1881)

All day long, at Scott's or Menzies', I await the gorging crowd,
Panting, penned within a pantry, with the blowflies humming loud.
There at seven in the morning do I count my daily cash,
While the home-returning reveller calls for 'soda and a dash'.
And the weary hansom-cabbies set the blinking squatters down,
Who, all night, in savage freedom, have been 'knocking round the
    town'.
Soon the breakfast gong resounding bids the festive meal begin,
And, with appetites like demons, come the gentle public in.
'Toast and butter!' 'Eggs and coffee!' 'Waiter, mutton chops for
    four!'
'Flatheads!' 'Ham!' 'Beef!' 'Where's the mustard?' 'Steak and
    onions!' 'Shut the door!'
Here sits Bandicoot, the broker, eating in a desperate hurry,
Scowling at his left-hand neighbour, Cornstalk from the Upper
    Murray,
Who with brandy-nose empurpled, and with blue lips cracked and
    dry,
In incipient delirium shoves the eggspoon in his eye.
'Bloater paste!' 'Some *tender* steak, sir?' 'Here, *confound* you,
    where's my chop?'
'Waiter!' 'Yessir!' '*Waiter*!' 'Yessir!!'—running till I'm fit to drop.
Then at lunch time—fearful crisis! In by shoals the gorgers pour,
Gobbling, crunching, swilling, munching—ten times hungrier than
    before.
'Glass of porter!' '*Ale* for me, John!' 'Where's my stick?' 'And
    where's my *hat*!'
'Oxtail soup!' '*I* asked for curry!' 'Cold boiled beef, and cut it fat!'
'Irish stew!' 'Some pickled cabbage!' 'What, no *beans*?' 'Bring *me*
    some pork!'
'Soup, sir?' 'Yes. You grinning idiot, can I eat it with a FORK?'
'Take care, waiter!' 'Beg your pardon.' 'Curse you, have you two
    left legs?'

'I asked for *bread* an hour ago, sir!' 'Now then, have you *laid* those
    eggs?'
'Sherry!' 'No, I called for *beer*—of all the fools I ever saw!'
'Waiter!' 'Yessir!' 'WAITER!!' 'Here, sir!' 'Damme, sir, this steak is
    RAW!'

Thus amid this hideous Babel do I live the livelong day,
While my memory is going, and my hair is turning grey.
All my soul is slowly melting, all my brain is softening fast,
And I know that I'll be taken to the Yarra Bend at last.
For at night from fitful slumbers I awaken with a start,
Murmuring of steak and onions, babbling of apple-tart.
While to me the Poet's cloudland a gigantic kitchen seems,
And those mislaid table-napkins haunt me even in my dreams
Is this right?—Ye sages tell me!—Does a man live but to eat?
Is there nothing worth enjoying but one's miserable meat?
Is the mightiest task of Genius but to swallow buttered beans,
And has Man but been created to demolish pork and greens?
Is there no *unfed* Hereafter, where the round of chewing stops?
Is the atmosphere of heaven clammy with perpetual chops?
Do the friends of Mr Naylor sup on spirit-reared cow-heel?
Can the great Alexis Soyer really say 'Soyez tranquille?'
Or must I bring spirit beefsteak grilled in spirit regions hotter
For the spirit delectation of some spiritual squatter?
Shall I in a spirit kitchen hear the spirit blowflies humming,
Calming spiritual stomachs with a spiritual 'Coming!'?
Shall—but this is idle chatter, I have got my work to do.
'WAITER!!' 'Yessir.' 'Wake up, stupid! Biled calves' feet for
    Number Two!'

Where the Pelican Builds

MARY HANNAY FOOTT

(1846–1918)

The horses were ready, the rails were down,
    But the riders lingered still—
        One had a parting word to say,
    And one had his pipe to fill.
Then they mounted, one with a granted prayer,
    And one with a grief unguessed.
        'We are going,' they said as they rode away,
    'Where the pelican builds her nest!'

They had told us of pastures wide and green,
    To be sought past the sunset's glow;
        Of rifts in the ranges by opal lit;
    And gold 'neath the river's flow.
And thirst and hunger were banished words
    When they spoke of the unknown West;
        No drought they dreaded, no flood they feared,
    Where the pelican builds her nest!

The creek at the ford was but fetlock deep
    When we watched them crossing there;
        The rains have replenished it twice since then,
    And thrice has the rock lain bare.
But the waters of Hope have flowed and fled,
    And never from blue hill's breast
        Come back—by the sun and the sands devoured—
    Where the pelican builds her nest.

Catching the Coach

ALFRED T CHANDLER ('SPINIFEX')

(1852–1941)

At Kangaroo Gully in 'Fifty-two
The rush and the scramble was reckless and rough;
'Three ounces a dish and the lead running true!'
Was whispered around concerning the stuff.

Next morning a thousand of fellows or more
Appeared for invasion along the brown rise,
Some Yankees, and Cockneys, and Cantabs of yore
And B.As from Oxford in blue-shirt disguise.

And two mornings later the Nugget saloon,
With billiards and skittles, was glaring with signs,
A blind fiddler, Jim, worried out a weak tune,
Beguiling the boys and collecting the fines.

Then tents started up like the freaks of a dream
While heaps of white pipeclay dotted the slope,
To 'Dern her—a duffer!' or 'Creme de la creme!'
That settled the verdict of languishing hope.

And bustle and jollity rang through the trees
In strange combination of humankind traits;
With feverish searchings and gay levities
The fires of excitement were fully ablaze.

Well, three mornings after, the stringybark gums
All rustled their leaves with further surprise;
They'd seen old stagers and limey new-chums,
But here were galoots in peculiar guise:

With nondescript uniform, booted and spurred,
A fierce-looking strap on the underneath lip,
An ominous shooter, a dangling sword,
A grim leather pouch above the right hip!

And maybe a dozen came cantering so,
All clanking and jaunty—authority vain—
When down through the gully rang out the word 'Joe',
And 'Joe' was sent on with a sneering refrain.

There was hunting for 'rights', and producing the same,
Or passing them on to a paperless mate,
Or hiding in bushes or down in the claim—
Such various expedients to baffle the State.

Then 'Who put him on?'—'Twig his illigant seat!'
'Cuss me, but it's purty!'—'The thing on the horse!'
'His first dacent clothes!'—'What surprise for his feet!'
Such volleys as these were soon fired at the Force.

But duty was duty. Just then through the scrub
A digger made off—he a culprit no doubt!
'Dismount you then, Wilson!' roared Sergeant Hubbub;
'Quick! follow the rascal and ferret him out.'

The sapling cadet, with budding moustache,
Then sprang to the ground in dauntless pursuit
And, filled up with zeal and a soldier-like dash,
He felt a true hero of saddle and boot.

The gully quick echoed with taunts that were real,
Keen chaff of defiance allied to revolt,
Such sharp wordy weapons as might have been steel
From skirmishers laughing on hillock and holt.

Away went the fugitive, spurred on by haste,
Escaping the undergrowth, leaping the logs,
Yet ne'er looking back—did he know he was chased?
Said Wilson, 'He's one of the worst of the dogs!

'Some greater misdeed must have blackened his hand;
I'll have him—promotion! Stop there, or I'll shoot!'
The other ahead didn't hear the command
But sprang on unheeding o'er dry branch and root.

The chase settled down to a heavy set-to;
They ran o'er the hill and across the clear flat;
And Wilson was chuckling—the villain he knew
Was making a bee-line for jail—Ballarat!

'I'll follow the rogue safely into the trap—
Confound him, he's speedy: I can't run him down;
But there, quite unconscious of any mishap,
I'll fix him up neatly in gay Canvas Town!'

Then over a creek where a line of sage-gums
All flourishing grew, then away to the right;
Their loud breathings mingled with strange forest hums,
And wallabies scampered with terror and fright.

And cockatoos screeched from the loftiest trees,
The minahs and magpies all fluttered and flew,
The drowsy old possums were roused from their ease,
The locusts and lizards quick stepped out of view.

But on went the pair, never noticing this,
For both had a serious business in hand.
With one there were feelings that prophesied bliss,
The other saw capture and glory so grand.

O'er hillside and creek, beyond hollow and spur,
Through brief strips of woodland, they hurried on still;
The trooper lost ground, but he wasn't a cur;
Besides, they were nearing on Bakery Hill.

Then suddenly broke on each sweltering sight
The thousand of tents in the city of gold;
And straight to the thick of them ran with delight
The chased and the chaser—what luck for the bold!

The coach was just starting for Melbourne that day
As Wilson rushed eagerly on to his man.
'I'll put you with care where you won't be so gay,'
The trooper in triumph already began.

'You've led me a dance in a lively hour's sun;
Now trip out your licence, or waltz off to jail!
What! got one? Oh, ho! Why the —— did you run?'
'To post this here letter for Nell by the mail.'

Narcissus and Some Tadpoles

VICTOR J DALEY

(1858–1905)

Scene I. THE RED PAGE ROOM.

[The RED PAGE EDITOR *discovered sitting,* en boucher, *in his shirt sleeves. Proof sheets of new Australian poems on his desk. Coils of more new Australian poems (in manuscript) hanging over back of his chair. He reads one of the latter, and mutters, shaking his head: 'Won't do. Lacks the indefinable something which is the soul of Poetry. Must define that one of these days.' Takes up another poem. Strikes out six verses and leaves two. Murmurs 'Pith in these—all the rest is padding,' and sweeps the refuse into the W.P. Basket. Hums softly—]*

The critic of the days of yore
(I aptly call him Blunderbore)
Ground bones of bards to make him bread—
I scoop their marrow out instead.

[Muses a few moments, then lilts loudly]

I am the Blender of the pure
Australian Brand of Literature.
No verse, however fine, can be
The radiant thing called Poetry
Unless it is approved by me.
I am the Critic set on high,
The Red Page Rhadamanthus I.
The Master, too, of the Event
Am I on this weird Continent:
This phrase I took from—thanks herewith!—
My little brother Meredith.
I make or mar. My daring hand
Explores the entrails of the land,
And finds, beneath a greasy hat,
An Austral Homer at Cow Flat.
I seize him by his shaggy hair,
And lift him high, and hold him there,
And wave him like a Habakkuk;
And yell to notify my luck.
Should any dare at me to jeer
And say 'His swan's a goose, we fear,'
I crown his head with laurel-wreath—
And promptly fling it in their teeth.

A primrose by a river's brim
A splendid sunflower is to him.

VOICE FROM W.P.B.

But he himself—bear this in mind!—
Must be the first that flower to find.

SEVERAL VOICES FROM PROOF-SHEETS (*conclusively*)

His simple task is to be good
To members of the Brotherhood.

R.P. EDITOR (*with gay irony*)

A month goes by. I drop him hard,
And take up with a newer bard—
The Shakespeare of Dead Dingo Swamp.
The Cow Flat Homer has to tramp.
The adjectives I decked him with,
I take them back to use on Smith—
Or Jones, or whatsoever name
The Shakespeare of the Swamp may claim—
And, like a kite without a tail,
He flops into the hollow vale.

The dog, ah! well he got a bait,
And thought he'd like to die,
So I buried him in the tucker box,
Nine miles from Gundagai.
Jack Moses, 'Nine Miles from Gundagai'

CHAPTER 3

Gundagai to Ironbark

'Them barber chaps what keeps a tote, by George, I've had enough,
One tried to cut my bloomin' throat, but thank the Lord it's tough.'
And whether he's believed or not, there's one thing to remark,
That flowing beards are all the go way up in Ironbark.
AB Paterson, 'The Man from Ironbark'

20/20   Currawong Bridgland

Nine Miles from Gundagai

JACK MOSES

(1860–1945)

I've done my share of shearing sheep,
Of droving and all that,
And bogged a bullock-team as well,
On a Murrumbidgee flat.
I've seen the bullock stretch and strain,
And blink his bleary eye,
And the dog sit on the tucker box,
Nine miles from Gundagai.

I've been jilted, jarred, and crossed in love,
And sand-bagged in the dark,
Till if a mountain fell on me
I'd treat it as a lark.
It's when you've got your bullocks bogged
That's the time you flog and cry,
And the dog sits on the tucker box,
Nine miles from Gundagai.

We've all got our little troubles,
In life's hard, thorny way.
Some strike them in a motor car
And others in a dray.
But when your dog and bullocks strike
It ain't no apple pie,
And the dog sat on the tucker box
Nine miles from Gundagai.

But that's all past and dead and gone,
And I've sold the team for meat,
And perhaps some day where I was bogged,
There'll be an asphalt street.
The dog, ah! well he got a bait,
And thought he'd like to die,
So I buried him in the tucker box,
Nine miles from Gundagai.

The Duke of Buccleuch

JA PHILP

(1861–1935)

There once was a bull named the Duke of Buccleuch
Whose hide it was shiny, whose blood it was blue,
He was shipped to Australia, stud-duty to do,
Was this highly-priced bovine, the Duke of Buccleuch.

And a lord-loving cableman sent out a line
To announce to Australia its visitor fine,
But if it was human, or if it was kine,
Was left quite in doubt—merely 'Duke of Buccleuch'.

And Sydney lickspittledom went off its head
As the news round the club-room like lightning did spread;
A jook, a live jook, and perhaps he ain't wed!
Let us hasten to welcome the Duke of Buccleuch!

When the steamer arrived, the crowd it was great,
And Circular Quay seemed to be quite en fête;
And the Gov. he was there in vice-regal state
To receive his old pal the Duke of Buccleuch.

And the Mayor was there too with a speech in his hand,
To read to the Duke as he stepped on the land
And spruce Dan O'Connor, a-smiling so bland,
All ready to cheer for the Duke of Buccleuch.

And Railway-Commissioner Eddy was there,
All properly clobbered, with nicely-brushed hair
And he had in his pocket—oh, courtesy rare—
A gilt-edged free pass for the Duke of Buccleuch.

· · · ·

There was horror, confusion, a frightful to-do—
How the larrikins laughed—and the jeers from the crew!
And the maidens and matrons shamefacedly flew
When they learned 'twas a bull—the great Duke of Buccleuch!

How We Drove the Trotter

WT GOODGE

(1862–1909)

Oh, he was a handsome trotter, and he couldn't be completer,
He had such a splendid action and he trotted to this metre,
Such a pace and such a courage, such a record-killing power,
That he did his mile in two-fifteen, his twenty in the hour.
When he trotted on the Bathurst road the pace it was a panter,
But he broke the poet's rhythm when he broke out in a canter—

As we were remarking the pace was a panter,
But just as we liked it he broke in a canter,
And rattled along with a motion terrific,
And scattered the sparks with a freedom prolific;
He tugged at the bit and he jerked at the bridle,
We pulled like a demon, the effort was idle,
The bit in his teeth and the rein in the crupper,
We didn't much care to get home to our supper.

> Then we went
> Like the wind,
> And our hands
> They were skinned,
> And we thought
> With a dread
> To go over his head,
> And we tugged
> And we strove,
> Couldn't say
> That we drove
> Till we found
> It had stopped
> And the gallop was dropped!

Then he dropped into a trot again as steady as a pacer,
And we thought we had a dandy that was sure to make a racer
That would rival all the Yankees and was bound to beat the British,
Not a bit of vice about him though he was a trifle skittish;
Past the buggies and the sulkies on the road we went a-flying,
For the pace it was a clinker, and they had no chance of trying,
But for fear he'd start a canter we were going to stop his caper
When he bolted like a bullet at a flying piece of paper—

Helter skelter,
What a pelter!
Such a pace to win a welter!
    Rush,
    Race,
    Tear!
  Flying through the air!
Wind a-humming,
Fears benumbing,
Here's another trap a-coming!
    Shouts!
    Bash!
    Crash!
Moses, what a smash!

Our Ancient Ruin

'CRUPPER D'

(19th century)

The new-chum leaned against the bar
And tapped his boot and tipped his beer,
Then, looking round, remarked: 'Er—ar—
One thing you chaps don't have out here!

'You've churches, chapels, pubs and halls—
Er—er—and such and so-and-so;
But you've no ivied abbey-walls,
No ancient ruins, don-cher-know!'

Then Jack the Shearer left the bar
(It might have been to dodge his shout!)—
They filled 'em up with Dick's three-star,
And scarcely noticed him go out.

He came back, lugging by the hair
Old Ned the Cook, all rags and beer—
'Er—er!' the joker said. 'Er—air—
'We've got *one* ancient ruin here!'

The Brucedale Scandal

MARY GILMORE

(1863–1962)

Himself and me put in the trap
    And daundered into town,
And there we found a whirlygig,
    A circus and a clown;
We took a ticket for the two,
    Without a thought of shame,
And never knew till we got home
    The loss of our good name.

'Twas Mrs Dinny met us first;
    Says she, 'What's this I hear?
Ye're gaddin' round like young gossoons
    Instid of sixty year!'
Says she, 'I heard a shockin' thing
    About a horse ye rid! ...'
Says I, 'The divel take your ears—
    I don't care if ye did!'

Says she, 'I've had respect for you;
    I've held ye up to all;
And now my heart is broke in two
    To think ye've had a fall;
For sure I never thought to find
    The frivolous in you ....'
Says I, for I was feelin' warm,
    'I don't care if ye do!'

We turned and left her where she stood,
    A poor astonished thing,
Whose wildest dissipation was
    A sober Highland Fling;
But when we came to Kelly's gate
    We got another knock,
For there was John O'Brien's Joe,
    Who looked his naked shock!

Says he (to Dan he whispers it)
    'They say—' says he, 'they say....'
'Be damned to what they say,' says Dan;
    Says I, 'Do asses bray?'

53

The poor misfortune stared at me
  As if he thought me daft,
But, me, I looked him eye for eye,
  Until he felt a draught.

But dear old Gran O'Shaughnessy
  She met us at the door,
And said, 'Since first I heard the news
  My foot's wore out the floor!
I never laughed so much,' says she,
  'Not once in all me days,
As when I heard that you and Dan
  Was took to shameless ways.

'I'm keepin' up the fire,' she said,
  'Through all this blessed day.
My wan eye on the kittle, and
  Me other up the way;
And when I heard ye on the road,
  And thought of what ye'd done,
I felt me longest years slip off
  For thinkin' of your fun!'

'Sure then,' says I, 'it's not myself
  That would begrudge the tale,
And jokes, like butter on the shelf,
  If left too long grow stale.'
I told her how I rid the horse
  In that there jig-ma-gee,
And when I said how I fell off,
  'A-w-w, did ye now!' says she.

The next was Mrs Tracy's Mick;
  Who said, 'I'm hearin' things!'
Says I, 'We'd never need to ride
  If gossipin' was wings!'
Says he, 'There's decency you know;
  Ye mustn't go too far.
I'm that much shocked ....' 'Tut, tut,' says I,
  'I don't care if ye are!'

I told her of the circus clown,
  And all the things he did.
She said, 'He wasn't half the fun
  Of that there horse ye rid;
And though my bones is eighty-six,
  I wisht I was wi' ye!'

Says I, 'Myself, I wisht it, too!'
　　'I bet ye did!' says she.

'Aw, girl,' she said, 'ye've had your day,
　　If Brucedale has the talk;
Ye've ate the apple to the core,
　　So let them chew the stalk!'
They chewed the stalk from Rapley's gate
　　To Cartwright's on the hill—
'Bedad,' says Dan, 'though years is gone,
　　There's some that's chewin' still!'

Since the Country Carried Sheep

HARRY MORANT ('THE BREAKER')

(1864–1902)

We trucked the cows to Homebush, saw the girls, and started back,
Went West through Cunnamulla, and got to the Eulo track,
Camped a while at Gonybibil—but, Lord! you wouldn't know
It for the place where you and Mick were stockmen long ago.

Young Merino bought the station, fenced the run and built a 'shed',
Sacked the stockmen, sold the cattle, and put on sheep instead,
But he wasn't built for Queensland; and every blessed year
One hears of 'labour troubles' when Merino starts to shear.

There are ructions with the rouseabouts, and shearers' strikes galore!
The likes were never thought of in the cattle days of yore.
And slowly, round small paddocks now, the 'sleeping lizards' creep,
And Gonybibil's beggared since the country carried sheep.

Time was we had the horses up ere starlight waned away,
The billy would be boiling by the breaking of the day;
And our horses—by Protection—were aye in decent nick,
When we rode up the 'Bidgee where the clearskins mustered thick.

They've built *brush-yards* on Wild Horse Creek, where in the
    morning's hush
We've sat silent in the saddle, and listened for the rush
Of the scrubbers—when we heard 'em, 'twas wheel 'em if you can,
While gidgee, pine and mulga tried the nerve of horse and man.

The mickies that we've branded there! the colts we had to ride!
In Gonybibil's palmy days—before the old boss died.
Could Yorkie Hawkins see his run, I guess his ghost would weep,
For Gonybibil's beggared since the country carried sheep.

From sunrise until sunset through the summer days we'd ride,
But stockyard rails were up and pegged, with cattle safe inside,
When 'twixt the gloamin' and the murk, we heard the well-known
    note—
The peal of boisterous laughter from the kookaburra's throat.

Camped out beneath the starlit skies, the tree-tops overhead,
A saddle for a pillow, and a blanket for a bed,
'Twas pleasant, mate, to listen to the soughing of the breeze,
And learn the lilting lullabies which stirred the mulga-trees.

Our sleep was sound in those times, for the mustering days were hard,
The morrows might be harder, with the branding in the yard.
But did you see the station now! the men—and mokes—they keep!
You'd own the place was beggared—since the country carried sheep.

The Man from Ironbark

AB PATERSON ('THE BANJO')

(1864–1941)

It was the man from Ironbark who struck the Sydney town,
He wandered over street and park, he wandered up and down,
He loitered here, he loitered there, till he was like to drop,
Until at last in sheer despair he sought a barber's shop.
' 'Ere! shave my beard and whiskers off, I'll be a man of mark,
I'll go and do the Sydney toff up home in Ironbark.'

The barber man was small and flash, as barbers mostly are,
He wore a strike-your-fancy sash, he smoked a huge cigar:
He was a humorist of note and keen at repartee,
He laid the odds and kept a 'tote', whatever that may be,
And when he saw our friend arrive, he whispered 'Here's a lark!
Just watch me catch him all alive, this man from Ironbark.'

There were some gilded youths that sat along the barber's wall.
Their eyes were dull, their heads were flat, they had no brains at all;
To them the barber passed the wink, his dexter eyelid shut,
'I'll make this bloomin' yokel think his bloomin' throat is cut.'
And as he soaped and rubbed it in he made a rude remark:
'I s'pose the flats is pretty green up there in Ironbark.'

A grunt was all reply he got; he shaved the bushman's chin,
Then made the water boiling hot and dipped the razor in.
He raised his hand, his brow grew black, he paused awhile to gloat,
Then slashed the red-hot razor-back across his victim's throat;
Upon the newly shaven skin it made a livid mark—
No doubt it fairly took him in—the man from Ironbark.

He fetched a wild up-country yell might wake the dead to hear,
And though his throat, he knew full well, was cut from ear to ear,
He struggled gamely to his feet, and faced the murderous foe:
'You've done for me! you dog, I'm beat! one hit before I go
I only wish I had a knife, you blessed murderous shark!
But you'll remember all your life the man from Ironbark.'

He lifted up his hairy paw, with one tremendous clout
He landed on the barber's jaw, and knocked the barber out.
He set to work with tooth and nail, he made the place a wreck;
He grabbed the nearest gilded youth, and tried to break his neck.
And all the while his throat he held to save his vital spark,
And 'Murder! Bloody murder!' yelled the man from Ironbark.

A peeler man who heard the din came in to see the show;
He tried to run the bushman in, but he refused to go.
And when at last the barber spoke, and said, ''Twas all in fun—
'Twas just a little harmless joke, a trifle overdone.'
'A joke!' he cried. 'By George, that's fine; a lively sort of lark;
I'd like to catch that murdering swine some night in Ironbark.'

And now while round the shearing floor the listening shearers gape,
He tells the story o'er and o'er, and brags of his escape.
'Them barber chaps what keeps a tote, by George, I've had enough,
One tried to cut my bloomin' throat, but thank the Lord it's tough.'
And whether he's believed or not, there's one thing to remark,
That flowing beards are all the go way up in Ironbark.

The Old Whim-Horse

EDWARD DYSON

(1865–1931)

He's an old grey horse, with his head bowed sadly,
And with dim old eyes and a queer roll aft,
With the off-fore sprung and the hind screwed badly
And he bears all over the brands of graft;
And he lifts his head from the grass to wonder
Why by night and day now the whim is still,
Why the silence is, and the stampers' thunder
Sounds forth no more from the shattered mill.

In that whim he worked when the night-winds bellowed
On the riven summit of Giant's Hand,
And by day when prodigal Spring had yellowed
All the wide, long sweep of enchanted land;
And he knew his shift, and the whistle's warning,
And he knew the calls of the boys below;
Through the years, unbidden, at night or morning,
He had taken his stand by the old whim bow.

But the whim stands still, and the wheeling swallow
In the silent shaft hangs her home of clay,
And the lizards flirt and the swift snakes follow
O'er the grass-grown brace in the summer day;
And the corn springs high in the cracks and corners
Of the forge, and down where the timber lies;
And the crows are perched like a band of mourners
On the broken hut on the Hermit's Rise.

All the hands have gone, for the rich reef paid out,
And the company waits till the calls come in;
But the old grey horse, like the claim, is played out,
And no market's near for his bones and skin.
So they let him live, and they left him grazing
By the creek, and oft in the evening dim
I have seen him stand on the rises, gazing
At the ruined brace and the rotting whim.

The floods rush high in the gully under,
And the lightnings lash at the shrinking trees,
Or the cattle down from the ranges blunder
As the fires drive by on the summer breeze.
Still the feeble horse at the right hour wanders

To the lonely ring, though the whistle's dumb, And with
hanging head by the bow he ponders
Where the whim-boy's gone—why the shifts don't come.

But there comes a night when he sees lights glowing
In the roofless huts and the ravaged mill,
When he hears again the stampers going
Though the huts are dark and the stampers still:
When he sees the steam to the black roof clinging
As its shadows roll on the silver sands,
And he knows the voice of his driver singing,
And the knocker's clang where the braceman stands.

See the old horse take, like a creature dreaming,
On the ring once more his accustomed place;
But the moonbeams full on the ruins streaming
Show the scattered timbers and grass-grown brace.
Yet he hears the sled in the smithy falling
And the empty truck as it rattles back,
And the boy who stands by the anvil, calling;
And he turns and backs, and he takes up slack.

While the old drum creaks, and the shadows shiver
As the wind sweeps by and the hut doors close,
And the bats dip down in the shaft or quiver
In the ghostly light, round the grey horse goes;
And he feels the strain on his untouched shoulder,
Hears again the voice that was dear to him,
Sees the form he knew—and his heart grows bolder
As he works his shift by the broken whim.

He hears in the sluices the water rushing
As the buckets drain and the doors fall back:
When the early dawn in the east is blushing,
He is limping still round the old, old track.
Now he pricks his ears, with a neigh replying
To a call unspoken, with eyes aglow,
And he sways and sinks in the circle, dying;
From the ring no more will the grey horse go.

In a gully green, where a dam lies gleaming,
And the bush creeps back on a worked-out claim,
And the sleepy crows in the sun sit dreaming
On the timbers grey and a charred hut frame,
Where the legs slant down, and the hare is squatting
In the high rank grass by the dried-up course,
Nigh a shattered drum and a king-post rotting
Are the bleaching bones of the old grey horse.

Where the Dead Men Lie

BARCROFT BOAKE

(1866–1892)

Out on the wastes of the Never-Never—
　That's where the dead men lie!
There where the heat waves dance for ever—
　That's where the dead men lie!
That's where the Earth's loved sons are keeping
Endless tryst: not the west wind sweeping
Feverish pinions can wake their sleeping—
　Out where the dead men lie!

Where brown Summer and Death have mated—
　That's where the dead men lie!
Loving with fiery lust unsated—
　That's where the dead men lie!
Out where the grinning skulls bleach whitely
Under the saltbush sparkling brightly;
Out where the wild dogs chorus nightly—
　That's where the dead men lie!

Deep in the yellow, flowing river—
　That's where the dead men lie!
Under the banks where the shadows quiver—
　That's where the dead men lie!
Where the platypus twists and doubles,
Leaving a train of tiny bubbles;
Rid at last of their earthly troubles—
　That's where the dead men lie!

East and backward pale faces turning—
　That's how the dead men lie!
Gaunt arms stretched with a voiceless yearning—
　That's how the dead men lie!
Oft in the fragrant hush of nooning
Hearing again their mother's crooning,
Wrapt for aye in a dreamful swooning—
　That's how the dead men lie!

Only the hand of Night can free them—
　That's when the dead men fly!
Only the frightened cattle see them—
　See the dead men go by!
Cloven hoofs beating out one measure,

Bidding the stockmen know no leisure—
That's when the dead men take their pleasure!
    That's when the dead men fly!

Ask, too, the never-sleeping drover:
    He sees the dead pass by;
Hearing them call to their friends—the plover,
    Hearing the dead men cry;
Seeing their faces stealing, stealing,
Hearing their laughter, pealing, pealing,
Watching their grey forms wheeling, wheeling
    Round where the cattle lie!

Strangled by thirst and fierce privation—
    That's how the dead men die!
Out on Moneygrub's farthest station—
    That's how the dead men die!
Hard-faced greybeards, youngsters callow;
Some mounds cared for, some left fallow;
Some deep down, yet others shallow;
    Some having but the sky.

Moneygrub, as he sips his claret,
    Looks with complacent eye
Down at his watch-chain, eighteen carat—
    There, in his club, hard by:
Recks not that every link is stamped with
Names of the men whose limbs are cramped with
Too long lying in grave mould, cramped with
    Death where the dead men lie.

Australia

BERNARD O'DOWD

(1866–1953)

Last sea-thing dredged by sailor Time from Space,
Are you a drift Sargasso, where the West
In halcyon calm rebuilds her fatal nest?
Or Delos of a coming Sun-God's race?
Are you for Light, and trimmed, with oil in place,
Or but a Will o' Wisp on marshy quest?
A new demesne for Mammon to infest?
Or lurks millennial Eden 'neath your face?

The cenotaphs of species dead elsewhere
That in your limits leap and swim and fly,
Or trail uncanny harp-strings from your trees,
Mix omens with the auguries that dare
To plant the Cross upon your forehead sky,
A virgin helpmate Ocean at your knees.

The Stockman's Cheque

EW HORNUNG

(1866–1921)

There's a hut in Riverina where a solitary hand
May weaken on himself and all that's his;
There's a pub in Riverina where they keep a smashing brand
Of every sort of liquor short o' fizz.
And I've been an' blued another fifty-pounder at the pub—
You're very sorry for me, I'll be bound!
But when a man is fit up free with hut, an' horse, an' grub,
What the blazes does he want with fifty pound?

Why the devil should he hoard his fifty quid?
Who would be a bit the better if he did?
Though they slithered in a week,
When I couldn't see or speak,
Do you think I'm here to squeak?
    Lord forbid.

The boss was in the homestead: when he give me good advice
I took my oath, but took his cheque as well.
And to me the moonlit shanty looked a pocket paradise,
Though the boss had just been calling it a hell.
Then the shanty-keeper's daughter, she's an educated lass,
And she bangs the new pianner all for me;
And the shanty-keeper's wife she sticks me up as bold as brass,
An' the shanty-keeper's wife is good to see.

Two petticoats between 'em whisk you far!
But the shanty-keeper smoked behind the bar.
Oh, his words were grave and few,
And he never looked at you,
But he just uncorked a new
    Gallon jar.

We fed and then we started in the bar at nine o'clock;
At twelve we made a move into the cool;
The shanty-keeper *he* was just as steady as a rock,
And me as paralytic as a fool.
I remember the veranda like a sinkin' vessel's deck,
And a brace of moons suspended in the sky . . .
And nothing more till waking and inquiring for my cheque,
And the oath of all them three I'd drunk it dry!

So that was all I got for fifty notes!
The three of 'em stood lying in their throats:
There was one that must have seen
I'd have beat him blue an' green
If I hadn't gone an' been
      Off my oats.

Thank the Lord I'm back at last— though back wrecked and whisky-logged!
Yet the gates have not come open that I shut,
And I've seen no broken fences, and I've found no weak sheep bogged,
An' my little cat is purring in the hut.
There's tea, too, for the billy-can, there's water in the tanks,
The ration-bags hang heavy all around;
An' my good old bunk an' blanket beat the bare veranda planks
Of the shanty where I blued my fifty pound!

Here I stick until I'm worth fifty more,
When I'll take another cheque from the store;
And with Riverina men
All the betting is that then
I shall knock it down again
      As before.

The Bullocky's Love-Episode

AF YORK

(19th century)

I sez to her—'Gee, Boxer, gee'—behind the shed last night,
'Old girl,' I says—'Come up, there, Star! I'll make you pull all right!' —
'I've saved a quid or two,' I says, 'and if you'll only say'—
'Gee, Boxer! Star! Come hither, Spot! Gee, Boxer! Come 'ee way!'—
'We might get'—'BRANDY! Bless my soul, such bullocks drive me mad!
I'll take the livin' hide off you in strips, I will, my lad!'—

'So, what d'yer think, old girl,' I says, 'just tell me fair and straight,
I'm tongue-tied like and'—'Holy Frost! they've caught the bloomin' gate!
You cross-eyed, jumped-up, wobblin' swine! What's set you all astray!
It's no good, boss; they *can't* go back—though there'll be hell to pay!
They can't back fifteen ton of load—the post must come away!
Stand back in case the rails should fly—stand back there up the bank.
I'll rouse 'em with the bleedin' butt along the bleedin' flank.
Gee there! you blank, dash, asterisks!—you sons of blankers! Blank!
There goes the boss's bran'-new gate!'—and then she says, says she,
'I can't think, George'—Gee, Boxer, gee!—'what you can see in me;
But if you're talkin' splice,' she says—'Whoa, Brandy!'—'I'll agree.'

But against the wall of Riley's pub the Bastard made a stand,
a nasty grin upon his dial; a bike-chain in each hand.
Anonymous, 'The Bastard from the Bush'

CHAPTER 4

Bastard and Bushranger

Ben Hall was out on the Lachlan side
With a thousand pounds on his head;
A score of troopers were scattered wide
And a hundred more were ready to ride
Wherever a rumour led.
Will H Ogilvie, 'The Death of Ben Hall'

20/20 Spotted Dove Buckstein

The Bastard from the Bush

ANONYMOUS

(19th century)

As night was falling slowly on city, town and bush,
from a slum in Jones's Alley came the Captain of the Push,
and his whistle, loud and piercing, woke the echoes of the Rocks,
and a dozen ghouls came slouching round the corners of the blocks.

Then the Captain jerked a finger at a stranger by the kerb,
whom he qualified politely with an adjective and verb.
Then he made the introduction: 'Here's a covey from the bush;
fuck me blind, he wants to join us, be a member of the Push!'

Then the stranger made this answer to the Captain of the Push:
'Why, fuck me dead, I'm Foreskin Fred, the Bastard from the Bush!
I've been in every two-up school from Darwin to the Loo;
I've ridden colts and blackgins; what more can a bugger do?'

'Are you game to break a window?' said the Captain of the Push.
'I'd knock a fucking house down!' said the Bastard from the Bush.
'Would you out a man and rob him?' said the Captain of the Push.
'I'd knock him down and fuck him!' said the Bastard from the
     Bush.

'Would you dong a bloody copper if you caught the cunt alone?
Would you stoush a swell or Chinkie, split his garret with a stone?
Would you have a moll to keep you; would you swear off work for
     good?'
Said the Bastard: 'My colonial silver-mounted oath I would!'

'Would you care to have a gasper?' said the Captain of the Push.
'I'll take that bloody packet!' said the Bastard from the Bush.
Then the Pushites all took council, saying, 'Fuck me, but he's game!
Let's make him our star basher; he'll live up to his name.'

So they took him to their hideout, that Bastard from the Bush,
and granted him all privileges appertaining to the Push.
But soon they found his little ways were more than they could
     stand,
and finally their Captain addressed the members of his band:

'Now listen here, you buggers, we've caught a fucking Tartar.
At every kind of bludging, that Bastard is a starter.
At poker and at two-up he's shook our fucking rolls;
he swipes our fucking likker and he robs our bloody molls!'

So down in Jones's Alley all the members of the Push
laid a dark and dirty ambush for that Bastard from the Bush.
But against the wall of Riley's pub the Bastard made a stand,
a nasty grin upon his dial; a bike-chain in each hand.

They sprang upon him in a bunch, but one by one they fell,
with crack of bone, unearthly groan, and agonising yell,
till the sorely battered Captain, spitting teeth and gouts of
        blood,
held an ear all torn and bleeding in a hand bedaubed with mud.

'You low polluted Bastard!' snarled the Captain of the Push,
'Get back where your sort belongs—that's somewhere in the bush.
And I hope heaps of misfortunes may soon tumble down on you;
may some lousy harlot dose you till your ballocks turn sky-blue!

'May the itching piles torment you; may corns grow on your feet!
May crabs as big as spiders attack your balls a treat!
And when you're down and outed, to a hopeless bloody wreck,
may you slip back through your arsehole and break your fucking
        neck!'

When Your Pants Begin to Go

HENRY LAWSON

(1867–1922)

When you wear a cloudy collar and a shirt that isn't white,
And you cannot sleep for thinking how you'll reach tomorrow night,
You may be a man of sorrow, and on speaking terms with Care,
But as yet you're unacquainted with the Demon of Despair;
For I rather think that nothing heaps the trouble on your mind
Like the knowledge that your trousers badly need a patch behind.

I have noticed when misfortune strikes the hero of the play
That his clothes are worn and tattered in a most unlikely way;
And the gods applaud and cheer him while he whines and loafs around,
But they never seem to notice that his pants are mostly sound;
Yet, of course, he cannot help it, for our mirth would mock his care
If the ceiling of his trousers showed the patches of repair.

You are none the less a hero if you elevate your chin
When you feel the pavement wearing through the leather, sock and skin;
You are rather more heroic than are ordinary folk
If you scorn to fish for pity under cover of a joke;
You will face the doubtful glances of the people that you know;
But—of course, you're bound to face them when your pants begin to go.

If, when flush, you took your pleasure, failed to make a god of Pelf—
Some will say that for your troubles you can only thank yourself;
Some will swear you'll die a beggar, but you only laugh at that
While your garments hang together and you wear a decent hat;
You may laugh at their predictions while your soles are wearing through—
But a man's an awful coward when his pants are going too!

Though the present and the future may be anything but bright,
It is best to tell the fellows that you're getting on all right.
And a man prefers to say it—'tis a manly lie to tell,
For the folks may be persuaded that you're doing very well;
But it's hard to be a hero, and it's hard to wear a grin,
When your most important garment is in places very thin.

Get some sympathy and comfort from the chum who knows you best,
Then your sorrows won't run over in the presence of the rest;
There's a chum that you can go to when you feel inclined to whine;
He'll declare your coat is tidy, and he'll say: 'Just look at mine!'
Though you may be patched all over he will say it doesn't show,
And he'll swear it can't be noticed when your pants begin to go.

Brother mine, and of misfortune! Times are hard, but do not fret,
Keep your courage up and struggle, and we'll laugh at these things yet.
Though there is no corn in Egypt, surely Africa has some—
Keep your smile in working order for the better days to come!
We shall often laugh together at the hard times that we know,
And get measured by the tailor when our pants begin to go.

The Fisher

RODERIC QUINN

(1867–1949)

All night a noise of leaping fish
Went round the bay,
And up and down the shallow sands
Sang waters at their play.

The mangroves drooped on salty creeks,
And through the dark,
Making a pale patch in the deep,
Gleamed, as it swam, a shark.

In streaks and twists of sudden fire
Among the reeds
The bream went by, and where they passed
The bubbles shone like beads.

All night the full deep drinking-song
Of nature stirred,
And nought beside, save leaping fish
And some forlorn night-bird.

No lost wind wandered down the hills
To tell of wide
Wild waterways; on velvet moved
The silky, sucking tide.

Deep down there sloped in shadowy mass
A giant hill;
And midway, mirrored in the tide,
The stars burned large and still.

The fisher, dreaming on the rocks,
Heard Nature say
Strange secret things that none may hear
Upon the beaten way,

And whisperings and wonder stirred,
And hopes and fears,
And sadness touched his heart, and filled
His eyes with star-stained tears:

And so, thrilled through with joy and love
And sweet distress,
He stood entranced, enchained by her
Full-breasted loveliness.

The Mystery Man

'NQ'

(19th century)

Going home in the dusk from the township
We passed an old man with his dog.
'Good evening,' said we, and 'Good evening,' said he,
Then turned down a track by a log,
A quiet old track by a log.
And somebody said, 'Well, who'd think it?'
And 'What would you think then?' I said.
'Why, that man going home with his dog,
Going down on the track by the log,
He's no one but Kelly, *the* Kelly,
Dan Kelly, the brother of Ned!'

'But how can you know that?' I asked him.
He said, 'It's as plain as your nose.
From nowhere he came, with a vague sort of name,
And a beard that nobody grows,
No, nowadays nobody grows.
And kiddies won't pass him at twilight
And he talks to his dog, so it's said,
And it's all about watches and gold
And things that shouldn't be told.
So he's no one but Kelly, *the* Kelly,
Dan Kelly, the brother of Ned.'

Now that was in one little township,
But many such townships there be
From Mansfield to Sale or the Acheron Vale,
And one point in common you'll see,
They've all the one bogey to see.
For someone's said, 'Well, he's a caution!'
'That little old man there?' I've said.
'Yes, there's loot in his hut,
So he keeps the door shut,
For he's no one but Kelly, *the* Kelly,
Dan Kelly, the brother of Ned.'

So bogeys will never be dead
While men get dreams in their head,
And an old chap ready for bed
And tired with the life he's led,
Shearing in shed after shed
Or mining or farming instead,
Has *got* to be Kelly, *the* Kelly,
Dan Kelly, the brother of Ned!

Emus

MARY FULLERTON
(1868–1946)

My annals have it so:
A thing my mother saw,
Nigh eighty years ago,
With happiness and awe.

Along a level hill—
A clearing in wild space.
And night's last tardy chill
Yet damp on morning's face.

Sight never to forget:
Solemn against the sky
In stately silhouette
Ten emus walking by.

One after one they went
In line, and without haste:
On their unknown intent,
Ten emus grandly paced.

She, used to hedged-in fields
Watched them go filing past
Into the great Bush Wilds
Silent and vast.

Sudden that hour she knew
That this far place was good,
This mighty land and new
For the soul's hardihood.

For hearts that love the strange,
That carry wonder;
The Bush, the hills, the range,
And the dark flats under.

The Death of Ben Hall

WILL H OGILVIE

(1869–1963)

Ben Hall was out on the Lachlan side
With a thousand pounds on his head;
A score of troopers were scattered wide
And a hundred more were ready to ride
Wherever a rumour led.

They had followed his track from the Weddin heights
And north by the Weelong yards;
Through dazzling days and moonlit nights
They had sought him over their rifle-sights,
With their hands on their trigger-guards.

The outlaw stole like a hunted fox
Through the scrub and stunted heath,
And peered like a hawk from his eyrie rocks
Through the waving boughs of the sapling box
On the troopers riding beneath.

His clothes were rent by the clutching thorn
And his blistered feet were bare;
Ragged and torn, with his beard unshorn,
He hid in the woods like a beast forlorn,
With a padded path to his lair.

But every night when the white stars rose
He crossed by the Gunning Plain
To a stockman's hut where the Gunning flows,
And struck on the door three swift light blows,
And a hand unhooked the chain—

And the outlaw followed the lone path back
With food for another day;
And the kindly darkness covered his track
And the shadows swallowed him deep and black
Where the starlight melted away.

But his friend had read of the Big Reward,
And his soul was stirred with greed;
He fastened his door and window-board,
He saddled his horse and crossed the ford,
And spurred to the town at speed.

You may ride at a man's or a maid's behest
When honour or true love call
And steel your heart to the worst or best,
But the ride that is ta'en on a traitor's quest
Is the bitterest ride of all.

A hot wind blew from the Lachlan bank
And a curse on its shoulder came;
The pine-trees frowned at him, rank on rank,
The sun on a gathering storm-cloud sank
And flushed his cheek with shame.

He reined at the Court; and the tale began
That the rifles alone should end;
Sergeant and trooper laid their plan
To draw the net on a hunted man
At the treacherous word of a friend.

False was the hand that raised the chain
And false was the whispered word:
'The troopers have turned to the south again,
You may dare to camp on the Gunning Plain.'
And the weary outlaw heard.

He walked from the hut but a quarter-mile
Where a clump of saplings stood
In a sea of grass like a lonely isle;
And the moon came up in a little while
Like silver steeped in blood.

Ben Hall lay down on the dew-wet ground
By the side of his tiny fire;
And a night-breeze woke, and he heard no sound
As the troopers drew their cordon round—
And the traitor earned his hire.

And nothing they saw in the dim grey light,
But the little glow in the trees;
And they crouched in the tall cold grass all night,
Each one ready to shoot at sight,
With his rifle cocked on his knees.

When the shadows broke and the dawn's white sword
Swung over the mountain wall,
And a little wind blew over the ford,
A sergeant sprang to his feet and roared:
'In the name of the Queen, Ben Hall!'

Haggard, the outlaw leapt from his bed
With his lean arms held on high.
'Fire!' And the word was scarcely said
When the mountains rang to a rain of lead—
And the dawn went drifting by.

They kept their word and they paid his pay
Where a clean man's hand would shrink;
And that was the traitor's master-day
As he stood by the bar on his homeward way
And called on the crowd to drink.

He banned no creed and he barred no class,
And he called to his friends by name;
But the worst would shake his head and pass
And none would drink from the bloodstained glass
And the goblet red with shame.

And I know when I hear the last grim call
And my mortal hour is spent,
When the light is hid and the curtains fall
I would rather sleep with the dead Ben Hall
Than go where that traitor went.

The Coachman's Yarn

EJ BRADY

(1869–1952)

This a tale that the coachman told,
As he flicked the flies from Marigold
And flattered and fondled Pharaoh.
The sun swung low in the western skies;
Out on a plain, just over a rise,
 Stood Nimitybell, on Monaro;

Cold as charity, cold as hell,
Bleak, bare, barren Nimitybell—
 Nimitybell on Monaro.

'Now this 'ere 'appened in 'Eighty-three,
The coldest winter *ever* we see;
Strewth, it *was* cold, as cold as could be,
 Out 'ere on Monaro;
It froze the blankets, it froze the fleas,
It froze the sap in the blinkin' trees,
It made a grindstone out of cheese,
 Right 'ere in Monaro.

'Freezin' an' snowin'—ask the old hands;
They seen, they knows, an' *they* understands.
The ploughs was froze, and the cattle brands,
 Down 'ere in Monaro;
It froze our fingers and froze our toes;
I seen a passenger's breath so froze
Icicles 'ung from 'is bloomin' nose
 Long as the tail on Pharaoh!

'I ketched a curlew down by the creek;
His feet was froze to his blessed beak;
'E stayed like that for over a week—
 That's *cold* on Monaro.
Why, even the *air* got froze that tight
You'd 'ear the awfullest sounds at night,
When things was put to a fire or light,
 Out 'ere on Monaro.

'For the *sounds* was froze. At Haydon's Bog
A cove 'e cross-cut a big back-log,
An' carted 'er 'ome ('e wants to jog—

Stiddy, go stiddy there, Pharaoh!).
As soon as his log begins to thaw
They 'ears the sound of the cross-cut saw
A-thawin' out. Yes, his name was Law.
    Old hands, them Laws, on Monaro.

'The second week of this 'ere cold snap
I'm drivin' the coach. A Sydney chap,
'E strikes this part o' the bloomin' map,
    A new hand 'ere on Monaro;
'Is name or game I never heard tell,
But 'e gets off at Nimitybell;
Blowin' like Bluey, freezin' like 'ell
    At Nimitybell on Monaro.

'The drinks was froze, o' course, in the bar;
They *breaks* a bottle of old Three Star,
An' the barman sez, "Now, there y' are,
    You can't beat *that* for Monaro!"
The stranger bloke, 'e was tall an' thin,
Sez, "Strike me blue, but I think *you* win;
We'll 'ave another an' I'll turn in—
    It's blitherin *cold* on Monaro."

' 'E borrowed a book an' went to bed
To read awhile, so the missus said,
By the candle-light. 'E must ha' read
    (These nights is long on Monaro)
Past closin' time. Then 'e starts an' blows
The candle out; but the wick 'ad froze!
Leastways, that's what folks round 'ere suppose,
    Old hands as lived on Monaro.

'So bein' tired, an' a stranger, new
To these mountain ways, they think he threw
'Is coat on the wick; an' maybe, too,
    Any old clothes 'e'd to spare. Oh,
This ain't no fairy, an' don't *you* fret!
Next day came warmer, an' set in wet—
There's some out 'ere as can mind it yet,
    The real old 'ands on Monaro.

'The wick must ha' thawed. The fire began
At breakfast time. The neighbours all ran
To save the pub ... an' forgot the man
    (Stiddy, go stiddy there, mare-oh).
The pub was burned to the blanky ground;

'Is buttons was all they ever found.
The blinkin' cow, *'e owed me a pound*—
　　From Cooma his blinkin' fare, oh!

'That ain't no fairy, not what I've told;
I'm gettin' shaky an' growin' old,
An' I hope *I* never again see cold,
　　Like that down 'ere on Monaro!' . . .
He drives his horses, he drives them well,
And this is the tale he loves to tell
Nearing the town of Nimitybell,
　　Nimitybell on Monaro.

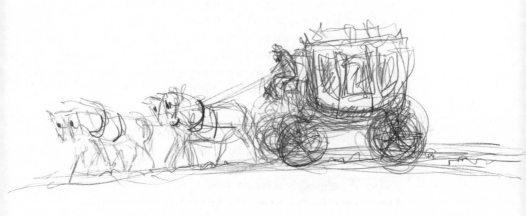

Fire in the Heavens, and Fire along the Hills

CHRISTOPHER BRENNAN

(1870–1932)

Fire in the heavens, and fire along the hills,
and fire made solid in the flinty stone,
thick-mass'd or scatter'd pebble, fire that fills
the breathless hour that lives in fire alone.

This valley, long ago the patient bed
of floods that carv'd its antient amplitude,
in stillness of the Egyptian crypt outspread,
endures to drown in noon-day's tyrant mood.

Behind the veil of burning silence bound,
vast life's innumerous busy littleness
is hush'd in vague-conjectured blur of sound
that dulls the brain with slumbrous weight, unless

some dazzling puncture let the stridence throng
in the cicada's torture-point of song.

The Orange Tree

JOHN SHAW NEILSEN

(1872–1942)

The young girl stood beside me. I
    Saw not what her young eyes could see:
—A light, she said, not of the sky
    Lives somewhere in the Orange Tree.

—Is it, I said, of east or west?
    The heartbeat of a luminous boy
Who with his faltering flute confessed
    Only the edges of his joy?

Was he, I said, borne to the blue
    In a mad escapade of Spring
Ere he could make a fond adieu
    To his love in the blossoming?

—Listen! the young girl said. There calls
    No voice, no music beats on me;
But it is almost sound: it falls
    This evening on the Orange Tree.

—Does he, I said, so fear the Spring
    Ere the white sap too far can climb?
See in the full gold evening
    All happenings of the olden time?

Is he so goaded by the green?
    Does the compulsion of the dew
Make him unknowable but keen
    Asking with beauty of the blue?

—Listen! the young girl said. For all
    Your hapless talk you fail to see
There is a light, a step, a call
    This evening on the Orange Tree.

—Is it, I said, a waste of love
    Imperishably old in pain,
Moving as an affrighted dove
    Under the sunlight or the rain?

Is it a fluttering heart that gave
    Too willingly and was reviled?

Is it the stammering at a grave,
    The last word of a little child?

—Silence! the young girl said. Oh, why,
    Why will you talk to weary me?
Plague me no longer now, for I
    Am listening like the Orange Tree.

Dummy Bridge

CJ DENNIS

(1876–1938)

'If I'd 'a' played me Jack on that there Ten,'
    Sez Peter Begg, 'I might 'a' made the lot.'
' 'Ow could yeh?' barks ole Poole. ' 'Ow could yeh, when
    I 'ad me Queen be'ind?' Sez Begg, 'Wot rot!
I slung away me King to take that trick.'
'*Which* one! Say, ain't yer 'ead a trifle thick?'

'Now, don't yeh see that when I plays me King
    I give yer Queen a chance, an' lost the slam.'
But Poole, 'e sez 'e don't see no sich thing,
    So Begg gits 'ot, an' starts to loose a 'Damn.'
'E twigs the missus jist in time to check,
An' makes it 'Dash,' an' gits red down 'is neck.

There's me an' Peter Begg, an' ole man Poole—
    Neighbours uv mine, that farm a bit close by—
Jist once a week or so we makes a school,
    An' gives this game uv Dummy Bridge a fly.
Doreen, she 'as 'er sewin' be the fire,
The kid's in bed; an' 'ere's me 'eart's desire.

'Ome-comfort, peace, the picter uv me wife
    'Appy at work, me neighbours gathered round
All friendly-like—wot more is there in life?
    I've searched a bit, but better I ain't found.
Doreen, she seems content, but in 'er eye
I've seen reel pity when the talk gits 'igh.

This ev'nin' we 'ad started off reel 'ot:
    Two little slams, an' Poole, without a score,
Still lookin' sore about the cards 'e'd got—
    When, sudden-like, a knock comes to the door.
'A visitor,' growls Begg, 'to crool our game.'
An' looks at me, as though I was to blame.

Jist as Doreen goes out, I seen 'er grin.
    'Deal 'em up quick!' I whispers. 'Grab yer 'and,
An' look reel occupied when they comes in.
    Per'aps they'll 'ave the sense to understand.
If it's a man, maybe 'e'll make a four;
But if'—Then Missus Flood comes in the door.

86

'Twas ole Mar Flood, 'er face wrapped in a smile.
    'Now, boys,' she sez, 'don't let me spoil yer game.
I'll jist chat with Doreen a little while;
    But if yeh stop I'll be ashamed I came.'
An' then she waves a letter in 'er 'and.
Sez she, 'Our Jim's a soldier! Ain't it grand?'

'Good boy,' sez Poole. 'Let's see. I make it 'earts.'
    'Doubled!' shouts Begg.... 'An' 'e's been in a fight,'
Sez Missus Flood, 'out in them furrin' parts.
    French, I suppose. I can't pronounce it right.
'E's been once wounded, somewhere in the leg....'
' 'Ere, Bill! Yeh gone to sleep?' asks Peter Begg.

I plays me Queen uv Spades; an' plays 'er bad.
    Begg snorts.... 'My boy,' sighs Missus Flood. 'My Jim.' ...
'King 'ere,' laughs Poole. 'That's the last Spade I 'ad.' ...
    Doreen she smiles: 'I'm glad yeh've 'eard from 'im.' ...
'We're done,' groans Begg. 'Why did yeh nurse yer Ace?' ...
'My Jim!' An' there was sunlight in 'er face.

'I always thought a lot uv Jim, I did,'
    Sez Begg. ' 'E does yeh credit. 'Ere, your deal.'
'That's so,' sez Poole. ' 'E was an all-right kid.
    No trumps? I'm sorry that's the way yeh feel.
'Twill take yeh all yer time to make the book.' ...
An' then Doreen sends me a wireless look.

I gets the S.O.S.; but Begg is keen.
    'My deal,' 'e yaps. 'Wot rotten cards I get.'
Ole Missus Flood sits closer to Doreen.
    'The best,' she whispers, 'I ain't told yeh yet.'
I strains me ears, an' leads me King uv Trumps.
'Ace 'ere!' grins Begg. Poole throws 'is Queen—an' thumps.

'That saves me Jack!' 'owls Begg. 'Tough luck, ole sport.' ...
    Sez Missus Flood, 'Jim's won a medal too
For doin' somethin' brave at Bullycourt.' ...
    'Play on, play on,' growls Begg. 'It's up to you.'
Then I reneges, an' trumps me partner's Ace,
An' Poole gets sudden murder in 'is face.

'I'm sick uv this 'ere game,' 'e grunts. 'It's tame.'
    'Righto,' I chips. 'Suppose we toss it in?'
Begg don't say nothin'; so we sling the game.
    On my wife's face I twigs a tiny grin.
'Finished?' sez she, su'prised. 'Well, p'r'aps it's right.
It looks to me like *'earts* was trumps to-night.'

An' so they was. An', say, the game was grand.
    Two hours we sat while that ole mother told
About 'er Jim, 'is letter in 'er 'and,
    An', on 'er face, a glowin' look that rolled
The miles all up that lie 'twixt France an' 'ere,
An' found 'er son, an' brought 'im very near.

A game uv Bridge it was, with 'earts for trumps.
    We was the dummies, sittin' silent there.
I knoo the men, like me, was feelin' chumps:
    Foolin' with cards while this was in the air.
It took Doreen to shove us in our place;
An' mother 'eld the lot, right from the Ace.

She told us 'ow 'e said 'e'd writ before,
    An' 'ow the letters must 'ave gone astray;
An' 'ow the stern ole father still was sore,
    But looked like 'e'd be soft'nin', day by day;
'Ow pride in Jim peeps out be'ind 'is frown,
An' 'ow the ole fool 'opes to 'ide it down.

'I knoo,' she sez. 'I never doubted Jim.
    But wot could any mother say or do
When pryin' folks asked wot become uv 'im,
    But drop 'er eyes an' say she never knoo.
Now I can lift me 'ead to that sly glance,
An' say, "Jim's fightin', with the rest, in France."

An' when she's gone, us four we don't require
    No gossipin' to keep us in imploy.
Ole Poole sits starin' 'ard into the fire.
    I guessed that 'e was thinkin' uv 'is boy,
'Oo's been right in it from the very start;
An' Poole was thinkin' uv a father's part.

An' then 'e speaks: 'This war 'as turned us 'ard.
    Suppose, four years ago, yeh said to me
That I'd sit 'eedless, starin' at a card
    While that ole mother told—Good Lord!' sez 'e
'It takes the women for to put us wise
To playin' games in war-time,' an' 'e sighs.

An' 'ere Doreen sets out to put 'im right.
    'There's games an' games,' she sez. 'When women starts
A hand at Bridge like she 'as played to-night
    It's Nature teachin' 'em to make it 'earts.
The other suits are yours,' she sez; 'but then,
That's as it should be, seein' you are men.'

'Maybe,' sez Poole; an' both gits up to go.
    I stands beside the door when they are gone,
Watchin' their lantern swingin' to an' fro,
    An' 'ears Begg's voice as they goes trudgin' on:
'If you 'ad led that Queen we might 'ave made ....'
'Rubbidge!' shouts Poole. 'You mucked it with yer Spade!'

Morning

HUGH McCRAE

(1876–1958)

The grand red sun has glistened in,
And through the curtain I can see
His disc upon the steeple-pin
(Just touching) of St Anthony.

The night mist on the window flows
In long, wet channels down the pane,
And from the distance slowly grows
The rattle of a country train.

But here, in this disordered room,
The dusty motes stand motionless
Above the glasses in the gloom
That rang last night with merriness.

A spotted spider walks between
The long white fingers of her glove,
Like feathers opened out, to preen,
By some proud thoughtless lady-dove.

Her little sober churchy hat,
Her month-old summer muslin gown,
The short half-stays I marvelled at—
A Frenchman's symphony in brown—

(These, set within a chair, are hid;
A mountain heaped up carelessly—
Sweets hiding other sweets amid
A cataract of lingerie.)

And she herself, still breathing sound,
Her passive eyes fast-closed in sleep,
Waits weary, in her bed, the round
Black Fortune means that she should keep.

Ah frail and sadly beautiful—
Above us in the blue-breast sky
Those stars at dusk most visible
Are now lost treasures to the eye.

And you, a mortal star on earth,
Perhaps, like that bright sisterhood,
So fair by night, may, at the birth
Of Day, be no more where you stood.

And so (that I may see you yet
As when across the lighted Place
Your beauty caught me in its net
And held me by its sovran grace)

I'll leave you softly to yourself
Before a second quarter-chime,
With this memento on the shelf
Until the purple evening time.

Sleep on—your glossy hair unrolled
Burns in my fingers, and I see
A ghostly lover in its gold
Look backward mockingly at me . . .

Another, and another—lo!
Each tress reveals a satyr-face . . .
But I must stop this play and go—
Or choke you with your pillow-lace!

CHAPTER 5

ભ

Drought, Dusk and War

20/20   Magpie Lark   Bridgford

Said Hanrahan

PJ HARTIGAN ('JOHN O'BRIEN')

(1879–1952)

'We'll all be rooned,' said Hanrahan
In accents most forlorn
Outside the church ere Mass began
One frosty Sunday morn.

The congregation stood about,
Coat-collars to the ears,
And talked of stock and crops and drought
As it had done for years.

'It's lookin' crook,' said Daniel Croke;
'Bedad, it's cruke, me lad,
For never since the banks went broke
Has seasons been so bad.'

'It's dry, all right,' said young O'Neil,
With which astute remark
He squatted down upon his heel
And chewed a piece of bark.

And so around the chorus ran
'It's keepin' dry, no doubt.'
'We'll all be rooned,' said Hanrahan,
'Before the year is out.

'The crops are done; ye'll have your work
To save one bag of grain;
From here way out to Back-o'-Bourke
They're singin' out for rain.

'They're singin' out for rain,' he said,
'And all the tanks are dry.'
The congregation scratched its head,
And gazed around the sky.

'There won't be grass, in any case,
Enough to feed an ass;
There's not a blade on Casey's place
As I came down to Mass.'

'If rain don't come this month,' said Dan,
And cleared his throat to speak—
'We'll all be rooned,' said Hanrahan,
'If rain don't come this week.'

A heavy silence seemed to steal
On all at this remark;
And each man squatted on his heel,
And chewed a piece of bark.

'We want an inch of rain, we do,'
O'Neil observed at last;
But Croke maintained we wanted two
To put the danger past.

'If we don't get three inches, man,
Or four to break this drought,
We'll all be rooned,' said Hanrahan,
'Before the year is out.'

In God's good time down came the rain;
And all the afternoon
On iron roof and windowpane
It drummed a homely tune.

And through the night it pattered still,
And lightsome, gladsome elves
On dripping spout and windowsill
Kept talking to themselves.

It pelted, pelted all day long,
A-singing at its work,
Till every heart took up the song
Way out to Back-o'-Bourke.

And every creek a banker ran,
And dams filled overtop;
'We'll all be rooned,' said Hanrahan,
'If this rain doesn't stop.'

And stop it did, in God's good time:
And spring came in to fold
A mantle o'er the hills sublime
Of green and pink and gold.

And days went by on dancing feet,
With harvest hopes immense,
And laughing eyes beheld the wheat
Nid-nodding o'er the fence.

And, oh, the smiles on every face,
As happy lad and lass
Through grass knee-deep on Casey's place
Went riding down to Mass.

While round the church in clothes genteel
Discoursed the men of mark,
And each man squatted on his heel,
And chewed his piece of bark.

'There'll be bushfires for sure, me man,
There will, without a doubt;
We'll all be rooned,' said Hanrahan,
'Before the year is out.'

The Victoria Markets Recollected in Tranquillity

FRANK WILMOT ('FURNLEY MAURICE')

(1881–1942)

I

Winds are bleak, stars are bright,
Loads lumber along the night:
Looming, ghastly white,
A towering truck of cauliflowers sways
Out of the dark, roped over and packed tight
Like faces of a crowd of football jays.

The roads come in, roads dark and long,
To the knock of hubs and a sleepy song.
Heidelberg, Point Nepean, White Horse,
Flemington, Keilor, Dandenong,
Into the centre from the source.

Rocking in their seats
The worn-out drivers droop
When dawn stirs in the streets
And the moon's a silver hoop;
Come rumbling into the silent mart,

To put their treasure at its heart,
Waggons, lorries, a lame Ford bus,
Like ants along the arms of an octopus
Whose body is all one mouth; that pays them hard
And drives them back with less than a slave's reward.

When Batman first at Heaven's command
Said, 'This is the place for a peanut-stand.'
It must have been grand!

II

'Cheap to-day, lady; cheap to-day!'
Jostling water-melons roll
From fountains of Earth's mothering soul.
Tumbling from box and tray
Rosy, cascading apples play
Each with a glowing aureole
Caught from a split sun-ray.
'Cheap to-day, lady, cheap to-day.'
Hook the carcases from the dray!
(*Where the dun bees hunt in droves*
Apples ripen in the groves.)

An old horse broods in a Chinaman's cart
While from the throbbing mart
Go cheese and celery, pears and jam
In barrow, basket, bag or pram
To the last dram the purse affords—
Food, food for the hordes.

Shuffling in the driven crush
The souls and the bodies cry,
Rich and poor, skimped and flush,
'Spend or perish, buy or die!'

Food, food for the hordes!
Turksheads tumble on the boards.

There's honey at the dairy produce stall
Where the strung saveloys festooning fall;
Yielding and yellow, the beautiful butter blocks
Confront the poultryman's plucked Plymouth Rocks.
The butcher is gladly selling,
Chopping and slaughtering, madly yelling.
A bull-like bellow for captured sales;
A great crowd surges around his scales.

Slap down the joint!
The finger point
Wobbles and comes alive,
Springs round to twenty and back to five.

No gracious burbling, nor arts to please,
No hypocritical felicities.
Buy and be damned to you! Sell and be damned also!
Decry the goods, he'll tell you where to go!

To him Creation's total aim
Is selling chops to a doubting dame.
And what will matter his steaks and joints,
The underdone and the overdone,
On the day when the old Earth jumps the points
And swings into the sun?

Along the shadows furtive, lone,
The unwashed terrier carries his week-end bone.
An old horse with a pointed hip
And dangling disillusioned under-lip
Stands in a harvest-home of cabbage leaves
And grieves.

A lady by a petrol case,
With a far-off wounded look in her face
Says, in a voice of uncertain pitch,
'Muffins' or 'crumpets,' I'm not sure which.
A pavement battler whines with half a sob,
'Ain't anybody got a bloody bob?'
Haunted by mortgages and overdrafts
The old horse droops between the shafts.
A smiling Chinaman upends a bag
And spills upon the bench with thunder-thud
(A nearby urchin trilling the newest rag)
Potatoes caked with loamy native mud.

Andean pinnacles of labelled jam.
The melting succulence of two-toothed lamb.
The little bands of hemp that truss
The succulent asparagus
That stands like tiny sheaves of purple wheat
Ready to eat!
Huge and alluring hams and rashered swine
In circular repetitive design.
Gobbling turkeys and ducks in crates,
Pups in baskets and trays of eggs;
A birdman turns and gloomily relates
His woes to a girl with impossible legs.

When Batman first at Heaven's command
Stuck flag-staffs in this sacred strand ...
We'll leave all that to the local band.

Rabbits skinned in a pink nude row,
Little brown kidneys out on show;
'Ready for the pot, mum, ready to bake!'
Buy them, devour them for pity's sake—
(*Trapped, 'neath the moon in a field of dream,*
Did anyone hear a bunny scream?)

'Cheap to-day, lady, cheap to-day.'
Slimy fish slide off the tray.
Women pondering with a sigh—
'Spend or perish, buy or die!'
Packed with babies and Brussels sprouts,
It's a ricketty pram for a woman to shove—
But tell me, lady, whereabouts
Is the long leisure of love

Flattened out on a trestle board
Somebody's trousers await their lord.

The populace takes a sidelong view
Of a coolie from one of the Orient boats,
With the help of the bo's'n and half the crew,
Trying on all of the sick-bob coats.
'Will these fit, Willie?' 'No, they're fours.'
'Oh, don't be silly, they're bigger than yours.'

'Midst iron and kitchenware,
In shameful, hidden nooks,
'Twixt wrenches and rakes and brackets at fourpence a pair,
Some dirty little crumpled books.
Pitiful they are—
'Dred' and 'A Mother's Recompense'
So pitiful and drab and far
From use or influence.
Dead gilt lettering in faded banners,
Dead laws, dead names, dead manners.
And yet I dare not touch
Their gritty spines, remembering, vaguely moved,
So many of their dear cousins that I have known and loved,
Possibly, at times, too much.
'Lost Gyp' and 'Garnered Sheaves'
Their curled and withered leaves
Stir in the faint draught of a passing dame;
Lift, fall, and again lift,
Till, parted, some pages drift
'Without a home,' without a name,
Far down the dusty aisle
Beyond the stocking stall and the man that's a bargain suit
And the girl with a loud, loud smile.
Alas! These pages originally
Were stolen from a Sunday School library,
Now 'tis their dismal fate to be
Crushed in the crimson saw-dust under a butcher's boot!

When Batman first at Heaven's command
Set foot on this square mile of land ...
Ah, no, he never would understand ...

III

Apples ripen in the groves
Where the dun bees hunt in droves

And the dainty blossom slips
Honey fetters on their lips.
Tumble down
Thistledown
Where the strawberries are sown.

Snowdrop pulls back from the bail.
Now the sickle's on the nail.
Now the plough is in the shed
And old Nugget paws his bed.
Steal away,
Gentle day;
Apples, ripen for the dray!

IV

Shuffling in the driven tide
The huddled people press,
Hoarding and gloating, having defied
Hunger, cold and nakedness
For a few days more—or less.
Is it nothing to you that pass?
Will you not pity their need?
Store beef fattens on stolen grass,
Brows grow dark with covetous greed.
Storm or manacle, cringe or pray,
There is no way but the money way.

Pouring sun, pouring heavens, pouring earth,
And the life-giving seas:
Treasure eternally flowing forth,
None greater than these!
Richness, colour and form,
Ripe flavours and juices rare!

Within men's hearts rises a deathless prayer
Deep as a spirit storm,
Giving thanks that earth has offered such
(So grateful to the eye, so rich to touch)
Miraculous varieties of fare.

And yet that lamb with the gentle eye
She had to die ...
There have been foolish dreams
Of fishes pulled from reedy streams
Of delicate earthly fruits

Being torn up by the roots—
But only the Mandragora screams.
Gentle curates and slaughtermen
Murder the cattle in the pen:
Body, Spirit, the Word, the Breath
Only survive by so much death.
The old horse with the pointed hip
And disillusioned under-lip
Stands in a drift of cabbage leaves
And grieves.

V

There is no wile to capture
Rugged and massive things
In all their fervent rapture
Soaring without wings.
No high vision can fashion
Bowed body, groping hand
Urged by a frenzy of passion
Difficult to understand;
Stripped of affected aversions
And muffling mannerliness
Which, like the laws of the Medes and Persians,
Cramp and oppress.

Grace is the power:
Only vision can flower
Into immortal song.
Art is mannered, pure and long—
These folk, accursed, can have no vital part
In schooled philosophies or templed art.
A force that throngs the by-ways and the streets
A dark, enormous influence that pours
Its passion through the light and vainly beats
On spired churches and closed college doors.
In love—the jealous pistol and the 'jug,'
In hate—the bottle-swinger and the thug,
In peace—some rows of figures and a graph,
In war—a motto on a cenotaph.
Now the plough is in the shed,
And old Nugget paws his bed.
    Steal away,
    Gentle day;
Apples, ripen for the dray!

Sea Music

WJ TURNER

(1884–1946)

Are there sounds in the sea
Fifty fathoms deep?
No, there is not a sigh
There, but like sheep
Valley-wandering on the mountain-side
Soft as the wool of sheep collide
Sister-sounding streams
In dumb clash of dreams.

There, where it is all light—
Jewel-boundaried, cool—
Nothing is dark or bright
There is no sound at all;
Running water is not heard,
Stone-babble, beak of bird
Wing-dip or trout-streak
In water, pool, or fall.

Inter-winding, never-ending
Over-topping, under-lapping
In foamless motion
Without crest crossing
Or opaque white tossing
Of billowless shadows
Thro' the fish-eyed meadows
Flows the herd-pasturing ocean.

Yet, there is music there,
Music the flounders hear,
Music lapping the ear
Of the sea anemone:
Music that flows around
Silence deep-fringed with sound,
Music whose still, bright curl
Sleeps in the oyster pearl.

What is the song of those
Fin-waving passengers
Still, as they rest afloat,
Eyes lidless, lives remote
Sending no messengers?

Voiceless the waves along
I hear that finny song
Into my heart it flows.

Strange is the thing it tells
Lovely and small
How a God once did dwell
In the sea's hall
How his harp hanging there
Now he is gone
Strung with his rainbow hair
Weeps all alone.

Cold is the grief that flows
Through the wide sea
Wordless its bloodless woes
Windless those hills where blows
No hope to be.
But there the living tone
Of the Unseen, Unknown
Is heard by me.

Dusk in the Domain

~

DOROTHEA MACKELLAR

(1885–1968)

~

Elf-light, owl-light,
Elfin-green sky;
Under the fig trees
Bats flit by;

Under the fig trees
Sprawl in a ring
Slim-limbed courtiers,
Brown Elf King.

Crowned with autumn's
Tawny gold,
Lizard-eyed, cricket-thighed,
Neither young nor old:

Like the fig-leaves'
Broad yellow wreath
Round each forehead—like
The waves beneath

Lipping the weed-hung
Low sea-wall—
Ageless, careless
Lords of all!

Grey rock-monsters
Out of the grass
Heaved; lie staring;
Moths drift past

On their business—
None have the elves,
Who hold high festival
By themselves.

•   •   •   •

So I saw them
Very plain,
Green-dusky Elfland,
Their Domain.

So I saw them
As I went through:
Seven slum children from
Wooloomooloo!

Kangaroo

DH LAWRENCE

(1885–1930)

In the northern hemisphere
Life seems to leap at the air, or skim under the wind
Like stags on rocky ground, or pawing horses, or
    springy scut-tailed rabbits.

Or else rush horizontal to charge at the sky's horizon,
Like bulls or bisons or wild pigs.

Or slip like water slippery towards its ends,
As foxes, stoats, and wolves, and prairie dogs.

Only mice, and moles, and rats, and badgers, and
    beavers, and perhaps bears
Seem belly-plumbed to the earth's mid-navel.
Or frogs that when they leap come flop, and flop to the
    centre of the earth.

But the yellow antipodal Kangaroo, when she sits up,
Who can unseat her, like a liquid drop that is heavy,
    and just touches earth.

The downward drip
The down-urge.
So much denser than cold-blooded frogs.

Delicate mother Kangaroo
Sitting up there rabbit-wise, but huge, plump-weighted,
And lifting her beautiful slender face, oh! so much more
    gently and finely lined than a rabbit's, or than a
    hare's,

Lifting her face to nibble at a round white peppermint
    drop which she loves, sensitive mother Kangaroo.

Her sensitive, long, pure-bred face.
Her full antipodal eyes, so dark,
So big and quiet and remote, having watched so many
    empty dawns in silent Australia.

Her little loose hands, and drooping Victorian shoulders.
And then her great weight below the waist, her vast
    pale belly
With a thin young yellow little paw hanging out, and
    straggle of a long thin ear, like ribbon,

Like a funny trimming to the middle of her belly, thin
    little dangle of an immature paw, and one thin ear.

Her belly, her big haunches
And, in addition, the great muscular python-stretch of
    her tail.

There, she shan't have any more peppermint drops.
So she wistfully, sensitively sniffs the air, and then
    turns, goes off in slow sad leaps
On the long flat skis of her legs,
Steered and propelled by that steel-strong snake of a
    tail.
Stops again, half turns, inquisitive to look back.
While something stirs quickly in her belly, and a lean
    little face comes out, as from a window,
Peaked and a bit dismayed,
Only to disappear again quickly away from the sight of
    the world, to snuggle down in the warmth,
Leaving the trail of a different paw hanging out.

Still she watches with eternal, cocked wistfulness!
How full her eyes are, like the full, fathomless, shining
    eyes of an Australian black-boy
Who has been lost so many centuries on the margins of
    existence!
She watches with insatiable wistfulness.
Untold centuries of watching for something to come,
For a new signal from life, in that silent lost land of the
    South.

Where nothing bites but insects and snakes and the
    sun, small life.
Where no bull roared, no cow ever lowed, no stag cried,
    no leopard screeched, no lion coughed, no dog
    barked,
But all was silent save for parrots occasionally, in the
    haunted blue bush.

Wistfully watching, with wonderful liquid eyes.
And all her weight, all her blood, dripping sack-wise
    down towards the earth's centre,
And the live little-one taking in its paw at the door of
    her belly.

Leap then, and come down on the line that draws to
    the earth's deep, heavy centre.

Women Are Not Gentlemen

HARLEY MATTHEWS

(1889–1968)

ﾻ

They said there was a woman in the hills
Behind us. All day long she watched for when
A man's head showed.
                              'It is like home. Off for a drink
While she's not looking.'
                                    The old soldier laughed.
You know that you are near it by the hum
Of talk. But not a word
You hear until you drink that long, first draught.
'They got into our trench to-day. We had
To bomb them out of it.' You break the scum.
There is your form beneath you in the pool,
Deep down. Dipping and filling, it grows blurred.
'Who says the navy is no help? The fool.'
'I do. And our artillery is as bad.
They've killed more of our own than Turks.' By some
Fresh fit of firing stirred
Your form down there is breaking
Into strange shapes. 'I say, that's near Lone Pine.
Hear the destroyer on our right join in?'
Shadows, not of your making,
Trouble the water. Fires into it come
And pass, and go. 'Our colonel has gone mad;
They're taking him away.'
'I wish they'd take ours, too. He's drunk all day.
Fewer of us get killed. But it's our rum.'
'A soldier, you? To talk
Of officers like that. Why, ours all say
We'll be across to Maidos in a week.'
'Yes, if the battleships go overland.'
More men crowd in. Lights shine.
The pool mirrors it all, not right, not wrong.
'She shot my mate to-day.' 'Here, that's my tin.'
'I tell you it is mine.'
'Clean out behind his eyes the bullet came—'
'Stop fighting, there. No war's down here. Get back,
You two, where you belong.'
New faces show as matches flame.

The cigarettes glow and the pool turns black.
'We buried him just now.'

　　All the way back it seemed the earth were waking
To a new life from some day-dream of Death's.
The slopes were deafening with fiery flowers,
Winds of all colours blew.
Forests of smoke rode by on unfelt breaths.
Lights crashed. Flames strode along the ridges, making
A world where nought was fixed, but all was true:
A time that had no hours,
No days, nor years;
A world where, a time when
Height called to height and kindred ears,
And, without speaking, men could speak to men.
Pallor bloomed dim as shapes came, carried by,
Towards ease at last. No moan was heard, no cry
Of pity. Pain was here an ecstasy
That held lips mute, made eyes too wide for tears.
And figures passed, heads high,
Walking as men should walk the earth,
Proud, without pride of birth,
Gentle, though unbeset by fears.

　　And in the morning still was Beauty there.
We lived. We could stand up and watch the sea,
Telling its dream. Then how
The wind would have it told another way:
See how the first light found
A new cape, a fresh tree;
The mist still hid a hollow, until now
Unguessed at.
　　　　　　　　We would hear again the sound
Of silence settling in from everywhere:
Then voices floating strangely in. Far-off
In front behind their lines the same cock crew.
And still his brother lived beneath the hill
To answer. Closer in the dog barked still.
We'd listen, straining towards the trench out there
To catch the same man's laugh, his comrade's cough.
We'd call good morning, then. And they'd call, too.

　　Deep in the hush somewhere
A rifle whispers, a spent bullet whirs
Past us. 'That is not hers.

It is too early for her yet. She knows
We'd see her rifle smoking in this light.'
The left is waking. As it stretches, stirs
Its limbs, things crash. It mutters now in fear
Of the time coming—'That is where the fight
Will be to-day. There—' Its full roar we hear
Of rifle, bomb, rifle. 'Look!
It's our men attacking. See the way
They're going over?' 'Here, let me
Up! Why, you'd think they're walking out to play
A game of football.' The rifle fire rushes
All to one spot, to one noise. In the trench
We crowd together, clambering up to see.
'Get down, men. It will be
Her time, soon.' Arms, heads, bodies drop to stay
Down. Every voice hushes.

    And still the battle shouts. The hill behind
Mimics it shrilly. 'They are never done,
Women, spoiling our fun,'
The old soldier mutters. 'I came here to get
Away from one.
For King and country, I told her. She swore
I went because I was a coward. True,
That was, truer than she knew.
Now here is this one saying the same thing yet:
"Sneak! Liar! Coward! You won't see the war."'
A youngster down the trench says: 'And I am here
Because a girl said I'm a coward, too.
She never even came to wave good-bye.'

    The firing stops for breath. Only the shout,
Shout from men's throats, strikes on that other ear
Of ours. 'You have an eye for women, son,
I have a way with them. Point this one out
And I'll soon show her it is not
Her war.' Bombs. Up there rifles snarl.
Leashes are slipped. New packs give tongue. 'They've got
Our fellows on the run.'

    And then, one morning, the young soldier raised
His rifle up. He cried: 'I've got her. Look!
There is her rifle lying beneath that bush.
I saw the sun shine on it when she took
Aim at somebody.' 'Get down. Quick!
You young fool. You shoot her? It's just a trick

Of hers.'
        Still he stood there and no shot came.
Then men began to push
Hats up on bayonets. Their arms grew tired
And let them fall while we looked on amazed.
A man stood up, and then another. Soon
We were all standing, and no rifle fired
At us. 'There, see it lying shining there.'
There was a wrinkled smile upon the sea.
The leaves across the valley gleamed. Below,
Uncringing, men went on their ways, as though
They knew already. 'It makes a man feel
The War is almost over.' 'God! For me
It is all over,' the old soldier said.
'What is there now to be afraid of?' 'Her!'
Our sergeant told him, 'We are going across
To-night to see if she is really dead.'
'What for? If she stays quiet I don't care.'
'The sergeant wants to get that money. Share
And share alike, I say.'
'But it's the boys' here.'
        'God! I wouldn't touch
The bloody stuff. Yes, yes, there's too much
Blood on it.'
        'We can play
For it, then.'
        Someone found
Two pennies. 'Let the sergeant toss.'
'Heads! Tails!' It went. 'Heads!'
        The old soldier won.

    We felt our way down; up. Our best guide was
To keep the uproar of the fight
Behind us. Bushes clutched, leaves felt our faces,
Then whispered us to pass.
Eyes told but little, blind with all the light
Of one bright instant, then the sudden dark.
Like that for hours we went. Our whispers grew
To mutterings—'We've long lost our landmark,
Sergeant. Let us go back.'
                'Come on! The place is
Somewhere between that hump there and that star.'
We crept behind him still, sick of it all,
Cold, tired. 'We can't be far

From it now. This way!'
           Then we heard him fall,
Snapping wood, cursing, 'Help me out of this.
Stop laughing up there. God, there's something soft
Under my foot. It's her.
Give me that torch. Yes, here she is.'
We leaned over. Then a man laughed. He coughed
With laughing, still—
             'Sergeant, she grew a strong
Beard, did that woman there.'
            'God,' a voice gasped,
'It was a man, poor bastard, all the time.'

'What,' the old soldier cried. 'But what about
My money? Turn the pockets out.'
'Here you are. Look!' There were
Some copper coins, a charm, a crust of bread.

   Nobody spoke till we began the climb
Back to the trench. Then the old soldier said,
'My luck with women never lasted long.'
Another laughed: 'Well, anyway, she's dead.'
Someone was humming to himself a song:
      'And my thoughts back there fly,
      To where I said good-bye.
      To my land, my own land, where the sky
      Is always blue,
      And blue her eyes are, too.
      Oh, I love her true,
      And she loves—'
            The young soldier's tawdry song
Told us that she would never die.

Day's End

LESBIA HARFORD

(1891–1927)

Little girls—
You are gay,
Little factory girls
At the end of day.

There you stand
Huddled close
On the back of a tram,
Having taken your dose.

And you go
Through the grey
And the gold of the streets
At the close of the day.

Blind as moles:
You are crude,
You are sweet—little girls—
And amazingly rude.

But so fine
To be gay,
Gentle people are dull
At the end of the day.

The Jester in the Trench

LEON GELLERT

(1892–1977)

'That just reminds me of a yarn,' he said,
And everybody turned to hear his tale.
He had a thousand yarns inside his head.
They waited for him, ready with their mirth
And creeping smiles—then suddenly turned pale,
Grew still, and gazed upon the earth.
They heard no tale. No further word was said.
And with his untold fun,
Half leaning on his gun,
They left him—dead.

On Having Grown Old

ERNEST G MOLL

(1900–1979)

Now are those peaks unscalable sierras
Against a darkening sky. I may not climb,
Sure of my skill, contemptuous of errors,
Their crags as gaily as once upon a time.
To reach those heights, now, even were I able,
Were but to push a faltering heart too far
And to be laid out at last on a stone table
Bare to the gaze of a mortician star.

No, never again! But from the dull plain counting,
Before dark blot them, every hazardous peak,
I'll let my eyes leap in a swift upmounting
To what I knew, and having known, still seek;
Then, on my slab, while stars put on their white
Uniforms, yield myself to absolute night.

And over the flat earth of empty farms
The monstrous continent of air floats back
Coloured with rotting sunlight and the black,
Bruised flesh of thunderstorms:
Kenneth Slessor, 'South Country'

CHAPTER 6
❦
Country
Story

I swept off like Miss Virtue
down dusty Roma Street,
and heard the goods trains whistle
WHO? WHOOOOOO? *in aching heat.*
Gwen Harwood, 'A Simple Story'

20/20   Satin Bowerbird Etching

South Country

༄

KENNETH SLESSOR

(1901–1971)

✦

After the whey-faced anonymity
Of river-gums and scribbly-gums and bush,
After the rubbing and the hit of brush,
You come to the South Country

As if the argument of trees were done,
The doubts and quarrelling, the plots and pains,
All ended by these clear and gliding planes
Like an abrupt solution.

And over the flat earth of empty farms
The monstrous continent of air floats back
Coloured with rotting sunlight and the black,
Bruised flesh of thunderstorms:

Air arched, enormous, pounding the bony ridge,
Ditches and hutches, with a drench of light,
So huge, from such infinities of height,
You walk on the sky's beach

While even the dwindled hills are small and bare,
As if, rebellious, buried, pitiful,
Something below pushed up a knob of skull,
Feeling its way to air.

Football Field: Evening

JAR McKELLAR

(1904–1932)

Cross bars and posts, the echo of distant bells,
The cool and friendly scent of whispering turf;
And in the air a little wind that tells
Of moonlit waves beyond a murmuring surf.

The glittering blue and verdant afternoon
Has locked up all its colours, leaving dearth,
Deserted, underneath a careless moon,
The glory has departed from this earth.

The goals stand up on their appointed lines,
But all their worth has faded with the sun;
Unchallenged now I cross their strict confines;
The ball is gone, the game is lost and won.

I walk again where once I came to grief,
Crashing to earth, yet holding fast the ball,
Symbol of yet another True Belief,
The last but surely not the least of all:

To strain and struggle to the end of strength;
To lean on skill, not ask a gift of chance,
To win, or lose, and recognize at length
The game the thing; the rest, a circumstance.

And now the teams are vanished from the field,
But still an echo of their presence clings;
The moon discovers what the day concealed,
The gracefulness and grief of passing things.

Quick as the ball is thrown from hand to hand
And fleetly as the wing three-quarters run,
Swifter shall Time to his defences stand
And bring the fastest falling one by one,

Until the moon, that looked on Stonehenge ground
Before the stones, will rise and sink and set
Above this field, where also will be found
The relics of a mystery men forget.

Country Places

AD HOPE

(1907–2000)

Hell, Hay and Booligal!
(Banjo Paterson)

I glean them from signposts in these country places,
Weird names, some beautiful, more that make me laugh.
Driving to fat-lamb sales or to picnic races,
I pass their worshippers of the golden calf
And, in the dust of their Cadillacs, a latter-day Habbakuk
Rises in me to preach comic sermons of doom,
Crying: 'Woe unto Tocumwal, Teddywaddy, Tooleybuc!'
And: 'Wicked Wallumburrawang, your hour has come!'

But when the Four Horsemen ride their final muster
And my sinful country sinks in the fiery rain
One name shall survive the doom and the disaster
That fell on the foolish cities of the plain.
Like the three holy children or the salamander
One place shall sing and flourish in the fire:
It is Sweet Water Creek at Mullengandra
And there at the Last Day I shall retire.

When Numbugga shrieks to Burrumbuttock:
'The curse of Sodom comes upon us all!'
When Tumbarumba calls for spade and mattock
And they bury Hell and Hay in Booligal;
When the wrath of God is loosed upon Gilgandra
And Gulargambone burns red against the west,
To Sweet Water Creek at Mullengandra
I shall rise and flee away and be at rest.

When from Goonoo Goonoo, Underbool and Grong Grong
And Suggan Buggan there goes up the cry,
From Tittybong, Drik Drik and Drung Drung,
'Help, Lord, help us, or we die!'
I shall lie beside a willow-cool meander, or
Cut myself a fly-whisk in the shade
And from Sweet Water Creek at Mullengandra
Fill my cup and whet my whistle unafraid.

When Boinka lies in ruins (more's the pity!),
And a heavenly trump proclaims the End of Grace,
With: 'Wombat is fallen, is fallen, that great city!'

Adding: 'Bunyip is in little better case;'
When from Puckapunyal and from Yackandandah
The cry goes up: 'How long, O Lord, how long?'
I shall hear the she-oaks sough at Mullengandra
And the Sweet Waters ripple into song:

Oh, there's little to be hoped for Grabben Gullen
And Tumbulgum shrinks and shudders at its fate;
Folks at Wantabadgery and Cullen Bullen
Have Buckley's chance of reaching Heaven's gate;
It's all up with Cootamundra and Kiandra
And at Collarenebri they know they're through;
But at Sweet Water Creek at Mullengandra
You may pitch your camp and sleep the whole night through.

God shall punish Cargellico, Come-by-Chance, Chinkapook;
They shall dance no more at Merrijig nor drink at Gentleman's
    Halt;
The sin of Moombooldool He shall in no wise overlook;
Wee Jasper and Little Jilliby, He shall not condone their fault;
But though I preach down Nap Nap and annihilate Narrandera,
One place shall yet be saved, this I declare:
Sweet Water Creek at Mullengandra
For its name and for my sake the Lord shall spare.

Coda

Alas! my beautiful, my prosperous, my careless country,
She destroys herself: the Lord will come too late!
They have cut down even their only tree at One Tree;
Dust has choked Honey Bugle and drifts over Creeper Gate;
The fires we lit ourselves on Mt Boothegandra
Have made more ruin than Heaven's consuming flame;
Even Sweet Water Creek at Mullengandra,
If I went there now, would it live up to its name?

They'll Tell You About Me

IAN MUDIE

(1911–1976)

Me, I'm the man that dug the Murray for Sturt to sail down,
I am the one that rode beside the man from Snowy River,
and I'm Ned Kelly's surviving brother (or did I marry his sister?
I forget which), and it was my thumbnail that wrote that Clancy
had gone a-droving and when wood was scarce I set the grass on
        fire
and ran with it three miles to boil my billy, only to find
I'd left the tea and sugar back with my tucker-bag,

and it was me, and only me, that shot through with the padre's
        daughter,
shot through with her on the original Bondi tram.
But it's a lie that I died hanging from a parrot's nest
with my arm in the hollow limb when my horse moved from under
        me;
I never die, I'm like the Leichhardt survivor I discovered
fifty years after the party had disappeared, I never die.
I'm Lasseter and Leichhardt both, I joined the wires of the O.T.
so that Todd could send the first message from Adelaide to Darwin;
I settled everywhere long before the explorers arrived,
my tracks criss-cross the Simpson Desert like city streets,
and I've hung my hat on Poeppel's Peg a thousand times.
It was me who boiled my billy under the coolibah,
told the bloke in the flash car to open his own flamin' gates,
put the goldfields pipeline through where the experts said nobody
        could,
wanted to know 'Who's robbing this coach, you or Ned Kelly?'
left the dog guarding my tucker-box outside of Gundagai,
yarned with Tom Collins while we fished for a cod someone'd
        caught years before,
and gave Henry Lawson the plots to make his stories from.
Me, I found a hundred wrecked galleons on the Queensland coast
dripping with doubloons, moidores and golden Inca swords,
and dug a dozen piles of guelders from a Westralian beach;
I was the one that invented the hollow woodheap,
and I built the Transcontinental, despite heat, dust, death, thirst.
        And flies.
I led the ragged thirteen, I fought at Eureka and Gallipoli and Lae,
and I was a day too early (or was it too late?) to discover
        Coolgardie,

lost my original Broken Hill share in a hand of cribbage,
had the old man kangaroo pinch my shirt and wallet,
threw fifty heads in a row in the big game at Kal,
took a paddle-steamer seventy miles out of the Darling on a heavy
    dew,
then tamed a Gippsland bunyip and sooled him on
to capture the Tantanoola Tiger and Fisher's Ghost
and became Billy Hughes's secretary for a couple of weeks.
Me, I outshore Jacky Howe, gave Buckley his chance,
seem to remember riding a white bull through the streets of
    Wagga,
and have had more lonely drinks than Jimmy Woods:
I jumped across Govett's Leap and wore an overcoat in Marble
    Bar,
sailed a cutter down the Kindur to the Inland Sea,
and never travelled till I went to Moonta.
Me, I was the first man ever to climb to the top of Ayers Rock,
pinched one of the Devil's Marbles for the kids to play with,
drained the mud from the Yarra, sold the Coathanger for a gold
    brick,
and asked for beer off the ice at Innamincka.

Me – yesterday I was rumour,
today I am legend,
tomorrow, history.
If you'd like to know more of me
inquire at the pub at Tennant Creek
or at any drover's camp
or shearing-shed
or shout any bloke in any bar a drink
or yarn to any bloke asleep on any beach,
they'll tell you about me,
they'll tell you more than I know myself.
After all, they were the ones that created me,
even though I'm bigger than any of them now
– in fact, I'm all of them rolled into one.
For anyone to kill me he'd have to kill
every single Australian,
every single one of them,
every single one.

Death of a Whale

JOHN BLIGHT

(1913–1995)

When the mouse died, there was a sort of pity:
the tiny, delicate creature made for grief.
Yesterday, instead, the dead whale on the reef
drew an excited multitude to the jetty.
How must a whale die to wring a tear?
Lugubrious death of a whale: the big
feast for the gulls and sharks; the tug
of the tide simulating life still there,
until the air, polluted, swings this way
like a door ajar from a slaughterhouse.
Pooh! pooh! spare us, give us the death of a mouse
by its tiny hole; not this in our lovely bay.
– Sorry, we are, too, when a child dies;
but at the immolation of a race, who cries?

A Country Song

DOUGLAS STEWART

(1913–1985)

Schute, Bell, Badgery, Lumby,
How's your dad and how'd your mum be?
What's the news, oh, far from here
Under the blue sky burning clear
Where your beautiful business runs
Wild as a dingo, fresh as a brumby?

Lumby, Badgery, Bell, Schute,
Pipe me a song, for I am mute,
Of red earth growing you hides and tallow,
Rivers wandering brown and shallow
And old grey gum-trees never dead
While magpies play them like a flute.

Bell, Lumby, Schute, Badgery,
How's the world in your menagerie?—
Hennessey's stallion and Hogan's bull
Sheds at Yass crammed full with wool
Heifers and vealers, rams and lambs,
From Nimmitabel to Wantabadgery.

Badgery, Schute, Lumby, Bell,
How's the world? The world goes well.
The auctioneer, that merry man,
Out in the sleet at Queanbeyan
Swigged his whisky neat from the bottle
And up went prices while buyers fell.

Schute, Bell, Badgery, Lumby,
Town's all stone and stone so dumb be.
Past Wee Jasper I remember
The ewes drew out through the green timber …
Oh what's your price for all that country
Wild as a dingo, fresh as a brumby?

Bullocky

JUDITH WRIGHT

(1915–2000)

Beside his heavy-shouldered team,
thirsty with drought and chilled with rain,
he weathered all the striding years
till they ran widdershins in his brain:

Till the long solitary tracks
etched deeper with each lurching load
were populous before his eyes,
and fiends and angels used his road.

All the long straining journey grew
a mad apocalyptic dream,
and he old Moses, and the slaves
his suffering and stubborn team.

Then in his evening camp beneath
the half-light pillars of the trees
he filled the steepled cone of night
with shouted prayers and prophecies.

While past the campfire's crimson ring
the star-struck darkness cupped him round,
and centuries of cattlebells
rang with their sweet uneasy sound.

Grass is across the waggon-tracks,
and plough strikes bone beneath the grass,
and vineyards cover all the slopes
where the dead teams were used to pass.

O vine, grow close upon that bone
and hold it with your rooted hand.
The prophet Moses feeds the grape,
and fruitful is the Promised Land.

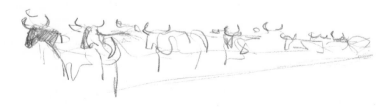

The Australian Dream

DAVID CAMPBELL

(1915–1978)

The doorbell buzzed. It was past three o'clock.
The steeple-of-Saint-Andrew's weathercock
Cried silently to darkness, and my head
Was bronze with claret as I rolled from bed
To ricochet from furniture. Light! Light
Blinded the stairs, the hatstand sprang upright,
I fumbled with the lock, and on the porch
Stood the Royal Family with a wavering torch.

'We hope,' the Queen said, 'we do not intrude.
The pubs were full, most of our subjects rude.
We came before our time. It seems the Queen's
Command brings only, "Tell the dead marines!"
We've come to you.' I must admit I'd half
Expected just this visit. With a laugh
That put them at their ease, I bowed my head.
'Your Majesty is most welcome here,' I said.
'My home is yours. There is a little bed
Downstairs, a boiler-room, might suit the Duke.'

He thanked me gravely for it and he took
Himself off with a wave. 'Then the Queen Mother?
She'd best bed down with you. There is no other
But my wide bed. I'll curl up in a chair.'
The Queen looked thoughtful. She brushed out her hair
And folded up *The Garter* on a pouf.
'Distress was the first commoner, and as proof
That queens bow to the times,' she said, 'we three
Shall share the double bed. Please follow me.'

I waited for the ladies to undress –
A sense of fitness, even in distress,
Is always with me. They had tucked away
Their state robes in the lowboy; gold crowns lay
Upon the bedside tables; ropes of pearls
Lassoed the plastic lampshade; their soft curls
Were spread out on the pillows and they smiled.
'Hop in,' said the Queen Mother. In I piled
Between them to lie like a stick of wood.
I couldn't find a thing to say. My blood

Beat, but like rollers at the ebb of tide.
'I hope your Majesties sleep well,' I lied.
A hand touched mine and the Queen said, 'I am
Most grateful to you, Jock. Please call me Ma'am.'

The Tomb of Lt. John Learmonth, A.I.F.

JOHN MANIFOLD

(1915–1985)

'*At the end on Crete he took to the hills, and said
he'ld fight it out with only a revolver. He was a
great soldier.*'
—One of his men in a letter.

This is not sorrow, this is work: I build
A cairn of words over a silent man,
My friend John Learmonth whom the Germans killed.

There was no word of hero in his plan;
Verse should have been his love and peace his trade,
But history turned him to a partisan.

Far from the battle as his bones are laid
Crete will remember him. Remember well,
Mountains of Crete, the Second Field Brigade!

Say Crete, and there is little more to tell
Of muddle tall as treachery, despair
And black defeat resounding like a bell;

But bring the magnifying focus near
And in contempt of muddle and defeat
The old heroic virtues still appear.

Australian blood where hot and icy meet
(James Hogg and Lermontov were of his kin)
Lie still and fertilise the fields of Crete.

O

Schoolboy, I watched his ballading begin:
Billy and bullocky and billabong,
Our properties of childhood, all were in.

I heard the air though not the undersong,
The fierceness and resolve; but all the same
They're the tradition, and tradition's strong.

Swagman and bushranger die hard, die game,
Die fighting, like that wild colonial boy—
Jack Dowling, says the ballad, was his name.

He also spun his pistol like a toy,
Turned to the hills like wolf or kangaroo,
And faced destruction with a bitter joy.

His freedom gave him nothing else to do
But set his back against his family tree
And fight the better for the fact he knew

He was as good as dead. Because the sea
Was closed and the air dark and the land lost,
'They'll never capture me alive,' said he.

O

That's courage chemically pure, uncrossed
With sacrifice or duty or career,
Which counts and pays in ready coin the cost

Of holding course. Armies are not its sphere
Where all's contrived to achieve its counterfeit;
It swears with discipline, it's volunteer.

I could as hardly make a moral fit
Around it as around a lightning flash.
There is no moral, that's the point of it,

No moral. But I'm glad of this panache
That sparkles, as from flint, from us and steel,
True to no crown nor presidential sash

Nor flag nor fame. Let others mourn and feel
He died for nothing: nothings have their place.
While thus the kind and civilised conceal

This spring of unsuspected inward grace
And look on death as equals, I am filled
With queer affection for the human race.

Song Cycle of the Moon-Bone

WONGURI–MANDJIGAI PEOPLE

(translated by Ronald M Berndt, 1916–1990)

North-eastern Arnhem Land

1

The people are making a camp of branches in that country at
  Arnhem Bay:
With the forked stick, the rail for the whole camp, the Mandjigai
  people are making it.
Branches and leaves are about the mouth of the hut: the middle is
  clear within.
They are thinking of rain, and of storing their clubs in case of a
  quarrel,
In the country of the Dugong, towards the wide clay-pans made by
  the Moonlight.
Thinking of rain, and of storing the fighting sticks.
They put up the rafters of arm-band-tree wood, put the branches on
  to the camp, at Arnhem Bay, in that place of the Dugong ...
And they block up the back of the hut with branches.
Carefully place the branches, for this is the camp of the Morning-
  Pigeon man,
And of the Middle-of-the-Camp man; of the Mangrove-Fish man;
  of two other head-men,
And of the Clay-pan man; of the Bayini-Anchor man, and of the
  Arnhem Bay country man;
Of the Whale man and of another head-man: of the Arnhem Bay
  Creek man;
Of the Scales-of-the-Rock-Cod man; of the Rock Cod man, and of
  the Place-of-the-Water man.

2

They are sitting about in the camp, among the branches, along the
  back of the camp:
Sitting along in lines in the camp, there in the shade of the paperbark
  trees:
Sitting along in a line, like the new white spreading clouds;
In the shade of the paperbarks, they are sitting resting like clouds.
People of the clouds, living there like the mist; like the mist sitting
  resting with arms on knees,
In here towards the shade, in this Place, in the shadow of paper-
  barks.

Sitting there in rows, those Wonguri-Mandjigai people, paperbarks
along like a cloud.
Living on cycad-nut bread; sitting there with white-stained fingers,
Sitting in there resting, those people of the Sandfly clan ...
Sitting there like mist, at that place of the Dugong ... and of the
Dugong's Entrails ...
Sitting resting there in the place of the Dugong ...
In that place of the Moonlight Clay Pans, and at the place of the
Dugong ...
There at that Dugong place they are sitting all along.

3

Wake up from sleeping! Come, we go to see the clay pan, at the
place of the Dugong ...
Walking along, stepping along, straightening up after resting:
Walking along, looking as we go down on to the clay pan.
Looking for lily plants as we go ... and looking for lily foliage ...
Circling around, searching towards the middle of the lily leaves to
reach the rounded roots.
At that place of the Dugong ...
At that place of the Dugong's Tail ...
At that place of the Dugong; looking for food with stalks,
For lily foliage, and for the round-nut roots of the lily plant.

4

The birds saw the people walking along.
Crying, the white cockatoos flew over the clay pan of the
Moonlight;
From the place of the Dugong they flew, looking for lily-root food;
pushing the foliage down and eating the soft roots,
Crying, the birds flew down and along the clay pan, at that place of
the Dugong ...
Crying, flying down there along the clay pan ...
At the place of the Dugong, of the Tree-Limbs-Rubbing-Together,
and of the Evening Star,
Where the lily-root clay pan is ...
Where the cockatoos play, at that place of the Dugong ...
Flapping their wings they flew down, crying, 'We saw the people!'
There they are always living, those clans of the white cockatoo ...
And there is the Shag woman, and there her clan:
Birds, trampling the lily foliage, eating the soft round roots!

5

An animal track is running along: it is the track of the rat …
Of the male rat, and the female rat, and the young that hang to her
   teats as she runs,
The male rat hopping along, and the female rat, leaving paw-marks
   as a sign …
On the clay pans of the Dugong, and in the shade of the trees,
At the Dugong's place, and at the place of her Tail …
Thus, they spread paw-mark messages all along their tracks,
In that place of the Evening Star, in the place of the Dugong …
Among the lily plants and into the mist, into the Dugong place, and
   into the place of her Entrails.
Backwards and forwards the rats run, always hopping along …
Carrying swamp-grass for nesting, over the little tracks, leaving
   their signs.
Backwards and forwards they run on the clay pan, around the place
   of the Dugong.
Men saw their tracks at the Dugong's place, in the shade of the trees,
   on the white clay;
Roads of the rats, paw-marks everywhere, running into the mist.
All around are their signs; and there men saw them down on the
   clay pan, at the place of the Dugong.

6

A duck comes swooping down to the Moonlight clay pan, there at
   the place of the Dugong …
From far away. 'I saw her flying over, in here at the clay pan …'
Floating along, pushing the pool into ripples and preening her
   feathers.
'I carried these eggs from a long way off, from inland to Arnhem
   Bay …'
Eggs, eggs, eggs; eggs she is carrying, swimming along.
She preens her feathers, and pulls at the lily foliage,
Drags at the lily leaves with her claws for food.
Swimming along, rippling the water among the lotus plants …
Backwards and forwards: she pulls at the foliage, swimming along,
   floating and eating.
This bird is taking her food, the lotus food in the clay plan,
At the place of the Dugong there, at the place of the Dugong's
   Tail …
Swimming along for food, floating, and rippling the water, there at
   the place of the Lilies.
Taking the lotus, the rounded roots and stalks of the lily; searching
   and eating there as she ripples the water,

'Because I have eggs, I give to my young the sound of the water.'
Splashing and preening herself, she ripples the water, among the
    lotus ...
Backwards and forwards, swimming along, rippling the water,
Floating along on the clay pan, at the place of the Dugong.

7

People were diving here at the place of the Dugong ...
Here they were digging all around, following up the lily stalks,
Digging into the mud for the rounded roots of the lily,
Digging them out at that place of the Dugong, and of the Evening
    Star,
Pushing aside the water while digging, and smearing themselves
    with mud...
Piling up the mud as they dug, and washing the roots clean.
They saw arm after arm there digging: people thick like the mist ...
The Shag woman too was there, following up the lily stalks.
There they saw arm after arm of the Mandjigai Sandfly clan,
Following the stalks along, searching and digging for food:
Always there together, those Mandjigai Sandfly people.
They follow the stalks of the lotus and lily, looking for food.
The lilies that always grow there at the place of the Dugong ...
At that clay pan, at the place of the Dugong, at the place of the lilies.

8

Now the leech is swimming along ... It always lives there in the
    water ...
It takes hold of the leaves of the lily and pods of the lotus, and
    climbs up on to their stalks.
Swimming along and grasping hold of the leaves with its head ...
It always lives there in the water, and climbs up on to the
    people.
Always there, that leech, together with all its clan ...
Swimming along towards the trees, it climbs up and waits for people.
Hear it swimming along through the water, its head out ready to
    grasp us ...
Always living here and swimming along.
Because that leech is always there, for us, however it came there:
The leech that catches hold of those Mandjigai Sandfly people ...

9

The prawn is there, at the place of the Dugong, digging out mud
    with its claws ...
The hard-shelled prawn living there in the water, making soft little
    noises.

It burrows into the mud and casts it aside, among the lilies ...
Throwing aside the mud, with soft little noises ...
Digging out mud with its claws at the place of the Dugong, the place
    of the Dugong's Tail ...
Calling the bone bukalili, the catfish bukalili, the frog bukalili, the
    sacred tree bukalili ...
The prawn is burrowing, coming up, throwing aside the mud, and
    digging ...
Climbing up on to the lotus plants and on to their pods ...

10

Swimming along under the water, as bubbles rise to the surface, the
    tortoise moves in the swamp grass.
Swimming among the lily leaves and the grasses, catching them as
    she moves ...
Pushing them with her short arms. Her shell is marked with designs,
This tortoise carrying her young, in the clay pan, at the place of the
    Dugong ...
The short-armed Mararba tortoise, with special arm-bands, here at
    the place of the Dugong ...
Backwards and forwards she swims, the short-armed one of the
    Mararba, and the Dalwongu.
Carrying eggs about, in the clay pan, at the place of the Dugong ...
Her entrails twisting with eggs ...
Swimming along through the grass, and moving her patterned shell.
The tortoise with her young, and her special arm-bands,
Swimming along, moving her shell, with bubbles rising;
Throwing out her arms towards the place of the Dugong ...
This creature with the short arms, swimming and moving her shell;
This tortoise, swimming along with the drift of the water ...
Swimming with her short arms, at the place of the Dugong ...

11

Wild-grape vines are floating there in the billabong:
Their branches, joint by joint, spreading over the water.
Their branches move as they lie, backwards and forwards,
In the wind and the waves, at the Moonlight clay pan, at the place of
    the Dugong ...
Men see them lying there on the clay pan pool, in the shade of the
    paperbarks:
Their spreading limbs shift with the wind and the water:
Grape vines with their berries ...
Blown backwards and forwards as they lie, there at the place of the
    Dugong.

Always there, with their hanging grapes, in the clay pan of the
    Moonlight ...
Vine plants and roots and jointed limbs, with berry food, spreading
    over the water.

12

Now the New Moon is hanging, having cast away his bone:
Gradually he grows larger, taking on new bone and flesh.
Over there, far away, he has shed his bone: he shines on the place of
    the Lotus Root, and the place of the Dugong,
On the place of the Evening Star, of the Dugong's Tail, of the
    Moonlight clay pan ...
His old bone gone, now the New Moon grows larger;
Gradually growing, his new bone growing as well.
Over there, the horns of the old receding Moon bent down, sank
    into the place of the Dugong:
His horns were pointing towards the place of the Dugong.
Now the New Moon swells to fullness, his bone grown larger.
He looks on the water, hanging above it, at the place of the Lotus,
There he comes into sight, hanging above the sea, growing larger
    and older ...
There far away he has come back, hanging over the clans near
    Milingimbi ...
Hanging there in the sky, above those clans ...
'Now I'm becoming a big moon, slowly regaining my roundness' ...
In the far distance the horns of the Moon bend down, above
    Milingimbi,
Hanging a long way off, above Milingimbi Creek ...
Slowly the Moon Bone is growing, hanging there far away.
The bone is shining, the horns of the Moon bend down.
First the sickle Moon on the old Moon's shadow; slowly he grows,
And shining he hangs there at the place of the Evening Star ...
Then far away he goes sinking down, to lose his bone in the sea;
Diving towards the water, he sinks down out of sight.
The old Moon dies to grow new again, to rise up out of the sea.

Up and up soars the Evening Star, hanging there in the sky.
Men watch it, at the place of the Dugong and of the Clouds, and of
    the Evening Star.
A long way off, at the place of Mist, of Lilies and of the Dugong.
The Lotus, the Evening Star, hangs there on its long stalk, held by
    the Spirits.
It shines on that place of the Shade, on the Dugong place, and on to
    the Moonlight clay pan ...
The Evening Star is shining, back towards Milingimbi, and over the
    Wulamba people ...
Hanging there in the distance, towards the place of the Dugong,
The place of the Eggs, of the Tree-Limbs-Rubbing-Together, and of
    the Moonlight clay pan ...
Shining on its short stalk, the Evening Star, always there at the clay
    pan, at the place of the Dugong ...
There, far away, the long string hangs at the place of the Evening
    Star, the place of the Lilies.
Away there at Milingimbi ... at the place of the Full Moon,
Hanging above the head of that Wonguri tribesman:
The Evening Star goes down across the camp, among the white gum
    trees ...
Far away, in these places near Milingimbi ...
Goes down among the Ngurulwulu people, towards the camp and
    the gum trees,
At the place of the Crocodiles, and of the Evening Star, away
    towards Milingimbi ...
The Evening Star is going down, the Lotus Flower on its stalk ...
Going down among all those western clans ...
It brushes the heads of the uncircumcised people ...
Sinking down in the sky, that Evening Star, the Lotus ...
Shining on to the foreheads of all those head-men ...
On to the heads of all those Sandfly people ...
It sinks there into the place of the white gum trees, at Milingimbi.

Because

JAMES McAULEY

(1917–1976)

My father and my mother never quarrelled.
They were united in a kind of love
As daily as the *Sydney Morning Herald,*
Rather than like the eagle or the dove.

I never saw them casually touch,
Or show a moment's joy in one another.
Why should this matter to me now so much?
I think it bore more hardly on my mother,

Who had more generous feelings to express.
My father had dammed up his Irish blood
Against all drinking praying fecklessness,
And stiffened into stone and creaking wood.

His lips would make a switching sound, as though
Spontaneous impulse must be kept at bay.
That it was mainly weakness I see now,
But then my feelings curled back in dismay.

Small things can pit the memory like a cyst:
Having seen other fathers greet their sons,
I put my childish face up to be kissed
After an absence. The rebuff still stuns

My blood. The poor man's curt embarrassment
At such a delicate proffer of affection
Cut like a saw. But home the lesson went:
My tenderness thenceforth escaped detection.

My mother sang *Because,* and *Annie Laurie,*
White Wings, and other songs; her voice was sweet.
I never gave enough, and I am sorry;
But we were all closed in the same defeat.

People do what they can; they were good people,
They cared for us and loved us. Once they stood
Tall in my childhood as the school, the steeple.
How can I judge without ingratitude?

Judgment is simply trying to reject
A part of what we are because it hurts.

The living cannot call the dead collect:
They won't accept the charge, and it reverts.

It's my own judgment day that I draw near,
Descending in the past, without a clue,
Down to that central deadness: the despair
Older than any hope I ever knew.

A Curse on Herod

AMY WITTING

(1918–2001)

May you live forever. In that eternity
may birdcries from the playground ring in your ear
incessantly. When you plan your forays, may
on your terrible blueprints starfish prints appear.

May short fierce arms be locked about your knees
wherever you turn, and small fists drag at your hem
while voices whine of weewee and icecream. These
are your children. You have made them. Care for them.

May you have no rest. May you wake at night with a cry
chilled by a nightmare that you can't dispel.
May the bogeyman be thirty inches high
and immortal. These are your children. Guard them well.

May they weary you till death appears to be
brighter than the walking doll or the tin drum,
the loveliest present on the Christmas tree—
but to the bad children, Christmas does not come.

A Simple Story

GWEN HARWOOD

(1920–1995)

A visiting conductor
    when I was seventeen,
took me back to his hotel room
    to cover the music scene.

I'd written a composition.
    Would wonders never cease—
here was a real musician
    prepared to hold my piece.

He spread my score on the counterpane
    with classic casualness,
and put one hand on the manuscript
    and the other down my dress.

It was hot as hell in the Windsor.
    I said I'd like a drink.
We talked across gin and grapefruit,
    and I heard the ice go clink

as I gazed at the lofty forehead
    of one who led the band,
and guessed at the hoarded sorrows
    no wife could understand.

I dreamed of a soaring passion
    as an egg might dream of flight,
while he read my crude sonata.
    If he'd said, 'That bar's not right,'

or, 'Have you thought of a coda?'
    or, 'Watch that first repeat,'
or, 'Modulate to the dominant,'
    he'd have had me at his feet.

But he shuffled it all together,
    and said, 'That's *lovely*, dear,'
as he put it down on the washstand
    in a way that made it clear

that I was no composer.
    And I being young and vain,
removed my lovely body
    from one who'd scorned my brain.

I swept off like Miss Virtue
    down dusty Roma Street,
and heard the goods trains whistle
    WHO? WHOOOOOO? in aching heat.

When children are born in Victoria
they are wrapped in the club-colours, laid in beribboned cots,
having already begun a lifetime's barracking.
Bruce Dawe, 'Life-Cycle'

CHAPTER 7

Melbourne
and Sydney

In a Federation bungalow beside Centennial Park,
With its joggers in the daytime, perves and muggers after dark,
Lived a famous author hostesses pretend that they have read;
A querulous curmudgeon with a tea-cosy on his head.
Barry Humphries, 'Threnody for Patrick White'

80/20   Willy Wagtail   Billystin

The Cliff

DAVID ROWBOTHAM

(1924–)

I remember the old joke,
Which isn't a joke now,
Of the drunk fallen at right-angles into the gutter.
Clinging with his finger-tips
To the edge, as to a cliff's edge,
He said to the passer-by,
'For Christsake help me up,
I can't hang on much longer.'
Laughter. Have another grog.
But life, not grog,
Tripped him into that illusion
With the boot of its reality.
You do not imagine cliffs unless there are cliffs.
You do not imagine death unless there is death.
Had I now been the passer-by
I would have helped him up
And turned away in horror at the rescue.
Had I been the drunk
I would have sat down at the edge of the cliff
And stared without a word of thanks,
Into the gutter.

20/25

Lament for St Maria Goretti

&

FRANCIS WEBB

(1925–1973)

&

Six o'clock. The virginal belly of a screen
Winces before the blade, the evening wind:
Diluted, a star
Twitches like a puddle on scoured hygienic stone.
All of the documents signed and countersigned
And truce to a cruel war:
Wreckage gesticulates, toothless broken ships,
Meteorite, cherubim. Horseman, in the wash of space
Round the petty bays of this child's face.

Teresa, it is easier now. But the choloroform
Comes like a stiletto to our gasping void:
Sometimes you look lovely swimming there beside me
I would take you into my hands to remould you, shape
    you,
But the pain, the pain ...
                    See Teresa, my father Luigi is coming
Out of the cemetery (but the chloroform holds)
    shouldering away
The earth. He touches his little Cross with his lips,
I am crying, and a flight of birds hangs like a rosary,
He is smiling, but the chloroform will dissolve him ...

Six o'clock. The bells of Nettuno chime
Angelus: Ave to Ave, hand to hand
The buckets of sound are passed in a slow time
Up to a thirsting land.
Again the breeze at the hospital window flutters in lace
Near the thirsting wilderness of this child's face.

Touch me, Teresa: you know you often asked me
Why I was in tears at Mass before the Communion:
I seemed to see Him there, heaving up to Golgotha,
And rising and falling, I stood there mocking Him
Like when I stole two spoonfuls of Angelino's polenta
(You haven't committed a sin, said the kind old priest):
Three times He fell: the last note of the Angelus
Falls with Him – I am falling with Him
– Must I fall with Him into chloroform?
Take up your cross. Touch me, Teresa, quickly ...

Six o'clock. There may be a moon tonight.
At dead Ferriere twitches the comatose star.
A peasant knows the early mosquito bite
Like a stiletto into his wincing ear.
The suave impersonal light
Trails its skirts over marshland: no mourners here,
And Nothing mourns at Nettuno: feel the embrace
Of Nothing scrambling ashore at this child's face.

Teresa, he's coming: *don't, you will go to Hell ...*
Teresa, I can still see you: Ferriere is closing in:
The chloroform works at you. Be dainty Corinaldo
Where I was born. I can hardly read or write:
But your breast is our little pet hill, your hair like shadows
Of clouds on our grain, your mouth like a watercourse.
Have you spoken? have words of water been truly uttered
To my thirst – it's this drumming, drumming in my ears.
Teresa, I am going. Teresa, to the last be Corinaldo,
All life writing me on earth:
Let my hands reach you – I can hardly sign my name:
My signature, my scrawl: now wait, Teresa, Teresa ...

Six o'clock. And the Miserere. Final Grace,
And Death and the Woman, strangely at one, will place
Ambiguous fingers on all of this child's face.

Stroke

VINCENT BUCKLEY

(1925–1988)

I

In the faint blue light
We are both strangers; so I'm forced to note
His stare that comes moulded from deep bone,
The full mouth pinched in too far, one hand
Climbing an aluminium bar.
Put, as though for the first time,
In a cot from which only a hand escapes,
He grasps at opposites, knowing
This room's a caricature of childhood.
'I'm done for.'

'They're treating you all right?'
We talk from the corners of our mouths
Like old lags, while his body strains
To notice me, before he goes on watching
At the bed's foot
His flickering familiars,
Skehan, Wilson, Ellis, dead men, faces,
Bodies, paused in the aluminium light,
Submits his answer to his memories,
'Yes, I'm all right. But still it's terrible.'

Words like a fever bring
The pillar of cloud, pillar of fire
Travelling the desert of the mind and face.
The deep-set, momentarily cunning eyes
Keep trying for a way to come
Through the bed's bars to his first home.
And almost find it. Going out I hear
Voices calling requiem, where the cars
Search out the fog and gritty snow,
Hushing its breathing under steady wheels.
Night shakes the seasonable ground.

II

Decorous for the dying's sake
The living talk with eyes and hands
Of football, operations, work;

The pussyfooting nurses take
Their ritual peep; the rule demands

I stand there with a stiff face
Ready, at a word or gleam,
To conjure off the drops of sweat.
So small a licit breathing-space
Brings each inside the other's dream.

Across the bright unechoing floors
The trolleys and attendants rove;
On tiptoe shine, by scoured walls,
The nearly speechless visitors
Skirt the precipice of love.

III

Oaks, pines, the willows with their quiet
Terror; the quiet terror of my age;
The seven-year-old bookworm sitting out
At night, in the intense cold, the horse
Tethered, the stars almost moving,
The cows encroaching on the night grass.
The frost stung my lips; my knees burned;
Darkness alone was homely. The hawthorn tree
Glimmered as though frost had turned to language
And language into sharp massy blossoms.
Once, I even scraped my father's hand
And glimpsed the white underside of poplars
That, moving, almost touched the flashing stars.
Squat, steep-browed, the Methodist Church nestled
Halfway between the distant police station
And the near barn; a whole world
Gave neither words nor heat, but merely
A geometry of the awakening sight.
I had forgotten that night, or nights;
And if I think back, there's nothing mythical:
A cross-legged kid with a brooding nose
His hands were too chilled to wipe,
A book whose pages he could hardly turn,
A silent father he had hardly learned
To touch; cold he could bear,
Though chill-blooded; the dark heat of words.
A life neither calm nor animal.
Now, in the deeper quiet of my age,
I feel thirty years

Turning my blood inwards; neither trees nor stars,
But a hush and start of traffic; spasms of sound
Loosening tram rails, bluestone foundations,
Manuscripts, memories; too many tasks;
A body shrinking round its own
Corruption, though a long way from dying.
We suit our memories to our sufferings.

IV

Every clod reveals an ancestor.
They, the spirit hot in their bodies,
Burned to ash in their own thoughts; could not
Find enough water; rode in a straight line
Twenty miles across country
For hatred jumping every wire fence;
With uillean pipes taunted the air
Ferociously that taunted them;
Spoke with rancour, but with double meanings;
Proud of muscle, hated the bone beneath;
Married to gain forty acres
And a family of bond servants; died bound.
I, their grandson, do not love straight lines,
And talk with a measured voice—in double meanings—
Remembering always, when I think of death,
The grandfather, small, loveless, sinister,
    ['The most terrible man I ever seen',
    Said Joe, who died thin as rice paper]
Horse-breaker, heart-breaker, whose foot scorches,
Fifty years after, the green earth of Kilmore.
It's his heat that lifts my father's frame
Crazily from the wheel-chair, fumbles knots,
Twists in the bed at night,
Considers every help a cruelty.

V

Indoors and out, weather and winds keep up
Time's passion: paddocks white for burning.
As usual, by his bed, I spend my time
Not in talk, but restless noticing:
If pain dulls, grief coarsens.
Each night we come and, voyeurs of decay,
Stare for minutes over the bed's foot,
Imagining, if we think at all,
The body turning ash, the near insane

Knowledge when, in the small hours,
Alone under the cold ceiling, above
The floor where the heating system keeps its pulse,
He grows accustomed to his own sweat
And sweats with helplessness, remembering
How, every day, at eight o'clock
The Polish nurse kisses him goodnight.
His arms are bent like twigs; his eyes
Are blown to the door after her; his tears
Are squeezed out not even for himself.
Where is the green that swells against the blade
Or sways in sap to the high boughs? To the root
He is dry wood, and in his sideways
Falling brings down lights. Our breath
Mingles,
Stirs the green air of the laurel tree.

VI

The roofs are lit with rain.
Winter. In that dark glow,
Now, as three months ago,
I pray that he'll die sane.

On tiles or concrete path
The old wheeling the old,
For whom, in this last world,
Hope is an aftermath,

And the damp trees extend
Branch and thorn. We live
As much as we believe.
All things covet an end.

Once, on the Kerrie road,
I drove with him through fire.
Now, in the burnt cold year,
He drains off piss and blood,

His wounded face tube-fed,
His arm strapped to a bed.

VII

At the merest handshake I feel his blood
Move with the ebb-tide chill. Who can revive
A body settled in its final mood?
To whom, on what tide, can we move, and live?

Later I wheel him out to see the trees:
Willows and oaks, the small plants he mistakes
For rose bushes; and there
In the front, looming, light green, cypresses.
His pulse no stronger than the pulse of air.

Dying, he grows more tender, learns to teach
Himself the mysteries I am left to trace.
As I bend to say 'Till next time', I search
For signs of resurrection in his face.

All Friends Together

RA SIMPSON

(1929–2002)

A survey of present-day Australian poetry

Charles and Bruce, Geoff and Ron and Nancy
May publish books this year: some hope they won't.
Tom and Les, Robert, Nan and John—
We live our lives quietly using words
And write of dragons and birds: we are our critics.
Asia, of course, is waiting, but somewhere else.

Max and Rod and Les, and someone else,
Are writing well, and so are Charles and John.
Who would have thought they knew so many words.
Who would have thought this country had such critics.
Mary may come good some day—she won't,
Of course. And yet we may all hear from Nancy.

Nan and Don are better now than Nancy.
Robert, too, writes well for all the critics—
And did you see that latest thing by John?
Nothing queer—the 'queers' are somewhere else
Painting paintings. And all our poems won't
Be anything but normal. We know our words

And buy anthologies to read our words—
David, Robert, Ron and Alex and Nancy.
And did you choke upon that thing by John?
Wasps and grass, magpies and something else
Have often made us write: I'm sure they won't
Seem overdone; they always please the critics.

The critics know (of course, we are the critics)
The qualities of Max and Geoff and Nancy.
And so we carry on with Charles and John,
Tom and Alex, Robert, and someone else—
Big thoughts about a myth, and simple words.
Perhaps you think we'll stop, and yet we won't.

Sometimes I think we'll stop, and yet we won't—
John and David, Bruce and Ron and Nancy,
Robert and Les, Rod and someone else,
Who love the words of friends, and please the critics

With neat anthologies and simple words—
Geoff and Max, Charles and Gwen and John.

Sometimes I think that Nancy, Don and John
And someone else are neither poets nor critics:
They won't like that. We only have our words.

Affair of the Heart

PETER PORTER

(1929–)

I have been having an affair
with a beautiful strawberry blonde.

At first she was willing to do anything,
she would suck and pump and keep on going.

She never tired me out and she flung
fireworks down the stairs to me.

What a girl I said over the telephone
as I worked her up to a red riot.

You are everywhere, you are the goddess
of tassels shining at my finger ends.

You set the alarm clock to remind us
to do it before leaving for the office.

You are classic like Roman gluttony,
priapic like St Tropez' lights.

She put up with a lot: I forgot about her
and went on the booze—I didn't eat or ring.

I borrowed from her in indigence.
I was frightened and fell back on her.

An experienced friend told me in his flat
among the press cuttings: they've got to play the field!

Of course, I said, but I knew where that was—
down my left arm, my left side, my windy stomach.

She was sometimes late and when alone
hammered me on the bed springs like a bell.

She was greedy as a herring gull and screamed
when my dreams were of Arcadian fellating.

I woke in her sweat; I had to do something,
so called in Dr Rhinegold and his machine.

Meanwhile, the paradigm was obvious:
it's me that's in you said a polar couple—

me, the love of hopeless meetings, the odd biter;
no, me, the wife by the rotary drier

with the ready hand. Dr Rhinegold moved
mountains for me and said the electric hearse

might not run. But you're sick, man, sick,
like the world itself waiting in Out Patients.

I know how the affair will end—
but not yet, Lord, not yet. It isn't hope,

it's being with her where the scenery's good,
going to concerts with her, eating Stravinsky.

It's something more. I haven't finished explaining
why I won't write my autobiography.

These poems are my reason. She knows
she can't leave me when the act's improving.

She could imagine our old age: a black-
fronted house in a Victorian Terrace

or a cat-piss Square. Working on Modernism
while the stark grey thistles push to the door.

She can't let me go with my meannesses intact,
I'll write her such letters she'll think it's

Flann O'Brien trapped in a windmill. I'll
say her the tropes of tenebrae (or Tannochbrae).

I'll squeal in fear at her feet—O, stay with me
I'll plead—look, the twentieth century

is darkening like a window; love is toneless
on the telephone with someone else to see—

only memory is like your tunnelling tongue,
only your fingers tinkering tell me I'm alive.

Life-Cycle

BRUCE DAWE

(1930–)

For Big Jim Phelan

When children are born in Victoria
they are wrapped in the club-colours, laid in beribboned
    cots,
having already begun a lifetime's barracking.

Carn, they cry, Carn ... feebly at first
while parents playfully tussle with them
for possession of a rusk: Ah, he's a little Tiger! (And they
    are ...)

Hoisted shoulder-high at their first League game
they are like innocent monsters who have been years
    swimming
towards the daylight's roaring empyrean

Until, now, hearts shrapnelled with rapture,
they break surface and are forever lost,
their minds rippling out like streamers

In the pure flood of sound, they are scarfed with light, a
    voice
like the voice of God booms from the stands
Ooohh you bludger and the covenant is sealed.

Hot pies and potato-crisps they will eat,
they will forswear the Demons, cling to the Saints
and behold their team going up the ladder into Heaven,

And the tides of life will be the tides of the home-team's
    fortunes
– the reckless proposal after the one-point win,
the wedding and honeymoon after the grand-final ...

They will not grow old as those from more northern States
    grow old,
for them it will always be three-quarter-time
with the scores level and the wind advantage in the final
    term,

That passion persisting, like a race-memory, through the
     welter of seasons,
enabling old-timers by boundary fences to dream of
     resurgent lions
and centaur-figures from the past to replenish continually
     the present,

So that mythology may be perpetually renewed
and Chicken Smallhorn return like the maize-god
in a thousand shapes, the dancers changing

But the dance forever the same – the elderly still
loyally crying Carn ... Carn ... (if feebly) unto the very
     end,
having seen in the six-foot recruit from Eaglehawk their
     hope of salvation.

Defeat

EVAN JONES

(1931–)

Huddled in overcoats,
High on the windy hill,
We nurse our injured throats
But stay on bravely still.

Out on the sodden field
They fumble and fall behind,
In all of their play revealed
The lag between body and mind.

Nothing more left to see,
We walk the chequered streets.
Later, about high tide,
Players, spectators, we
Lie between chilly sheets,
Bruised and undignified.

Bequest

PHILIP MARTIN

(1931–2006)

To those who never read, I leave my writings,
Just what they never wanted, tunes for the deaf,
Skywriting for the blind. To plagiarists,
A style, if not the taste for it. To critics,
Pushing aside their flagons to despatch
The work of half a life in half an hour,
This Christian hope: May they not wake in Limbo
Blushing. To the politicians of my birthplace
Who, not being God, do not provide: in time
Of drought, a cup of muddy water. And
To my coolest mistress, my electric blanket.

Balmoral Summer '66

VIVIAN SMITH

(1933–)

All day the weight of summer and the shrill
spaced flight of jet planes climbing north.
The news at half past twelve brought further crimes.
Insane dictators threaten new disasters.

The light of summer with its bone-white glare
and pink hibiscus in the yacht club garden.
The beach is strewn with bodies of all sizes.
How the sight of human nudity surprises —
cleft buttock, shaved armpit, nipple hair.

The heat haze hovers over Grotto Point
and skiers skim the violent flat water.
Incredible the feats that art demands.

Submarines surface to refuel
around this headland in a small bay's stillness.
History encroaches like an illness.
And children chase the gulls across the sand.

Early Discoveries

DAVID MALOUF

(1934–)

I find him in the garden. Staked tomato-plants are what
he walks among, the apples of paradise. He is eighty
and stoops, white-haired in baggy serge and braces. His moustache,

once warrior-fierce for quarrels in the small town of Zahle,
where honour divides houses, empties squares, droops and is thin
from stroking. He has come too far from his century to care

for more than these, the simplest ones: Webb's Wonders, salad-harmless,
stripped by the birds. He pantomimes a dervish-dance
among them and the birds creak off; his place at evening filled

by a stick that flares and swipes at air, a pin-striped waistcoat stuffed
with straw. It cuffs and swivels, I'm scared of it. Such temper-tantrums
are unpredictable; blind buffeting of storms that rattle

venetians, hiss off pavements in the sun. Grandpa is milder,
but when he hefts us high his white hairs prickle and the smell
is foreign. Is it garlic or old age? They are continents

I have not happened on, there time will come. Meanwhile he mutters
his blessings, I watch him practise his odd rites, hatchet in hand
as he martyrs chickens in the woodblock's dark, an old man struggling

with wings, or shakes a sieve while bright grain showers in a heap
and blown chaff flies and glitters, falling to the other mouths.
He comes and goes with daylight. He is the lord of vegetables,

the scourge of birds and nuns, those shoo-black crows his sullen daughters
taunt him with. His black-sheep son feeds rabbits live to greyhounds
in a cage behind choko-vines. The girls too go to the bad

in a foreign land, consorting with Carmelites, on hot nights tossing
on their high beds in a riot of lace doilies, painted virgins,
unwed. They dwell in another land. As I do, his eldest

grandson, aged four, where I nose through dusty beanstalks searching
for brothers under nine-week cabbages. He finds me there
and I dig behind his shadow down the rows. This is his garden,

a valley in Lebanon; you can smell the cedars on his breath
and the blood of massacres, the crescent flashing from ravines
to slice through half a family. He rolls furred sage between

thumb and stained forefinger, sniffs the snowy hills: bees shifting
gold as they forage sunlight among stones, churchbells wading
in through pools of silence. He has never quite migrated,

the weather in his head still upside-down as out of season
snow falls from his eyes on Queensland's green, and January's
midwinter still. These swelling suns are miracles. Tomatoes

in invisible glass-houses sweat in the heat of his attention,
like islands Columbus happens on. And me, whom he also finds
squatting, egg-plant tall and puzzled by his dark hands parting

the leaves. Where am I? This is Brisbane, our back yard. We let him
garden here behind a lattice wall. This house is ours
and home. He comes like a stranger, warrior-mustachioed,

un-Englished. These days I find him at all turns. One morning early
in Chios, I raise the shutter, and his garden, re-discovered,
shines: cucumbers, spinach, trellised vines. The old man finds me

watching; smiles and nods. Later, fresh on the marble step
in yesterday's newspaper (words of a tongue I cannot read)
his offering: two heads of new spring cabbage. I look under

the leaves (an ancient joke), there's nothing there. Just a sprinkling
of black soil on the headlines of another war, shaken
from the roots. That night I eat them, boiled, with oil and vinegar.

Threnody for Patrick White

BARRY HUMPHRIES

(1934–)

In a Federation bungalow beside Centennial Park,
With its joggers in the daytime, perves and muggers after dark,
Lived a famous author hostesses pretend that they have read;
A querulous curmudgeon with a tea-cosy on his head.

He had a vulnerable *hauteur*, he was arrogant and shy,
He had the visage of a dowager with a beady light blue eye,
He wrote at least two masterpieces, his correspondence flowed in
    torrents
With Firbank in one pocket, in the other D. H. Lawrence.

He was generous to young artists; often petty, never mean,
He was a typical high-minded, interbellum, stage-struck queen.
Before the war he would have queued to hear Bea Lillie sing,
One imagined him in private dragging like Douggie Byng*.

He had a few friends, (mostly female) whom he wrote to all their
    lives,
And he loved his male friends too until they traded in their wives.
Then he cut them and he dropped them and defamed them on the
    page
You felt he'd once been dropped so cruelly he had to share the pain
    and rage.

He dropped Sid and Geoff and Lawrence, he dropped Bruce, and
    Brett and me.
He preferred those lisping toadies who wouldn't dare to disagree.
With lickspittle round his table he was the Venerated Crank
But the malady was in his bones and he shrank and shrank and
    shrank ...

Now his writing light is switched off, though his wall-eyed dogs
    still bark
In that Federation garden beside Centennial Park,
Home of the family picnic and the jogger and the mugger;
Oh I pray God doesn't drop *you*, you miserable old bugger.

---

*Douglas Byng: 1893–1987 cabaret artiste and female impersonator of the '30s.

Melbourne

⤫

CHRIS WALLACE-CRABBE

(1934–)

⤬

Not on the ocean, on a muted bay
Where the broad rays drift slowly over mud
And flathead loll on sand, a city bloats
Between the plains of water and of loam.
If surf beats, it is faint and far away;
If slogans blow around, we stay at home.

And, like the bay, our blood flows easily,
Not warm, not cold (in all things moderate),
Following our familiar tides. Elsewhere
Victims are bleeding, sun is beating down
On patriot, guerrilla, refugee.
We see the newsreels when we dine in town.

Ideas are grown in other gardens while
This chocolate soil throws up its harvest of
Imported and deciduous platitudes,
None of them flowering boldly or for long;
And we, the gardeners, securely smile
Humming a bar or two of rusty song.

Old tunes are good enough if sing we must;
Old images, re-vamped *ad nauseam*,
Will sate the burgher's eye and keep him quiet
As the great wheels run on. And should he seek
Variety, there's wind, there's heat, there's frost
To feed his conversation all the week.

Highway by highway, the remorseless cars
Strangle the city, put it out of pain,
Its limbs still kicking feebly on the hills.
Nobody cares. The artists sail at dawn
For brisker ports, or rot in public bars.
Though much has died here, little has been born.

At the baths

GRAEME KINROSS SMITH

(1936–)

Fuck . . . fuck . . . fuckin' . . .
fuck . . . fuck,
and so on,
he said into the dun
and resolute lockers
in the boys' dressing-shed gloom
while we struggled
with towels and then shorts
on wet boards that sucked at the concrete.
The walls dripped
from the pool above, and the toilets
were a festering dark
of lime and stickiness –
careful not to drop your pocket-money!

Fuck . . . fuckin' . . . fuck . . .
fuck . . . fuck,
etcetera,
he was saying to his scrawny friends
as we kicked the door open
with sandalled feet and came outside,
our ears flattened by the horror of it
like squashed cans.

We did not really know
just how it touched us, where
the deep dye of it lay;
only that it had to do
with the rubber things
out in the park.

Above,
the last swimmers drowned
in their own splashings and cries
in the shadows of the cypresses.
And now – fuck . . . fuck –
he was coming out.
But the sun draped itself
tranquilly over his shoulders

and he walked unscathed
up the pitted, non-slip path
and through the footpool.
And by the time he'd reached
the upper level of running feet
and eager-smelling privet hedge
he'd stopped.

We watched.
He walked out through the turnstile,
under the noses of God
and the white-shirted baths manager
and away into the trimmed Eden of the gardens
and no-one touched him.

A Lifetime Devoted to Literature

JUDITH RODRIGUEZ

(1936–)

In your twenties you knew with elegiac certainty
you would die young. Your father's heart attack
tallied, a verification.

Thirty was your worst year: the thirties fatal to genius,
and genius undeclared by the would-be oracles.
You gave thought to publication;

then a news item—friend dropped dead in the street—
co-eval, a get-up-and-go editorial
viceroy at thirty-four—

cheered you somehow. You planned aloud and in detail,
publishers ventured for you, reviews came your way
as you learned to joke and your hair thinned,

and several thromboses onward you inhabit unruffled
an active advisory presence: a sitter on Boards
preparing to live for ever.

Sprawl leans on things. It is loose-limbed in its mind.
Reprimanded and dismissed
it listens with a grin and one boot up on the rail
of possibility. It may have to leave the Earth.
Les Murray, 'The Quality of Sprawl'

CHAPTER 8
❧

Beyond
Sprawl

Grey-coated, solitary stranger, hail!
Thou harbinger of summer's lusty days,
tracing through country parks thy mazy trail,
or lingering by some brook to catch the gaze
Vicki Raymond, 'On Seeing the First Flasher'

20/20 Black Swan Benedict

The Quality of Sprawl

LES MURRAY

(1938–)

Sprawl is the quality
of the man who cut down his Rolls-Royce
into a farm utility truck, and sprawl
is what the company lacked when it made repeated efforts
to buy the vehicle back and repair its image.

Sprawl is doing your farming by aeroplane, roughly,
or driving a hitchhiker that extra hundred miles home.
It is the rococo of being your own still centre.
It is never lighting cigars with ten-dollar notes:
that's idiot ostentation and murder of starving people.
Nor can it be bought with the ash of million-dollar deeds.

Sprawl lengthens the legs; it trains greyhounds on liver and beer.
Sprawl almost never says Why not? with palms comically raised
nor can it be dressed for, not even in running shoes worn
with mink and a nose ring. That is Society. That's Style.
Sprawl is more like the thirteenth banana in a dozen
or anyway the fourteenth.

Sprawl is Hank Stamper in Never Give an Inch
bisecting an obstructive official's desk with a chain saw.
Not harming the official. Sprawl is never brutal
though it's often intransigent. Sprawl is never Simon de Montfort
at a town-storming: Kill them all! God will know his own.
Knowing the man's name this was said to might be sprawl.

Sprawl occurs in art. The fifteenth to twenty-first
lines in a sonnet, for example. And in certain paintings;
I have sprawl enough to have forgotten which paintings.
Turner's glorious Burning of the Houses of Parliament
comes to mind, a doubling bannered triumph of sprawl —
except, he didn't fire them.

Sprawl gets up the nose of many kinds of people
(every kind that comes in kinds) whose futures don't include it.
Some decry it as criminal presumption, silken-robed Pope Alexander
dividing the new world between Spain and Portugal.
If he smiled *in petto* afterwards, perhaps the thing did have sprawl.

Sprawl is really classless, though. It's John Christopher Frederick Murray
asleep in his neighbours' best bed in spurs and oilskins

but not having thrown up:
sprawl is never Calum who, in the loud hallway of our house,
reinvented the Festoon. Rather
it's Beatrice Miles going twelve hundred ditto in a taxi,
No Lewd Advances, No Hitting Animals, No Speeding,
on the proceeds of her two-bob-a-sonnet Shakespeare readings.
An image of my country. And would that it were more so.

No, sprawl is full-gloss murals on a council-house wall.
Sprawl leans on things. It is loose-limbed in its mind.
Reprimanded and dismissed
it listens with a grin and one boot up on the rail
of possibility. It may have to leave the Earth.
Being roughly Christian, it scratches the other cheek
and thinks it unlikely. Though people have been shot for sprawl.

Bring Me the Sweat of Gabriela Sabatini

CLIVE JAMES

(1939–)

Bring me the sweat of Gabriela Sabatini
For I know it tastes as pure as Malvern water,
Though laced with bright bubbles like the *aqua minerale*
That melted the kidney stones of Michelangelo
As sunlight the snow in spring.

Bring me the sweat of Gabriela Sabatini
In a green Lycergus cup with a sprig of mint,
But add no sugar –
The bitterness is what I want.
If I craved sweetness I would be asking you to bring me
The tears of Annabel Croft.

I never asked for the wristbands of Maria Bueno,
Though their periodic transit of her glowing forehead
Was like watching a bear's tongue lap nectar.
I never asked for the blouse of Françoise Durr,
Who refused point-blank to improve her soufflé serve
For fear of overdeveloping her upper arm –
Which indeed remained delicate as a fawn's femur,
As a fern's frond under which cool shadows gather
So that the dew lingers.

Bring me the sweat of Gabriela Sabatini
And give me credit for having never before now
Cried out with longing.
Though for all the years since TV acquired colour
To watch Wimbledon for even a single day
Has left me shaking with grief like an ex-smoker
Locked overnight in a cigar factory,
Not once have I let loose as now I do
The parched howl of deprivation,
The croak of need.

Did I ever demand, as I might well have done,
The socks of Tracy Austin?
Did you ever hear me call for the cast-off Pumas
Of Hana Mandlikova?
Think what might have been distilled from these things,
And what a small request it would have seemed –

It would not, after all, have been like asking
For something so intimate as to arouse suspicion
Of mental derangement.
I would not have been calling for Carling Bassett's knickers
Or the tingling, Teddy Tinling B-cup brassiére
Of Andrea Temesvari.

Yet I denied myself.
I have denied myself too long.
If I had been Pat Cash at that great moment
Of triumph, I would have handed back the trophy
Saying take that thing away
And don't let me see it again until
It spills what makes this lawn burst into flower:
Bring me the sweat of Gabriela Sabatini.

In the beginning there was Gorgeous Gussie Moran
And even when there was just her it was tough enough,
But by now the top hundred boasts at least a dozen knockouts
Who make it difficult to keep one's tongue
From lolling like a broken roller blind.
Out of deference to Billie-Jean I did my best
To control my male chauvinist urges –
An objectivity made easier to achieve
When Betty Stove came clumping out to play
On a pair of what appeared to be bionic legs
Borrowed from Six Million Dollar Man.

I won't go so far as to say I harbour
Similar reservations about Steffi Graf –
I merely note that her thigh muscles when tense
Look interchangeable with those of Boris Becker –
Yet all are agreed that there can be no doubt
About Martina Navratilova:
Since she lent her body to Charles Atlas
The definition of the veins on her left forearm
Looks like the Mississippi river system
Photographed from a satellite,
And though she may unleash a charming smile
When crouching to dance at the ball with Ivan Lendl,
I have always found to admire her yet remain detached
Has been no problem.

But when the rain stops long enough for the true beauties
To come out swinging under the outshone sun,
The spectacle is hard for a man to take,

And in the case of this supernally graceful dish –
Likened to a panther by slavering sports reporters
Who pitiably fail to realize that any panther
With a topspin forehand line drive like hers
Would be managed personally by Mark McCormack –
I'm obliged to admit defeat.

So let me drink deep from the bitter cup.
Take it to her between any two points of a tie-break
That she may shake above it her thick black hair,
A nocturne from which the droplets as they fall
Flash like shooting stars –
And as their lustre becomes liqueur
Let the full calyx be repeatedly carried to me.
Until I tell you to stop,
Bring me the sweat of Gabriela Sabatini.

Smalltown memorials

❧

GEOFF PAGE

(1940–)

❧

No matter how small
Every town has one;
Maybe just the obelisk,
A few names inlaid;
More often full-scale granite,
Marble digger (arms reversed),
Long descending lists of dead:
Sometimes not even a town,
A thickening of houses
Or a few unlikely trees
Glimpsed on a back road
Will have one.

1919, 1920:
All over the country;
Maybe a band, slow march;
Mayors, shire councils;
Relatives for whom
Print was already
Only print; mates,
Come back, moving
Into unexpected days;
A ring of Fords and sulkies;
The toned-down bit
Of Billy Hughes from an
Ex-recruiting sergeant.
Unveiled;
Then seen each day –
Noticed once a year;
And then not always,
Everywhere.

The next bequeathed us
Parks and pools

But something in that first
Demanded stone.

The old colonist

ANDREW TAYLOR

(1940–)

1

Our old tomcat, with his weak heart,
anything over eighty, though once
menace of the whole district, prefers
to piss in the sink, in the frypan,
on the vegetables.
Anything but go out in the rain
and cold. Anything
than go at all. We house him
now in the laundry, on an old cushion
on the antique copper. He pisses
on the soap, finally on the cushion.
The laundry was a hazard of stale shit. Yet
when we scrubbed it with disinfectant,
hosed out the stink, encouraged clean air in,
he was neither grateful nor malcontent,
but with ravelled, unwashed dignity,
intelligent eyes, and ears alert,
from great age and its obscurity
pissed on the ironing with deliberate intent.

2

six days later

Too old at last even to wash himself
his only thought was to be comfortable.
Mostly on the table under the vine
he lay on his side, watching all his years
slip quietly from him, kittens prowl
backyard and lane that had been once his pride.
His tail was a tattered skipping-rope,
his haunches rejects of an Op-Shop coat:
you almost thought the moths would pass him by
he was so tattered. Hardly weighed a pound.
He had stopped eating, would sniff milk, take
barely a bite to eat then turn away,
content that we had offered him the choice,
would purr when we coaxed him, but still turn away.

And yet he had his spirit to the end.
We used his table for our lunch, and found
him comfortable among the cutlery
minutes before the guests arrived – not once
but three times. Lunchtime yesterday. Our last
sight of him was a scornful rickety leap
over the fence, tail raised in a vague
vanishing salute. This afternoon
we found him, dead, ants beginning to swarm,
stretched in the sun, warrior to the last,
sprawled like an insult on the mayor's front path.

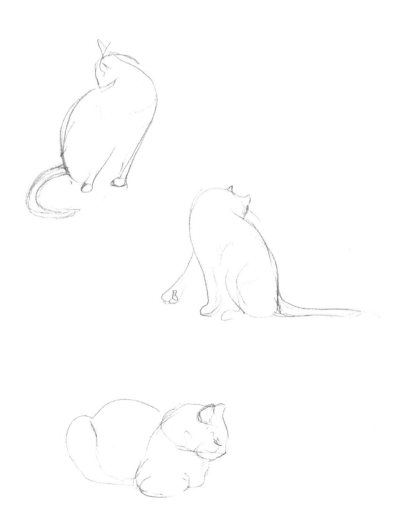

The old rifle

GEOFFREY LEHMANN

(1940–)

In the long school holidays in summer
I'd be out in the orchard
with an old rifle Mr Long fixed up,
shooting at rosellas
that were raiding fruit.
As each bird fell I'd watch
where the blue and red flickered down,
then I'd drop the rifle and run.
That way I stocked my aviary
with broken-winged rosellas.
And somewhere in my childhood
I dropped and forgot that rifle.

A year of grass grew over it.
Men were working in the orchard one day,
and my brother, the dentist, four years old,
was playing in the grass and found the rifle,
rusted all over – a wreck –
as though it had lain there for years.
My brother knew how to hold a gun
and pointing it at Jim Long, said,
'I'll shoot you Mr Long.'
He said, 'Oh don't shoot me, Barry –
shoot Bill over there.'
Barry pointed the gun at Bill.
'I'll shoot you Uncle Bill.'
'Don't shoot me, Barry,' Bill said,
'Shoot Ted here.' And Ted said,
'Why not shoot Jip?'

Jip was a good sort of dog,
my black and white fox terrier cross,
who was racing around the orchard,
looking for rabbits.
Barry dropped to one knee and squinting
took aim.
Jip dropped dead on the spot.
They buried him, telling no one,
but in their haste

made the hole too shallow,
and a few days later the story came out
when the fowls scratched him up.

'You know, Barry's quite a fair shot,'
Mr Long said,
out in the bush with Barry and me.
'My word I am,' said Barry.
'I can hit anything.'
'Can you, Barry, well – see what you can do.'
Barry took the rifle,
went down on one knee
and aimed at Mr Long's billy hanging
from a distant branch.
He fired,
and a stream of brown tea came spurting out.

The Blizzard

ROGER McDONALD

(1941–)

A man blew away.

His clothes gulped wind like sails.
He rotated—his burberry capped with ice
gripping, gripping, gripping
each faint revolution.

Now he's under the liquid ice
which never sets hard, but is
churned to a vast granita.

This was late summer, when all animal life
headed north, leaving a riddle:
'In what respect is the penguin
in other than dress
like man?'

'When she lays an egg
in this terrible wind
and puts a stone on top—
for the effort breaks
your heart, watching.'

M-----n, the meteorologist, posed this
re-entering the hut, his face clamped hard with ice
like a sculpted pie,
one eye and his mouth
and the words an abstraction of pain.

I too went out in the blizzard
at midnight, in weather twenty-five below,
when down the wind
a bird shrieked gliding at head-height,
beak and eyes and white-pinioned trunk
a heartbeat, straining.

I dreamed of that wind-rider
later, back in the hut, where the temperature sputtered
seven above freezing ...
warmed by coal, in my fur sack, I thought
no, the bird was never the blown man coming back
but could have been.

                    Later that year during sledging

I saw how death and thoughts like this
glided together, and to be brave
was to be persistently
dull, if you could,
in the face of such beauty,
and I was glad for reciting Robert W. Service
at our celebration dinners—
though at the end, and the very end,
all polar hands die under gas lamps
in lifting fog, the scrape of leaves at a window,
and a full scoop of anthracite
red in the grate.

When the blown man suddenly froze
I thought of that.

Here the driven snow will polish rusted chains in a week
and rub aluminium saucepans thin.
It blew the gust-meter down
at two hundred miles an hour (estimated)
howling with open mouth
until the sky parted and God looked down
with a cold deep face.

Anyone Home?

JOHN TRANTER

(1943–)

I can hear the stop-work whistle
down at the Club, can I go home now?
Then I see Grace Kelly,
    the young Grace Kelly!
'Starlet Fever', that's what it is.
I keep hearing the word 'workaholic'.
Echoing, echoing. The Doc says
    take a tablet.
How do you feel down there? Okay?
Take a dive. Bite the bullet. It's
the jim-jams, I've got the jim-jams.
I think he said 'phenomenology'.
I keep hearing jackhammers, it's
the jackhammers, that's what it is.

Do you know Jacky Rackett?
    Do I know Jacky Rackett?
Lovely type of a feller. Dropped his packet.
I keep hearing syllables, polysyllables.
Do I know Sherelle? Young Sherelle?

Then I hear an Appaloosa, getting closer,
the clip-clop racket in the bracken, then
a clattering gallop on the gravel,
    I hear the hullabaloo.
How d'you do, sir. Jacky Rackett?
Top o'the Paddock, sir, the witch's cat.
Then I can see Grace Kelly again,
up close, it's getting warmer.

Down here in Third Class it's getting warmer.
Pull the toggle. No, blow the whistle.
I keep hearing the word 'histrionic'.
Is that better? Snug in a rug?
    Clacketty-clack.

Do you know Gary Langer? Barry Langer?
They were both practising solicitors.
I keep hearing polysyllables,
    then jackhammers.

Now that's a clavier sonata!
That's the cat's pyjamas! No,
it's the Appaloosa! Barry! Gary!
How are you going, you old bastard!
I keep hearing these unpredictable
polysyllables, it's like the Name of God.
Isn't God indelible? Indivisible?

I can see a Californian kitchen, I'm
visiting Gidget, isn't she cute?
I can almost reach out and touch her,
gently. I pour us a Coke and it bubbles.
Is this Paradise? Is it really Paradise?

Hey, there's Jack Napier. Jack Napier!
Absolute type of a gentleman. Wouldn't
hurt you with a barge pole. Jack's
a jumper. Jack invented the calculus.
Then I hear a rustling noise,
        highly magnified.
I think I snapped the tape
at the pain threshold, then stumbled.
Oh Sherelle, will it ever diminish?
Will it ever diminish, and fade away?
Gidget, I'm carrying Gidget, on the beach,
and I stumble! Bugger it!

Down at the Club, the Workers' Club,
the stop-work whistle, should I go home now?
Spots in front of me, spots all over,
Black Friday, Over, for Black Friday
read Man Friday, Man Overboard.
Do you read me? Try again.

I keep hearing 'intelligent,
        very intelligent'.
Push the toggle-button, the green one,
the illuminated one, no, not that,
the other one! You'll feel
worse at first, considerably worse
at first, until the medicine. Oh boy,
some party! Were you there?
        Was I there?
I keep hearing 'medical, paramedical'.
Don't you think it's time to pull the plug?
Push the button? I can see Paul de Man,

Paul de Man, is he in Heaven?
I keep hearing 'shoot, parachute'.

Okay, what odds would you give me?
Push the toggle-button, bird-brain.
This one, or that one?
Go home, time to go home.
Quick, put on the Nazi uniform.
He says 'Quick, Sherelle, do as I say!'
Why should I?
   Why should I?
Who do you think I am? He says—
famous Chinese proverbs—he says
'Quick philosopher, dead solicitor!'
Who do you think I am? Paul de Man?

I can hear a whistle, an emergency whistle.
Now I can see the tropical effluent.
I think it's moving in our direction.
Dark stain.
   Dog paddle! Back-pedal!

That's funny, I can't hear a thing.
Ding-dong.
        Anyone home?

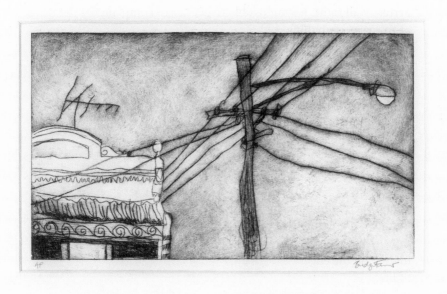

In Departing Light

ROBERT GRAY

(1945–)

My mother all of ninety has to be tied up
to her wheelchair, but still she leans far out of it sideways;
she juts there brokenly,
able to cut
with the sight of her someone who is close. She is hung
like her hanging mouth
in the dignity
of her bleariness, and says that she is
perfectly all right. It's impossible to get her to complain
or to register anything
for longer than a moment. She has made Stephen Hawking look
    healthy.
It's as though
she is being sucked out of existence sideways through a porthole
and we've got hold of her feet.
She's very calm.
If you live long enough it isn't death you fear
but what life can still do. And she appears to know this
somewhere,
even if there's no hope she could speak of it.
Yet she is so remote you think of an immortal – a Tithonus
    withering
forever on the edge
of life,
though with never a moment's grievance. Taken out to air
my mother seems in a motorcycle race, she
the sidecar passenger
who keeps the machine on the road, trying to lie far over
beyond the wheel.
Seriously, concentrated, she gazes ahead
towards the line,
as we go creeping around and around, through the thick syrups
of a garden, behind the nursing home.

Her mouth is full of chaos.
My mother revolves her loose dentures like marbles ground upon
    each other,
or idly clatters them,

broken and chipped. Since they won't stay on her gums
she spits them free
with a sudden blurting cough, that seems to have stamped out of her
an ultimate breath.
Her teeth fly into her lap or onto the grass,
breaking the hawsers of spittle.
What we see in such age is for us the premature dissolution of a body
that slips off the bones
and back to protoplasm
before it can be decently hidden away.
And it's as though the synapses were almost all of them broken
between her brain cells
and now they waver about feebly on the draught of my voice
and connect
at random and wrongly
and she has become a surrealist poet.
'How is the sun
on your back?' I ask. 'The sun
is mechanical,' she tells me, matter of fact. Wait
a moment, I think, is she
becoming profound? From nowhere she says, 'The lake gets dusty.'
    There is no lake
here, or in her past. 'You'll have to dust the lake.'
It could be
that she is, but then she says, 'The little boy in the star is
    food,'
or perhaps 'The little boy is the star in food,'
and you think, More likely
this appeals to my kind of superstition – the sleepless, inspiring
homunculus.
It is all a tangle and interpretation,
and hearing amiss,
all just the slipperiness
of her descent.

We sit and listen to the bird-song, which is like wandering lines
of wet paint –
it is like an abstract expressionist at work, his flourishes and
then
the touches
barely there,
and is going on all over the stretched sky.
If I read aloud skimmingly from the newspaper, she immediately
    falls asleep.

I stroke her face and she wakes
and looking at me intently she says something like, 'That was
a nice package.' In our sitting about
she has also said, relevant of nothing, 'The desert is a tongue.'
'A red tongue?'
'That's right, it's a
it's a sort of
you know – it's a – it's a long
motor car.'
When I told her I might be in Cambridge for a time, she told me,
    'Cambridge
is a very old seat of learning. Be sure –'
but it became too much –
'be sure
of the short Christmas flowers.' I get dizzy,
nauseous,
when I try to think about what is happening inside her head. I
    keep her
out there for hours, propping her
straight, as
she dozes, and drifts into waking; away from the stench and
the screams of the ward. The worst
of all this, to me, is that despite such talk, now is the most peace
I've known her to have. She reminisces,
momentarily, thinking I am one of her long-dead
brothers. 'Didn't we have some fun
on those horses, when we were kids?' she'll say, giving
her thigh a little slap. Alzheimer's
is nirvana, in her case. She never mentions
anything of what troubled her adult years – God, the evil passages
of the Bible, her own mother's
long, hard dying, my father. Nothing
at all of my father,
and nothing
of her obsession with religion, that he drove her to. She says the
    magpie's song,
that goes on and on, like an Irishman
wheedling to himself,
which I have turned her chair towards,
reminds her of
a cup. A broken cup. I think that the chaos in her mind
is bearable to her because it is revolving
so slowly – slowly
as dust motes in an empty room.

The soul? The soul has long been defeated, and is all but gone.
    She's only productive now
of bristles on the chin, of an odour
like old newspapers on a damp concrete floor, of garbled
    mutterings, of
some crackling memories, and of a warmth
(it was always there,
the marsupial devotion), of a warmth that is just in the eyes, these
    days, particularly
when I hold her and rock her for a while, as I lift her
back to bed – a folded
package, such as,
I have seen from photographs, was made of the Ice Man. She says,
'I like it
when you – when
when
you ...'
I say to her, 'My brown-eyed girl.' Although she doesn't
    remember
the record, or me come home
that time, I sing it
to her: 'Da
da-dum, de-dum, da-dum ... And
it's you, it's you,' – she smiles up, into my face – 'it's you, my
    brown-eyed girl.'

My mother will get lost on the roads after death.
Too lonely a figure
to bear thinking of. As she did once,
one time at least, in the new department store
in our town; discovered
hesitant among the aisles; turning around and around, becoming
a still place.
Looking too kind
to reject even a wrong direction,
outrightly. And she caught my eye, watching her,
and knew I'd laugh
and grinned. Or else, since many another spirit will be arriving
    over there, whatever
those are – and all of them clamorous
as seabirds, along the walls of death – she will be pushed aside
easily, again. There are hierarchies in Heaven, we remember; and
    we know
of its bungled schemes.

Even if 'the last shall be first,' as we have been told, she
could not be first. It would not be her.
But why become so fearful?
This is all
of your mother, in your arms. She who now, a moment after your
    game, has gone;
who is confused
and would like to ask
why she is hanging here. No – she will be safe. She will be safe
in the dry mouth
of this red earth, in the place
she has always been. She
who hasn't survived living, how can we dream that she will survive
    her death?

Sestina on taking a bus into Perth past the Narrows Bridge

HAL COLEBATCH

(1945–)

The bus is turning. Beside the sunny river I love
new trees are stuck in sandhills. Between flying concrete
and an artificial lake, is a waterfall against the blue
river, and quaint plastic bridges. Dust on the afternoon
light flies minutely with the spinning wind,
blurring against the flat and turning panes of glass.

Now our world is heavy with something seen through glass,
with some hindsight of innocence. It is something to love
even a small part of the City. In the warm summer wind
grandparents and refugees walk, threading the concrete
into the new park below the white office blocks of afternoon.
The bus is turning. It seems a bubble holds us in the blue.

The city's towers are waiting together under the blue
sky. Above the river the trembling cliffs of glass
are ranked to face beyond the Western afternoon.
From the riverside the city holds more to love,
despite the wounded trucks and roaring concrete.
Machines are shooting grass-seeds against the wind.

Now the new yellow sand flicks the small wind.
Elderly refugees throw bread to ducks on the blue
of the toy lake. For the benefit of the gentle concrete-
dwelling people, moving together below the glass,
saffron mystics in the city sell incense sticks with love
at ten times the retail price, a function of long afternoon.

Here parks are still being made in the Western afternoon.
Cheap apocalypse shambles on. Smiling against the wind
requires a measure of courage. We know that love
is not enough to save us, waiting against the blue
emptiness of this kindly West. We see through dusty glass,
taking the careful roads of new-laid sand and concrete.

Now here at the end of the West the concrete
thing is slipping away. But in this dust of waiting afternoon
there is no history between the City and the glass
of the river. Little girls hold kittens. The wind
chases butterfly yachts. Like comfort, small red and blue
wrapped presents are put on Christmas trees. Such banal love

is still something concrete. In this wind
is more than afternoon. Sharp into the blue
air hangs the city of glass. We can come to terms with love?

Kidding Myself in Kuta, Bali: A Pantoum

ALAN SMITH

(1945–)

They've hired too many actors for the scene
The piles of bodies really are a laugh
The wounds are so extreme that they're obscene
With limbs ripped off and bodies cut in half

The piles of bodies really are a laugh
The blood however excellently done
With limbs ripped off and bodies cut in half
While all around the crimson rivers run

The blood however excellently done
Confused? Concussed? A little drunk perhaps
While all around the crimson rivers run
I am the one in shock who laughs and claps

Confused? Concussed? A little drunk perhaps
At last it dawns, there is no camera crew
I am the one in shock who laughs and claps
Hawaiian shirt with blood now streaming through

At last it dawns, there is no camera crew
A laugh chokes in my throat, I'm sobbing now
Hawaiian shirt with blood now streaming through
A man in white sticks something on my brow

A laugh chokes in my throat, I'm sobbing now
The frantic search for living victims starts
A man in white sticks something on my brow
He smiles and whispers sorry and departs

The frantic search for living victims starts
A second man comes close, and shakes his head
He smiles and whispers sorry and departs
I can't accept I'm very nearly dead

A second man comes close, and shakes his head
I do not want to face my life's conclusion
I can't accept I'm very nearly dead
It's just a film: my final self-delusion

I do not want to face my life's conclusion
They've hired too many actors for the scene
It's just a film: my final self-delusion
The wounds are so extreme that they're obscene

Learning to Write

❧

GARY CATALANO

(1947–2002)

❧

At sixty-five my grandfather
is learning to write his name,
one hand flat
on the oilcloth covered table–
the other grappling

with a pen, guiding it
slowly over the paper.
He checks each
uncertain curve and stroke
against his master copy.

The only fine work
his fingers know
is thinning young lettuces
with a bent flange
of tin, or neatly

extricating ripe cues
from their imprisoning web.
To this kind of work
he's a stranger. As I
monitor his progress

I run the blunt edge of a knife
over the cloth
and watch the marks
bite,
deepen

then vanish. His one hope
is that those painful signs
will be recognised as his
by all who can read.
When he's finished

he leans back
and admires the miracle,
pleased to see a new
late shoot
emerging from its seed.

Profiles of My Father

RHYLL McMASTER

(1947–)

I

The night we went to see the Brisbane River
break its banks
my mother from her kitchen corner
stood on one foot and wailed, 'Oh Bill,
it's *dangerous*.'
'Darl,' my father reasoned,
'don't be Uncle Willy,'

And took me right down to the edge
at South Brisbane, near the Gasworks,
the Austin's small insignia winking
in the rain.

A policeman helped a man load
a mattress on his truck.
At a white railing we saw the brown water
boil off into the dark.
It rolled midstream higher than its banks
and people cheered when a cat on a crate,
and a white fridge whizzed past.

II

Every summer morning at five-thirty in the dark
I rummaged for my swimming bag
among musty gym shoes and Mum's hats from 1940
in the brown hall cupboard.

And Dad and I purred down through the sweet, fresh
    morning
still cool, but getting rosy
at Paul's Ice Cream factory,
and turned left at the Gasworks for South Brisbane Baths.

The day I was knocked off my kickboard
by an aspiring Olympian aged ten
it was cool and quiet and green down on the bottom.
Above in the swaying ceiling limbs like pink logs,
and knifing arms churned past.
I looked at a crack in the cream wall
as I descended and thought of nothing.

When all of a sudden
Dad's legs, covered in silver bubbles,
his khaki shorts and feet in thongs
plunged into view like a new aquatic animal.

I was happy driving home;
Dad in a borrowed shirt with red poinsettias
and the Coach's light blue, shot-silk togs.

Barbecue

PETER KOCAN

(1947–)

Which of us will one day sit alone
In that last isolation nothing mends,
Remembering a long-lost afternoon
And a casual gathering of friends?

The women, milky-breasted, beautiful,
Watching their children toddle on the grass;
The men, skylarking with a bat and ball
Until the Sunday sun begins to pass ...

Decades on, this sun will re-emerge
With aching clarity in someone's mind,
To shake and grieve them in their senile age
And shine the brighter when the eyes are blind.

For one amongst us will outlive the rest
And weep to think, perhaps at ninety-five,
About this knife-edged brilliance of the past
When all of us were happy and alive.

And so, my friends, let's cling together now
Against the future that we cannot see.
Let's love each other, for we cannot know
Who the condemned survivor is to be.

My Grandmother's Ghost

KATE JENNINGS

(1948–)

I asked my father about your girlhood, how you met
my grandfather, but he had forgotten, or never knew,

and so it goes; I have to cosset my few thin facts.
I loved to rummage in your dressing-table drawers,

a busy spy sending puffs of pink face powder
into the air and finding cards with panels of muslin

stitched with violets, and snaps of the ruins of Baalbeck,
souvenirs of my grandfather's travels courtesy the Kaiser.

You were raised in a house with clay floors, and it was
your job to damp the dirt down with wet tea leaves.

(This you told me when I complained about housework.)
You were nearly blinded by sandy blight and flinched

at the telling. I imagined an unrelenting dust storm,
a furious wall of grit, and you flailing, your arms

outstretched, eyes blasted in biblical retribution.
I was numb with anger at the world's injustices

when you died, so I failed to mourn or even miss you.
Later, I needed to talk with you, but I couldn't find

your headstone in the whiskery cemetery grass. Instead
you visited me on Forty-Eighth Street in New York,

a standard-issue ghost, soft around the edges and alive
with a sweet glow. 'You've come a long way,' I said.

You answered, 'And so have you. But not far enough.'
Then you faded, and I slept, untroubled.

Ballade for Alan Gould

ALAN WEARNE
(1948–)

What's in a name?
> —Alan Shakespeare

Dear Alan, with benignest aims
(you're telling me indeed *What's in ...*)
I give you not immodest claims,
nor self promotion's wincing din
(non-Alans need to bear this, grin,
unless you're one you'll never know)
our king of names demands it so:
with simple maximised endeavour
watch my ballade's blazon flow:
We Alans always stick together.

No minnows in the name big pond:
Turing, Lomax, Greenspan, Fels,
even our black sheep Jones and Bond;
the world takes note and something jells:
there's that big-heartedness which tells
we're democratic by the gallons,
just reinvent yourselves as Alans,
give the past a mighty sever
Ahmed, Boris, tip the balance,
join the name that sticks together!

Near holy writ, you know it pal,
like in a movie starring Ladd
that sheer delight in being Al:
the word gets out how, man, we're baaaaad!
Chicks just swarm to Alan's pad.
Or we're a Test team led by Border
who'll willingly obey this order
(seize the willow, whack the leather!)
in mateship pure (there's little broader)
we Alans always stick together.

Claudes make way! Move over Jasons!
We lay it wide and lay it thick.
You'd think we were a mob of masons
to see backscratching do the trick:
when poesy meets biopic

who'll play the Curnows, Ginsbergs, Tates?
Why Messrs Alda, Rickman, Bates.
(Met any poet first name Trevor?
His lonely, untuned, tin ear grates.)
Muses and Alans stick together.

Piss off Con 'n' Don 'n' Ron,
the world has not seen lesser beaux.
Like Monsieur ('ow you say?) Delon,
there's one way for a name to go:
ditch that Edgar, Mr Poe,
join *my* friends Alans Wayman, Murphy:
airborne, waterlogged or earthy
their word is law to end of tether.
Backsliders? Hardly! What a furphy,
both they and us will stick together!

Pettersson, Musgrave, Jeans and Price
all helped to build the Alan pie.
For kudos, though, please give that twice
since be it known that you and I
can only hold up half the sky,
and needing those who'll share our vistas
— since there's a Ms for all the misters
(Kyle has Kylie, Heath has Heather)
four simple words adorn our sisters:
Alannahs always stick together!

And since our name's the sweetest fate
here be our slogan, better, motto
If he's an Alan he's a mate.
(Who'd ever be a Merv or Otto?)
Like endless First Division Lotto
our deal is trumps, our crown is jewelled.
And furthermore all gods have ruled:
from big bang to the twelfth of never
(no need to tell *you* Brother Gould)
we Alans always stick together.

From yoohoo unto toodle-oo
your days are over Jean-Paul, Lou,
our cause is a when not whether.
One 1, two ls, a, e, u
(oh band of brothers! happy few!)
we Al(l)a(e)(u)ns always stick together.

Pliers

ⅇ

ALAN GOULD

(1949–)

ⅇ

Fist to grip the slippery, twist-easing
the recalcitrant, little mastiff nosing
into the crannies of blind manipulations.
The clench we reach for in tight situations.
As once, did Miss Tarbuck, a hard-nosed, roughly
middle-aged science teacher who took us briefly.

It was the period before lunch; *muscle forms
in earthworms.* Earthworms led to tapeworms,
and one of Miss T's field trips, bottling species
in a jungle hut (Dahomey or one of the Guineas).
Times were late colonial when tapeworms could
grow long as garden hoses. She had one, she said.

It grew, and grew snug in her intestinal miles,
shared her meals. *Uncompanionably,* she smiled.
*Prospect of starving. No medicines. But pliers,
I had pliers. Also meat, a pair of mirrors,
and I like to think, my nerves. For a week I fasted
let the meat grow foul, O very foul indeed,*

*then, on a day, arranged my mirrors, the view
not, ahem! flattering* (a snigger or two
though most of us were too agog), *I squatted,
cheeks distended, pliers in hand, waited
O, not long, for whatever might come out,
Sure enough. A head! No, more a puckered snout!*

Unpretty! I chose my moment. Then ... Snap! I bagged it
(unsqueamish fellows jumped in their seats). *I tugged it.
Quite a tussle.* (Blokes who played in the scrum
were turning green as they imaged this grim
alimentary pull-through. Tarbuck, unfazed
stuck with the facts, if anything surprised

by our pallor.) *Useful gadgets, pliers. Of course
I bottled it. Ha ha, no, not the pliers, MacInnes,
... and here ...* (rummaging under her trestle)
... it is. She flourished briefly a large vessel
above her head, placed it with a bang.
Inspect it as you leave. Then the school bell rang

for a lunch now suddenly more complex. We filed
past the pale, well-nourished horror, coiled
in its urinous solution, this worm, flattened
like white pantyhose loosely filled with sand;
it crammed the entire jar. And in the pocket
of her white coat we noted the pliers. Useful gadget,

we agreed, an opposable thumb with uncommon nip
for the use of anyone not wishing to lose their grip.

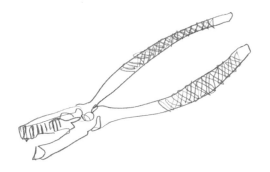

On Seeing the First Flasher

VICKI RAYMOND

(1949–)

Grey-coated, solitary stranger, hail!
Thou harbinger of summer's lusty days,
tracing through country parks thy mazy trail,
or lingering by some brook to catch the gaze
of passing schoolgirl, who, with scornful eye,
remarks upon thy manhood's lack of length,
then vanishing, before her angry cry
shall summon to her aid the studded strength
of forty skinheads, or, with deadly aim,
her dainty foot shall plunge into thy crotch —
when shalt thou find a partner to thy game,
a maid whose pleasure is to stand and watch?
As soon, alas, as poets shall enthrall
commuter crowds, or fill the Albert Hall.

CHAPTER 9

☙

The Generation of XYZ

Ode to Karl Marx

JOHN FORBES

(1950–1998)

Old father of the horrible bride whose
wedding cake has finally collapsed, you

spoke the truth that doesn't set us free—
it's like a lever made of words no one's

learnt to operate. So the machine it once
connected to just accelerates & each new

rap dance video's a perfect image of this,
bodies going faster and faster, still dancing

on the spot. At the moment tho' this set up
works for me, being paid to sit and write &

smoke, thumbing through Adorno like New Idea
on a cold working day in Ballarat, where

adult unemployment is 22% & all your grand
schemata of intricate cause and effect

work out like this: take a muscle car &
wire its accelerator to the floor, take out

the brakes, the gears the steering wheel
& let it rip. The dumbest tattooed hoon

—mortal diamond hanging round the Mall—
knows what happens next. It's fun unless

you're strapped inside the car. I'm not,
but the dummies they use for testing are.

Fantasia on a Theme by Thomas Tallis

෧

STEPHEN EDGAR

(1951–)

෧

This must be it: the gales, like an invasion
        Of Huns,
Storm through the island. Big trees strip
Off limbs against the grating sky's abrasion
And drag their roots; the whack of blown light stuns
   The flanks of sheds;
        Flags rip
Themselves daylong on flexing poles to shreds

Atop the flexing bravado of office blocks.
        All round,
Peeled-up roofing and cladding slams
Back and forth like the writhings of a fox,
Dementedly ensnared, that can smell the hound.
   (A brick wall halts
        A pram's
Attempt at the land speed record, with somersaults.)

The very air is a monstrous luffing sail,
        Within
Which all these forms and their loud claims
Are strands in a fabric tested till it fail.
One snapped thread and the fancied discipline
   Will burst apart,
        In flames
Of rags, a wound of absence at its heart.

At home behind the bending glass, aghast,
        Agog,
I sway to *Spem in Alium*
By Tallis, voices in a gale swept past,
Or through me, voices swelling like a drogue,
   And threatened by
        The thrum
Of air, as are the wind-warped hills and sky.

O holy voices! Not one word or wound,
        One shred
Of their doxology can sway

Me to belief. In faith, I am not tuned
In all this turbulence to a thing they've said.
    And how much less
        Do they
Then sing to me, whom they cannot address?

But in that less is the voice I'm listening for,
        When all
The solaces on which we're buoyed
Have burst, the last funds of belief in store
Ripped like the petty fabrics in a squall,
    Tatters about
        A void
That forms the throat through which all this cries out.

The Members of the Orchestra

✦

KEVIN HART

(1954–)

✦

walk onto the dark stage dressed for a funeral
or a wedding and we, the anxious ones, quieten
as we wait to discover which it will be tonight:

they sit or stand before thin books written
in a foreign script, more alien than Chinese,
but its secret contents will be revealed now

as at the reading of a dead relation's will,
for the last member has entered, slightly late
as befits his honour, like a famous lecturer

with a new theory and a pointer to make it clear.
Alas, he too cannot talk except in the language
of the deaf and dumb, but as he waves his hands

the members of the orchestra commence their act
of complicated ventriloquism, each making
his instrument speak our long-forgotten native tongue.

Now one violin reaches above the rest, rehearsing
the articulate sorrow of things in this world
where we have suddenly woken to find a music

as curious as the relation between an object
and its name. We are taken by the hand and led
through the old darkness that separates us

from things in themselves, through the soft fold
of evening that keeps two days apart. And now
each instrument tells its story in details

that become the whole, the entire forest contained
within a leaf: the orchestra is quickly building
a city of living air about us where we can live

and know our selves at last, for we have given up
our selves, as at our wedding or our funeral,
to take on something new, something that was always there.

The Ferris Wheel

&

JENNIFER HARRISON

(1955–)

&

Well, little wheel, spoked rose,
here we are – with a sense of memory mined
as though you've almost reached beyond yourself
and a fibro shack lurks always behind.

Up and over life's highest point,
you're moving down towards the dirt and the ground;
      towards cumulous friends, their upturned faces
like beds, your mother's eyes, strangers' mouths

and landscapes, too, returning holographically,
like 3-D birthday cards: a garden of thin-lipped irises;
a blown-about, blowsy hibiscus;
      pelicans toe-walking through oestrus mist.

Simple memories – talk-faded, grainier –
      answering back the long syllabic tricks
of scientists repairing the daisy-chained genes.
The fear of what we will fix.

The sensation one of falling, as though planing
down through a slick perpendicular dormitory
      as though, if you believed in height,
surfaces must pass you by this matter-of-factly,

      leaving you in the wooden cradle
the swing-boat of love. You're thinking that you
mustn't imagine the wheel as a circle
but as a music releasing the mind from its curfew.

      You remember the produce hall
all the mini-Australias fashioned from melons and figs,
bananas arranging Queensland – a child there, too,
wondering how the farmers grew the pumpkins so big.

You recall the crushed smell of peanut-shell floors,
the flair of brumbies from Scone or Penrith.
      You never wore a little white vest, nor marched
in fringe-time, flicking the air with a horse-hair whip

      but you wanted the big-bear life hammered
to the top of a bell; the torn-thumb fizzer

to reach the carousel's horses and lunge with them,
leisurely as the sea, around and around with the *Winterreise*.

You've not forgotten the nipple pinchers,
     those lovers of the ghost-house without sun –
the children's fluorescent screams,
mothers outside, listening, chatting, thinking *what fun*.

But careful now, or you'll see only plywood,
     the wheel as a vicious, ruinous form; a view
of emptiness across empty houses,
across nail-clipped streets to the far away lip of blue

where the sea grazes gauzy, white-duned Maroubra.
     Were you dreaming you'd missed the summit
and were coming down the icier side of a mountain,
when the cogs skipped – that's why you'd stopped –

just long enough to know how the runt feels
     on the outskirts of the litter;
long enough to know the exact chilliness
of a prison, how cold a metallic bar feels to the fingers?

     But then the cage shivers and begins again
to move, the faces below becoming huge, arriving
so fast you can see the mechanic's greasy overalls,
his loose-limbed boredom, his flashy ruby ring.

     And you remember, are remembering,
the way your father stood there in the dazzling sun
laughing at the way you never want to get off, even though
the wheel had stopped to let more children on.

The Domesticity of Giraffes

JUDITH BEVERIDGE

(1956–)

She languorously swings her tongue
like a black leather strap as she chews
and endlessly licks the wire for salt
blown in from the harbour.
Bruised-apple eyed she ruminates
towards the tall buildings
she mistakes for a herd:
her gaze has the loneliness of smoke.

I think of her graceful on her plain —
one long-legged mile after another.
I see her head framed in a leafy bonnet
or balloon-bobbing in trees.
Her hide's a paved garden of orange
against wild bush. In the distance, running
she could be a big slim bird just before flight.

Here, a wire-cripple —
legs stark as telegraph poles
miles from anywhere.
She circles the pen, licks the wire,
mimics a gum-chewing audience
in the stained underwear of her hide.
This shy Miss Marigold rolls out her tongue

like the neck of a dying bird.
I offer her the fresh salt of my hand
and her tongue rolls over it
in sensual agony, as it must
over the wire, hour after bitter hour.
Now, the bull indolently
lets down his penis like a pink gladiolus
drenching the concrete.

She thrusts her tongue under his rich stream
to get moisture for her thousandth chew.

When I consider

GIG RYAN

(1956–)

When I consider what my life has been
the tightening streets that stuck me to their side
the turning penitential globe inscribed
with gold and thorn, I picket what I've seen
as if the will were new, the heart were keen
before despair became where you abide
alone with cold ideals and clinging pride
acts and dreams spread out across the screen
I pause at the silky prolonged sunset
that death or god should taper off and shrink
as all the city's woe and all the skies
say not to remember but to forget
and chafing through the cars I fall to think
how sorrows lift and pleasures cauterize

Sky Writing

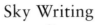

SARAH DAY

(1958–)

Things fall apart. Across a summer sky
the emblematic Coca Cola script
above the uproar, miles long, a mile high

dissolves like cirrus before the squinting eye,
until all that's left's a vaporous postscript.
Things fall apart. Across a summer sky,

once, subtler heavenly signs might testify
foreshadowing the end of Rome or Egypt
above the uproar, miles long, a mile high.

That titanium on blue could edify ...
there's a lofty riddle to decrypt.
Things fall apart. Across a summer sky

now wind-drift pulls the letters all awry
the pilot banks, the plane signs off, wings dipped
above the uproar, miles long, a mile high.

See how the characters emulsify
into the blue, now vacuous, nondescript.
Things fall apart. Across a summer sky
above the uproar, miles long, a mile high.

Life

KATHLEEN STEWART

(1958–)

The boys get together and do what makes them feel good.
The girls drift along the street writing.
The boys get successful.
The boys leave the girls for the other girls.
The girls drift along the street writing.
They have more to write about now.

The Big Goanna

PHILIP HODGINS

(1959–1995)

Who could have guessed the big surprise
in store for Bernie Wells the day
he chased the big goanna up the tree.
If someone else had told me this
I would have said no way
a thing like that could all be true
but curiously enough for me
I was there, I saw it with my own eyes.
It happened years ago one afternoon
on Bernie's uncle's farm near Boho South
where Bernie and myself had gone
out with the twenty-twos to bring a few
rabbits home, the idea being that we
were going to make a rabbit stew
that night. But though we both
had fired at least a dozen shots
we hadn't bagged a single one.
Eventually I'd said if that's
how good we are we may as well
go home and we were just walking down a lane
not far from Bernie's uncle's house
there at the bottom of the hill
when suddenly this big goanna shot out
across the lane in front of us
and scrambled up a gum tree
on the other side. It got about
two-thirds of the way up and then
looked down at us as if to be
two-thirds of the way up that gum tree
was some sort of guarantee
of immunity from captivity. But Bernie
Wells had other things in mind and soon
he had his boots and trousers off and ran
across the lane and climbed the tree
almost as nimbly as the big goanna had.
It stayed there watching Bernie climb
until he got within about a yard
and then it crawled out on the highest limb

which would have been about thirty feet up.
It must have thought it had him beat
but good old Bernie didn't stop.
He kept on climbing right up to the top
then out along the limb towards his prey.
The big goanna watched him come
and when he wasn't far away
it simply pushed out off the branch
and plummeted towards the sticks
and leaves below and landed, crunch!,
unhurt but pretty mad, and started to flex
its tail around in a mean way the likes
of which I'd never seen before.
And instead of pissing off the bloody thing
began to climb back up the tree again!
Its tail kept making those sharp little flicks
as if it had a scorpion-like sting
while from the other end there came
a low continuous unpleasant hiss.
Poor Bernie didn't like the looks
of what he saw and he liked it even less
when the big goanna got up with him
on the branch and moved in for the bite.
There didn't seem to be any way out,
the big goanna had him stumped.
He was up about thirty feet
and too close to it for me to shoot,
but then just at the end he jumped.

Holy Sydney

HARRY CUMMINS

(1961–)

Sylvia was dying so I returned to Australia,
Travelling with a friend.
It was the end
Of a beautiful friendship. I took the spare bedroom, forcing
      his parents to sleep with each other.
His mother,
I think, complaining of her husband's snoring,
Woke me up to this.
So worried that I woke to fear at four o'clock each morning,
As homeless and as formless as the mist.

There was a fresh forest wind off the sea,
The wind
Of gums and heady wetness.
The silver perfume of the sun, the muscles of the sun
Are in that wind;
A wind that splashed the schizophrenic deadness
Of the town like honey or a swarm of native bees.

Holy Sydney, Godly Sydney;
The most beautiful city on earth;
A virgin birth;
To live there is like living in a tree;
Rome, Paris, are the slagheaps of a pigmy:
Your life, like God's, descends in heresies.

Kristallnacht

✍

JEMAL SHARAH

(1969–)

✍

Alone in the bush.
Before, they had been singing,
when the car was given a great push
off the road; rain tinkling.

And then she got a fright —
the only one awake;
the others' eyes stayed shut tight
no matter how she'd shake

and shove their arms.
She didn't think of death —
sleep wasn't any harm —
and there was her father's breath,

though harsh, asthmatic, sore.
Locked in a foggy sleep
it might have been a snore.
Except it seemed so deep.

And she — she was awash
with cubes of window-glass,
with one leg safely squashed
in a metal cast;

with such neatly shattered crystal.
Her father loved to buy
goblets, clear as the distilled
water from an eye.

Its rhinestones chained her wrists.
She waited as time passed:
one car sped by — missed
seeing them, it went so fast.

And no-one came to help
in spite of all her cries;
she was stuck there herself,
and adult blandishments were lies —

that to cry help was the proof
against perverts, loss, distress,
that the boy who had cried wolf
was gobbled through excess.

Vague rain, sickness in tides;
neither offered any answers.
Nor, later, did the pride
of howling ambulances.

After Wendy Cope

✎

STEPHEN McINERNEY

(1976–)

✎

Bloody Men!

I think I am in love with Wendy Cope.
Perhaps you have discerned this from the title.
Last night I dreamed that I and A.D. Hope
Arrived to hear her very last recital.
A renowned womaniser, Alec said:
'I bet I'll be the first one to befriend her,
The first one here to get her into bed.
To prove it I will pocket a suspender!'
'Mr Hope,' I said, 'Have you lost your wits?
Men like you are the problem! Can't you see?
If you would raise your eyes above her tits
You'd realise that she needs someone like me.'
She caught my eye: 'Alas,' she said, 'It's you,
The one whose love could prove my verse untrue.'

Biographies

CR

1/8   Four Australian Water Birds   Bridget Parr

FRANCIS MACNAMARA ('Frank the Poet'; 1811–1880) was born in Ireland, and was transported to Australia in 1832 after being convicted of stealing a plaid. His poems were not published in his lifetime, but were circulated orally, though he wrote them down in fine copperplate for his friends to read. After several escapes, floggings, spells on the treadmill and in solitary, and much hard labour in leg irons, he was finally released from Port Arthur in 1857. He died in obscurity.

CHARLES HARPUR (1813–1868) was born in Windsor, New South Wales, and worked as a post office clerk, farmer, teacher and Gold Commissioner. He had political aspirations which came to nothing, and saw himself as Australia's first poet. He died of tuberculosis.

CHARLES R THATCHER (1831–1878) was born in England, and joined the gold rush to Victoria in 1852. He did not find gold, but made a living instead as a singer and entertainer, writing and performing his own songs. He returned to England, where he died in 1869.

ADAM LINDSAY GORDON (1833–1870) was born in the Azores and raised in England from the age of seven. In 1853 his father, a retired army officer, sent him to Adelaide because he would not pursue a military career. He joined the Mounted Police, became a horse-trainer, was briefly a Member of the South Australian Parliament, and was known as much for his horsemanship as for his poetry. He once rode three steeplechase winners in a day in Melbourne. In debt and suffering from injuries after a riding accident, he shot himself at Brighton, Victoria, the day after his fourth book of verse was published.

JAMES BRUNTON STEPHENS (1835–1902) was born in Scotland and migrated to Queensland in 1866. He was a teacher before he joined the civil service, rising to act as under-secretary to the Colonial Secretary in Brisbane. He was a regular contributor to the *Bulletin*, published poetry, plays and fiction, and was seen for a time as the leading literary figure in Australia.

HENRY KENDALL (1839–1882) was born at Kirmington on the New South Wales south coast, and grew up on both the north and south coasts of the state. At the age of sixteen he went to sea for two years, then worked as a shop assistant, solicitor's clerk and civil servant. He was only twenty-three when his first book was published, to some acclaim, but at thirty he was reduced to an alcoholic ruin, ending up in the Gladesville asylum. He was rescued by the Fagan family of timber merchants, working in their North Coast timber mill, before Sir Henry Parkes, an aspiring poet, appointed him Inspector of Forests at Cundletown. He died a year later of tuberculosis.

JOSEPH FURPHY ('Tom Collins'; 1843–1912) was born at Yering in Victoria and worked at different times as a farmer, farm labourer and bullocky in country Victoria and the Riverina. He is best known as the author of the novel *Such Is Life*, but he also wrote poems, short stories and sketches, many of which were published in the *Bulletin* from the late 1880s on. He moved to Western Australia in 1905, to be with his sons, and built what is now known as Tom Collins House in Swanbourne.

THOMAS E SPENCER (1845–1910) was born in London and moved to Sydney in 1875. He was a successful builder and contractor as well as being a popular writer, publishing a novel, several short stories and much ballad-style verse, which first appeared in the *Bulletin*.

MARCUS CLARKE (1846–1881) was born and educated in London, where Gerard Manley Hopkins was one of his school friends. His emigration to Australia at the age of seventeen was arranged by his cousin, who had been a Member of the Victorian Parliament. Clarke is remembered now as the author of the convict novel *For the Term of His Natural Life*, but for a time he was an immensely productive journalist, playwright, poet and member of Melbourne's café society. He was bankrupt when he died at an early age.

MARY HANNAY FOOTT (1846–1918) was born in Glasgow and was brought to Australia by her parents in 1853. She married TW Foott in 1874, and lived on his Queensland farm until he died ten years later. She then became a journalist and literary editor of the *Queenslander*.

ALFRED T CHANDLER ('Spinifex'; 1852–1941) was born in Geelong, and worked as a journalist in Victoria, South Australia and Western Australia.

VICTOR J DALEY (1858–1905) was born in Ireland and educated in England. He came to Australia in 1878 and worked first as a clerk and then as a freelance journalist. He was a regular contributor to the *Bulletin*'s Red Page, referred to in his poem in this collection. He died of tuberculosis in Waitara, New South Wales.

JACK MOSES (1860–1945) was born in Sydney and spent most of his life as a salesman in the wine industry. He was a friend of Henry Lawson, and a regular contributor to the *Bulletin*.

JA PHILP (1861–1935) was born in Scotland and educated in New Zealand before he came to Australia and worked as a journalist and as a sub-editor at the *Bulletin*. He wrote short stories as well as verse.

WT GOODGE (1862–1909) was born in London, and went to sea in 1882, only to leave his ship in Sydney. He roamed the outback for a dozen years before becoming a journalist and a regular contributor to the *Bulletin*.

'CRUPPER D' is a pseudonymous author about whom nothing is known.

MARY GILMORE (1863–1962) was born near Goulburn, New South Wales, and worked as a teacher in country schools before moving to Sydney. She became a friend of Henry Lawson, who proposed marriage to her without success. With a group of fellow utopians led by William Lane, who intended to create a 'New Australia', she moved to Paraguay; while she was there, in 1897, she married WA Gilmore. After her poetry began to appear in the *Bulletin* in 1903 it achieved such widespread acclaim that she was made a Dame of the British Empire in 1937.

HARRY MORANT ('The Breaker'; 1864–1902) was born in England and came to Australia in 1883. Less than a year after his arrival he married the woman later to become well known as Daisy Bates, but the marriage only lasted a few weeks. He lived a nomadic life as a drover and horsebreaker, but contributed sixty poems to the *Bulletin* over a decade from 1891. He enlisted in the SA Mounted Rifles to go to the Boer War, and was then court-martialled for the murder of some prisoners, and executed by firing squad.

ANDREW BARTON PATERSON ('The Banjo'; 1864–1941) was born near Orange, New South Wales and grew up in the Yass area before completing his education at Sydney Grammar School. He began work in a lawyer's office and qualified as a solicitor, but the success of the verse he began publishing in the *Bulletin* meant that he was able to give up the law for journalism. Apart from his writing, he was a crocodile hunter, a buffalo shooter, a pearl diver and a war correspondent.

EDWARD DYSON (1865–1931) was born near Ballarat and worked in the gold mines and in a factory before he became a journalist. He wrote many novels and short stories as well as two collections of verse.

BARCROFT BOAKE (1866–1892) was born in Sydney and was educated at Sydney Grammar School. He worked as a surveyor's assistant, and then as a drover and boundary-rider. Like Adam Lindsay Gordon, he was obsessed with horses and horsemanship and, like Gordon, he committed suicide, hanging himself with his stockwhip.

BERNARD O'DOWD (1866–1953) was born in Beaufort, Victoria, and grew up in Ballarat. He gained university degrees in arts and law, worked as a teacher, and then joined the civil service, rising to become Chief Parliamentary Draftsman for the State of Victoria. He was known as much for his radical political views, expressed in contributions to the *Bulletin*, as for his poetry.

EW HORNUNG (1866–1921) was born and lived most of his life in England, where he is well known as one of the founders of the crime-writing genre, the creator of the character 'Raffles', and as a prolific and popular novelist. However, he did spend two years in Australia from 1884, where he wrote several poems and stories.

AF YORK is a writer about whom nothing is known.

The ANONYMOUS author of 'The Bastard from the Bush' has been rumoured to be Henry Lawson, though the poem's somewhat crude rhymes and scansion could be seen as proof the poem was written by a more amateur poet.

HENRY LAWSON (1867–1922) was born in a tent on the goldfields at Grenfell, New South Wales, and grew up in the country, leaving school at fourteen. When his mother, Louisa, a journalist and precursor of the feminist movement, founded the newspaper *Dawn* he began to write for it, and he also began to write for the *Bulletin* and to travel widely in Australia and New Zealand. He married in 1896, and in 1900 took his wife and children to London, where two of his books were published. He returned to Australia in 1902, and began to drink heavily, spending much of the last two decades of his life in poverty, in and out of jail for drunkenness, and living on the streets of Sydney. When he died he was given a state funeral.

RODERIC QUINN (1867–1949) was born in Sydney and attended the Marist Brothers School along with EJ Brady, and St Ignatius College along with Christopher Brennan. He studied law briefly, and then became a freelance writer and journalist, contributing regularly to the *Bulletin*.

'NQ', author of 'The Mystery Man', is himself a mystery.

MARY FULLERTON (1868–1946) was born in a bark hut at Glenmaggie, Victoria, and published poetry and fiction in Australian newspapers before she left to live in London in 1922. She was a friend of Miles Franklin, who gave her the idea of publishing much of her writing, which included several novels, under pseudonyms; the best known of these was 'E', but she also published one novel as 'Robert Gray'.

WILL H OGILVIE (1869–1963) was born in Scotland and came to Australia at the age of twenty, inspired by the story of Adam Lindsay Gordon and a love of horses. He spent twelve years in the outback as a drover and horse-breaker, while contributing verse regularly to the *Bulletin*. He returned to Scotland in 1901, and his Scottish folk ballads were admired by Hugh McDiarmid, but he died in obscurity.

EJ BRADY (1869–1952) was born in Carcoar, New South Wales, and educated at first in the United States and then at the Marist Brothers School in Sydney. He worked as a shipping clerk before becoming a freelance journalist and writer; many of his poems appeared in the *Bulletin*. He was a friend of Henry Lawson.

CHRISTOPHER BRENNAN (1870–1932) was born in Sydney and attended St Ignatius College before studying classics and philosophy at Sydney University. He went to Berlin on a travelling scholarship, and married his German landlady's daughter, who returned to Australia with him. He worked for the New South Wales Public Library for more than a decade before he gained a position at Sydney University as a lecturer in modern literature in 1909; in 1922 he was awarded a professorship in German and comparative literature. By this time his marriage had failed, and he began living with a woman called Violet Singer, who was killed by a tram in 1925. Soon after her death, he was dismissed by the university and his remaining years were spent in poverty and alcoholism.

JOHN SHAW NEILSEN (1872–1942) was born in Penola, South Australia, and moved with his family to the Wimmera region of Victoria when he was nine. He had only two and a half years of formal education, though his father had some repute as a bush poet. He worked as a rural labourer until he was in his mid-fifties, though he had begun to publish poems in the *Bulletin* in 1896; his eyesight began to fail when he was in his early thirties, so that his poems, composed in his head, would be dictated to his sometimes bemused fellow labourers. In 1928 his literary admirers helped find him a job in Melbourne as a messenger with the Country Roads Board, but he produced little verse once he began living in the city.

CJ DENNIS (1876–1938) was born in Auburn, South Australia, and educated at the Christian Brothers College in Adelaide. He worked as a journalist and editor in Adelaide before moving to Melbourne in 1906; he then moved again, to Toolangi, near Healesville, living at first in a tent, to work on his writing. It was not until the publication of *The Songs of a Sentimental Bloke* in 1915 that he found success; the book sold 60,000 copies in less than eighteen months.

HUGH McCRAE (1876–1958) was born in Melbourne, the son of the now forgotten poet George Gordon McCrae, an associate of Henry Kendall, Marcus Clarke and Adam Lindsay Gordon. He first worked as an architect, then tried to make a living as a freelance writer, illustrator and actor. He moved to the United States in 1914 to try to find work as an actor, but returned to live in Sydney two years later. He was a popular character, acquainted with figures ranging from the *Bulletin*'s JF Archibald and AG Stephens, to artists Norman Lindsay and Will Dyson, and poets such as Kenneth Slessor and Mary Gilmore.

PJ HARTIGAN ('John O'Brien', 1879–1952) was born at Yass, New South Wales, and was a Catholic priest who wrote verse under a pseudonym. For many years he was the parish priest at Narrandera, New South Wales.

FRANK WILMOT ('Furnley Maurice', 1881–1942) was born in Collingwood and worked in a bookshop for thirty-five years, rising from errand boy to manager, before becoming the manager of Melbourne University Press. He devised the pseudonym he usually wrote under by conflating the sound of two of his favourite Melbourne suburbs, Ferntree Gully and Beaumaris.

WJ TURNER (1884–1946) was born in Melbourne, but left Australia at the age of twenty-one. He lived most of his life in London, where he was highly respected as a music critic, editor, writer and broadcaster. He was a significant member of the Bloomsbury Group, and was acquainted with WB Yeats, TS Eliot, Robert Graves and Virginia Woolf, though he made an enemy of Lady Ottoline Morrell by portraying her in his novel *The Aesthetes*.

DOROTHEA MACKELLAR (1885–1968) was born in Sydney and educated at Sydney University. At the age of nineteen she wrote the poem originally titled 'Core of My Heart', which remains perhaps the best known of all Australian poems. 'My Country' has been omitted from this collection because it is expected that most readers have it already by heart.

DH LAWRENCE (1885–1930), the celebrated English novelist, spent less than four months in Australia in 1922, but in that time he collaborated on one novel (*The Boy in the Bush*, with Molly Skinner) and wrote another, *Kangaroo*, which should not be confused with his poem of the same title.

HARLEY MATTHEWS (1889–1968) was born in St Leonards, New South Wales, and qualified as a solicitor before serving in the First World War at Gallipoli and other places. After the war he became a wine-maker: his vineyard was at Moorebank, now a suburb of Sydney, and is the place referred to in Kenneth Slessor's most famous poem 'Five Bells' ('the night we came to Moorebank in slab-dark'). In the

Second World War Matthews was falsely accused of belonging to a subversive organisation and was imprisoned for six months, in which time his vines were ruined. He was paid seven hundred pounds as compensation, but did not return to Moorebank, living for the rest of his life on a small farm at Ingleburn.

LESBIA HARFORD (1891–1927) was born in Melbourne. Despite a congenital heart defect, she was one of the first women to graduate in law from Melbourne University. Though qualified as a solicitor, she chose to work in factories as a machinist due to her sympathy for workers as a member of the radical Industrial Workers of the World movement. In 1920 she married an artist named Harford, but the marriage was short-lived. She died of an infection of the heart.

LEON GELLERT (1892–1977) was born in Walkerville, South Australia, and worked as a teacher before joining the services in the First World War; he was wounded at Gallipoli. After the war he taught, and then worked in journalism, becoming literary editor of the *Sydney Morning Herald*.

ERNEST G MOLL (1900–1979) was born in Murtoa, Victoria, and educated in schools in New South Wales. In 1920 he moved to the United States, and from 1928 to 1966 he was professor of English at the University of Oregon.

KENNETH SLESSOR (1901–1971) was born in Orange, New South Wales, and educated at Sydney Church of England Grammar School (Shore). While still at school, he had a poem published in the *Bulletin*. All of his working life was spent as a journalist, including four years as an Official War Correspondent during the Second World War. After the war, as he put it, he had 'no more use for the Muse', though he continued to be a prolific book reviewer, editor and supporter of younger poets. His best known poem, 'Five Bells', does not appear in this collection because it has already been so habitually anthologised.

JAR McKELLAR (1904–1932) was born at Dulwich Hill, New South Wales, and left school at the age of fifteen to work in a bank. He had begun to earn a reputation for his poetry, encouraged by Kenneth Slessor and Hugh McCrae, when he died of pneumonia.

AD HOPE (1907–2000) was born in Cooma, New South Wales, and attended schools in Hobart, Bathurst and Sydney. He completed a degree at Sydney University, and in 1928 went to Oxford on a scholarship. He worked first as a schoolteacher before becoming a lecturer in English at Melbourne University; in 1951 he was appointed Professor of English at the Australian National University, and he remained in Canberra for the rest of his life with an office in the university building that was named in his honour.

IAN MUDIE (1911–1976) was born in Hawthorn, South Australia, and educated at Scotch College, Adelaide. He worked as a journalist, book editor and a lecturer in creative writing, but he mainly made a living as a prolific author of histories and biographies. His poem 'They'll Tell You about Me' could be seen as a precursor to Les Murray's 'The Quality of Sprawl'.

JOHN BLIGHT (1913–1995) was born in Unley, South Australia, and educated at Brisbane High School. He qualified as an accountant, worked as a public servant and then became director of a timber company with sawmills on the north-west coast of Queensland. His poetry first appeared in the *Bulletin* in 1939, and for many years he was known for his tightly structured sonnets about the sea.

DOUGLAS STEWART (1913–1985) was born in Eltham, New Zealand, and moved to Australia in 1938 to take up a position as assistant editor on the Red Page of the *Bulletin*. He was made editor of the page in 1940, and remained there until the Red Page was closed by the magazine's new owner in 1961. He then spent a decade as an editor at Angus & Robertson.

JUDITH WRIGHT (1915–2000) was born near Armidale, New South Wales, and educated partly by correspondence. She attended lectures at Sydney University, though she was not a formally enrolled student. While working as a secretary at the University of Queensland, she met JP McKinney, a freelance writer and philosopher, who she came to live with and, eventually, to marry. Her early collections of poetry were highly praised by Douglas Stewart in the *Bulletin*. In her maturity she became involved in the conservation and Aboriginal land rights movements.

DAVID CAMPBELL (1915–1978) was born near Adelong, New South Wales, and educated at the Kings School, Parramatta, and then at Jesus College, Cambridge. At university he became close to John Manifold, and was such an outstanding rugby player that he was selected for both England and Scotland in a Test match between the two countries; he chose to play for Scotland. In the Second World War he won the DFC as a pilot with the RAAF; afterwards, he spent his life as a farmer in the Monaro district of New South Wales.

JOHN MANIFOLD (1915–1985) was born in Melbourne and educated at Geelong Grammar School. He became a communist in his last year at school after being told by his wealthy pastoralist father that his less gifted younger brothers would inherit the family property. He went to Jesus College, Cambridge, formally joined the Communist Party, and for much of his life received financial support from Moscow, even while serving in the British army in the Second World War.

RONALD M BERNDT (1916–1990) was for many years professor of anthropology at the University of Western Australia.

JAMES McAULEY (1917–1976) was born in Lakemba, New South Wales, and educated at Fort Street High School and Sydney University. While serving in the army during the Second World War he helped invent the hoax poet Ern Malley as a satirical comment on some of the English poets of the 1930s, such as Dylan Thomas and David Gascoigne, and their Australian imitators. In 1956 he founded the magazine *Quadrant*, and five years later he took up a position in the English department at the University of Tasmania. He died of cancer.

JOAN LEVICK ('Amy Witting', 1918–2001) was born in Annandale, New South Wales, and attended Sydney University, where she was a friend of James McAuley. She was diagnosed with tuberculosis in her twenties, but made a complete recovery. She worked as a teacher for many years, and married Les Levick, a fellow teacher, but it was only after her retirement that she gained prominence as a novelist. She died of cancer.

GWEN HARWOOD (1920–1995) was born in Taringa, Queensland, and grew up in Brisbane. She was a musician and church organist before she married Bill Harwood in 1945. When he was appointed to a lectureship in the English department at the University of Tasmania she was sorry to leave Brisbane, but she came to love Tasmania, and became a close friend of James McAuley. In the early 1960s she published poems under a series of pseudonyms (Walter Lehmann and Francis Geyer in particular) because she felt Vincent Buckley, poetry editor of the *Bulletin*, was prejudiced against female poets. Later, she became one of Buckley's greatest admirers. She died of cancer.

DAVID ROWBOTHAM (1924–) was born in Toowoomba, Queensland, and educated at Toowoomba Grammar School and the University of Queensland, as well as Sydney University. He served with the RAAF in the Second World War, and has worked as a journalist and, briefly, as a lecturer in English at the University of Queensland. For many years he was literary editor of the *Courier-Mail* in Brisbane.

FRANCIS WEBB (1925–1973) was born in Adelaide, and educated at two different Christian Brothers' schools in Sydney. He served with the RAAF in the Second World War, then worked for a publisher in Canada before his lifelong mental illness became disabling. He was diagnosed with schizophrenia, and spent most of his life in and out of psychiatric hospitals in Victoria and New South Wales; he died at Callan Park Hospital.

VINCENT BUCKLEY (1925–1988) was born in Romsey, Victoria, and boarded at St Patrick's College, Melbourne, before he attended Melbourne University. He studied at Cambridge University at the same time as Sylvia Plath, with whom he performed at poetry readings. Most of his working life was spent in the English department of Melbourne University, where he held a personal chair, though he did serve a term as poetry editor of the *Bulletin*.

RA SIMPSON (1929–2002) was born in Melbourne and worked for many years as a lecturer in fine art at what is now Monash University. He was poetry editor of the *Bulletin* for three years, and then was poetry editor of the *Age* for more than two decades.

PETER PORTER (1929–) was born in Brisbane and educated at Brisbane Church of England Grammar School (which he later referred to as 'Auschwitz on the River') and Toowomba Grammar School. He was briefly a cadet journalist in Brisbane before moving to London in 1951. He did not return to Australia until 1974. Since then he has made more frequent visits while continuing to live in London. He has worked in advertising and as a journalist, and is regarded as one of the leading poets in England.

BRUCE DAWE (1930–) was born in Geelong and attended Northcote High School, though he left school early. He worked in a factory and as a postman before he joined the RAAF; by the time he completed a university degree as a mature-age student he had already published two collections of poetry. He continued his studies and eventually earned a PhD; he became professor of literary studies at the University of Southern Queensland in Toowoomba.

EVAN JONES (1931–) was born in Preston, Victoria, and completed a degree at Melbourne University before winning a writing scholarship to Stanford University in the United States. He has been a lecturer in both the History and English departments at Melbourne University.

PHILIP MARTIN (1931–2006) was born in Richmond, Victoria, and educated at Xavier College and Melbourne University. He taught in the English department at Melbourne University at first, and then for many years at Monash University. In 1988, after reading a favourable review of his work in the *Age*, he suffered a severe stroke from which he never fully recovered.

VIVIAN SMITH (1933–) was born in Hobart and attended the University of Tasmania, where he became a lecturer in the French department. After ten years he moved to Sydney and was appointed to the English department at Sydney University, a position he retained for the rest of his working life.

DAVID MALOUF (1934–) was born in Brisbane and graduated from the University of Queensland. After living in Europe for almost a decade, he was appointed to the English department at Sydney University in 1968. The success of his first novel, *Johnno*, and subsequent writings have enabled him to pursue a career as a full-time writer since 1977.

BARRY HUMPHRIES (1934–) was born in Melbourne and educated at Melbourne Grammar School and Melbourne University, where among other extracurricular activities he joined a group of aspiring poets, which included Chris Wallace-Crabbe, Philip Martin and Fay Zwicky. According to the latter, Humphries was clearly the most promising poet in the group. He has since achieved such renown in other fields that his writing is sometimes overlooked.

CHRIS WALLACE-CRABBE (1934–) was born in Richmond, Victoria, and educated at Scotch College and Melbourne University. He qualified as a metallurgist before he joined the English department at Melbourne University, where most of his working life was spent.

GRAEME KINROSS SMITH (1936–) was born and educated in Melbourne. For many years he was a teacher of English and Creative Writing at what is now Deakin University in Geelong.

JUDITH RODRIGUEZ (1936–) was born in Perth and grew up in Brisbane, where she completed a degree at the University of Queensland, becoming a friend of David Malouf in the process, before going on to graduate from Cambridge. While teaching English at the University of the West Indies she met her first husband, Fabio Rodriguez. She was a lecturer in the English department at La Trobe

University for sixteen years, then later taught Creative Writing at the Victoria College in Melbourne. Her second husband is the poet Thomas W Shapcott.

LES MURRAY (1938–) was born at Nabiac and brought up at Bunyah, both on the north coast of New South Wales. Though he did not go to school until the age of nine, he attended Sydney University, where his poetry appeared on the syllabus before he finally completed a degree. He worked as a railway porter, a translator and as a civil servant in the Prime Minister's Department before retiring to become a full-time poet.

CLIVE JAMES (1939–) was born in Sydney and was a student at Sydney University at the same time as Les Murray. Like Barry Humphries, his literary skills have been overshadowed by his fame in other, more public, areas, but since he retired from television he has written a great deal of poetry.

GEOFF PAGE (1940–) was born at Grafton on the north coast of New South Wales, and was educated at the Armidale School and the University of New England. For many years he was a teacher at Narrabundah College in Canberra. He is a grandson of the former Australian prime minister Sir Earl Page.

ANDREW TAYLOR (1940–) was born in Warrnambool, Victoria, and educated at Scotch College and Melbourne University. He taught in the English department at Melbourne University and then at Adelaide University, before becoming professor of English at Edith Cowan University in Perth.

GEOFFREY LEHMANN (1940–) was born in Sydney, and educated at Sydney Church of England Grammar School (Shore) and Sydney University, where he met Les Murray. His first collection of poetry, *The Ilex Tree*, was shared with Murray. Lehmann practised as a solicitor, then taught law at the University of New South Wales, before becoming a partner in Price Waterhouse Coopers, specialising in tax law. He has written fiction, art criticism, children's books, and non-fiction works about tax and family law.

ROGER McDONALD (1941–) was born in Young, New South Wales, and educated at Scots College and Sydney University. He worked for the ABC and in publishing before the success of his first novel, *1915*, enabled him to become a full-time writer. He is also the recipient of the Miles Franklin award.

JOHN TRANTER (1943–) was born in Cooma, New South Wales, and educated at Hurlstone Agricultural High School and Sydney University. He has worked in publishing and for the ABC, but for much of his career he has been a full-time writer. He was poetry editor of the *Bulletin* for a time in the 1990s.

ROBERT GRAY (1945–) was born in Sydney and brought up at Coffs Harbour on the North Coast of New South Wales. He worked in an advertising agency in Sydney with the son of Dylan Thomas, and then for many years he was a buyer in the Sydney bookshop owned by the grandson of Lady Gregory, patron of WB Yeats.

HAL COLEBATCH (1945–) was born in Perth, and has degrees in Arts and Law from the University of Western Australia. He has worked as a journalist and a lawyer, and has been an unsuccessful Liberal Party candidate in a state election. Like John Blight, he has written many poems about the sea.

ALAN SMITH (1945–) was born in Sydney and educated at Sydney Technical Boys High School and Sydney Teachers College. He worked as a high school mathematics teacher before joining the navy, where he rose to the rank of commander. His career was cut short by the onset of Parkinsons Disease.

GARY CATALANO (1947–2002) was born in Brisbane and educated at Trinity Grammar School in Sydney. He moved to Melbourne in the mid-1970s, and in 1985 he became art critic of the *Age*, having already published several books of art criticism. He died of cancer.

RHYLL McMASTER (1947–) was born in Brisbane and had poems published in the *Bulletin* when she was still at school. She married Roger McDonald, and for more than a decade her literary output was sparse. Since the end of her marriage, she has become a prolific poet, as well as writing a prize-winning novel.

PETER KOCAN (1947–) was born in Newcastle and grew up in Melbourne, where he came to national attention before he had written a poem, as he attempted to assassinate the leader of the Federal Opposition in 1966. He spent the next decade in a psychiatric hospital, where he began to write poetry. Since his release he has written several novels, and won several literary prizes.

KATE JENNINGS (1948–) was born in Temora, New South Wales, and educated at Griffith High School and Sydney University. In the early 1970s she was prominent in the feminist movement and edited an anthology of women's poetry, *Mother I'm Rooted*, where many soon-to-be-famous writers made their first appearance in print. In 1979 she moved to New York, where she worked as an editor and, later, as a corporate speechwriter. In the 1990s she was for a time poetry editor of the *Bulletin*, while still living in New York.

ALAN WEARNE (1948–) was born in Melbourne and attended Blackburn South High School and Monash University before he graduated from La Trobe University. He has worked as a relief teacher, and has been an unsuccessful Labor Party candidate in a state election. He now teaches Creative Writing at Wollongong University and has written two verse novels, *The Nightmarkets* and *The Lovemakers*.

ALAN GOULD (1949–) was born in London and came to Australia at the age of seventeen, settling in Canberra, where he attended the Australian National University and became acquainted with AD Hope and David Campbell. He has worked as a relief teacher, but has lived mainly as a full-time writer.

VICKI RAYMOND (1949–) was born in Daylesford, Victoria, but was educated in Tasmania, graduating from the University of Tasmania. She moved to London in 1981, and for some years worked as a secretary at Australia House in Piccadilly.

JOHN FORBES (1950–1998) was born in Melbourne and grew up in New Guinea and Malaya before he graduated from Sydney University. He lived in Sydney and worked as a furniture removalist when he was not being supported by the Literature Board; some of his friends believe this strenuous work contributed to the heart attack from which he died in Melbourne.

STEPHEN EDGAR (1951–) was born and grew up in Sydney; when he finished school he moved to London, where he became acquainted with Clive James. In 1974 he moved to Tasmania and completed a degree in Classics and English at the University of Tasmania. He has worked as a librarian, an editor and proofreader. In 2005 he moved back to Sydney, where his partner is the poet Judith Beveridge.

KEVIN HART (1954–) was born in London and moved to Brisbane with his family at the age of ten. He attended the Australian National University in Canberra, where he became associated with Alan Gould. He also attended Stanford University in California and Melbourne University. After graduating, he considered becoming a Catholic priest before pursuing an academic career – he taught at Melbourne University, Deakin University and Monash University. In 2007 he became a professor at the University of Virginia in the United States.

JENNIFER HARRISON (1955–) was born in a motorbike shop in Liverpool, New South Wales. She has degrees in medicine and psychiatry, and works as a child psychiatrist at the Alfred Hospital in Melbourne.

JUDITH BEVERIDGE (1956–) was born in London but came to Australia at the age of four. She grew up in the western suburbs of Sydney, and attended the University of Technology Sydney. She has worked in libraries, and taught Creative Writing at Sydney University, but most of her career has been devoted to poetry.

GIG RYAN (1956–) was born in London, where her Australian father had gone to complete his qualifications as a surgeon. She arrived in Australia as a small child and was educated at Loreto Mandeville Hall in Melbourne, later attending both Sydney and Melbourne universities. She has been a singer with a rock band. She succeeded RA Simpson as poetry editor of the *Age*.

SARAH DAY (1958–) was born in Upholland, Lancashire, and came to Tasmania as a child. She attended the University of Tasmania and has worked as a librarian and as a teacher of Creative Writing.

KATHLEEN STEWART (1958–) was born in Sydney, and educated at Loreto Normanhurst. She has been a singer with a rock band, and for a time she lived in Berlin; on her return to Australia she became a prolific novelist, as well as publishing poetry.

PHILIP HODGINS (1959–1995) grew up on a farm at Katandra West, near Shepparton, Victoria, and attended Geelong College as a boarder. He was working in publishing when, at the age of twenty-four, he was diagnosed with leukaemia and told he had only a few years to live. He outlived his diagnosis by a decade, and in that time produced a body of work other poets might need a normal lifespan to achieve; he also completed a degree at Melbourne University, married and had two daughters, and, with his wife Janet Shaw, built a mud-brick house near Maryborough, Victoria, where he lived until his health finally declined.

HARRY CUMMINS (1961–) was born in Townsville, Queensland, but moved to London with his parents as a child. He graduated from University College, London, and for many years he was a senior official with the British Council.

JEMAL SHARAH (1969–) was born in Canberra and moved to Sydney after the death of her father in the car accident described in her poem 'Kristallnacht' in 1975. She was educated at Sydney Girls High School and Sydney University, and has worked for the Department of Foreign Affairs, with postings to the Solomon Islands and the Middle East.

STEPHEN McINERNEY (1976–) was born in Kiama, on the south coast of New South Wales, and attended St Josephs College, Hunters Hill, as a boarder before he graduated from the Australian National University. He considered becoming a Catholic monk, and entered a monastery in a remote area of the United States, then changed his mind and completed a doctorate at Sydney University. He is now a lecturer in English at Campion College in Sydney.

Credits

☙